Best wishes

Gary

[signature]

wembley
The FA Cup Finals
1923-2000

introduction
by Glen Isherwood

Wembley Stadium was a place which held so many memories for millions of people. My own personal fascination developed from watching Cup Finals on television during the seventies. It was a magical place and everything that happened there was a historic moment.

Even in later years, when other finals were played there, the stadium still held a certain mystique, whoever the teams involved, and whatever the competition. The sense of occasion was always there, as the players made the long walk from the tunnel to the halfway line. They stood for the National Anthem, met the special guest and, at the end of the game, climbed the steps to the Royal Box to receive the trophy and medals.

All of these rituals were steeped in traditions which went right back to the early days of the stadium, and its classic design with those magnificent twin towers ensured that this majestic concrete structure would forever remain in the memories of all those privileged to have experienced it.

Back in 1983, I began collecting details from all of Wembley's games. When it closed its doors for the last time, in 2000, there had been over 750 played under the twin towers, but it was the 72 F.A. Cup Finals which made the stadium famous and it is these games which are the focal point of this book.

Each person has their own particular favourite final, so I have sought to capture all the important events of the day. Plus, to give each final its appropriate place in history, I have documented each competing team's fortunes both before and after their Wembley visit. Thus, the significance of the game to each competing club is revealed.

Of course, some of these games are great moments in sporting history. The very first Wembley final, in 1923, was almost a national disaster. Wembley was world famous from day one. In 1953, the story of Stanley Matthews (knighted 1965) captured the nation's hearts with its fairytale ending. Sunderland's 1973 victory was the classic triumph of David over Goliath. 1979 gave us an incredible final twist, when Arsenal threw it away, only to snatch it back again.

These moments are etched forever in people's minds and it is my great privilege to be given the opportunity to present them to you.

wembley
The FA Cup Finals
1923-2000

A Britespot Publication

First Published in Great Britain by
Britespot Publishing Solutions Limited
Chester Road, Cradley Heath, West Midlands B64 6AB

© Britespot July 2003

ISBN 1 904103 17 0

Cover design and layout
© Britespot Publishing Solutions Limited

Printed and bound in Dubai, U.A.E.

The Author would like to thank Colin Timbrell for supplying me with masses of Wembley info over the years, to Chris Warren for the monumental binding of the complete record, to Jim Cadman and Tom Rowe for the pictures and memorabilia and to Tracy, Chloe and Max for understanding and supporting this obsession of mine!

Many thanks to Roger Marshall, Paul Burns, Linda Perkins, Chris Sweet and Chris Russell of Britespot Publishing for making the publishing of this book possible.

The Publishers would like to thank Nationwide Building Society for endorsing this publication, Jen Little of Empics, Tom Rowe, Jim Cadman and Ian Nannestad.

contents

Wembley Greats

The crowd swarms onto the Wembley pitch in 1923 before the first F.A. Cup Final to be played at the Empire Stadium, only to be quelled by PC George Scorey on Billy the white horse (right of picture). The game would now forever be known as 'The White Horse Final'.

Chapter One

The decade in which the Wembley story begins, saw Adolf Hitler gain a following for the fledgling Nazi party in Germany, the death of Lenin in the Soviet Union, whilst the United States was hit by the Wall Street crash. Britain, meanwhile, lost an Empire but gained a Commonwealth, and the General Strike of 1926 brought the country to a standstill.

Against this depressing backdrop, the world of football continued to flourish as a hugely popular distraction from the times. The new offside law generated a large increase in the number of goals, and records were set that still stand today. Dixie Dean netted 60 First Division goals in one season, Huddersfield Town became the first club to win three successive Football League Championships and the decade ended with the first World Cup. Without British involvement, it was hosted and won by Uruguay.

Wembley Stadium was built in 15 months, between January 1922 and the first event in April 1923. The dramatic scenes of overcrowding at the 'White Horse' Cup Final ensured that the stadium made front-page news right from the start. The British Empire Exhibition the following year put Wembley on the map, although it had an uncertain future until Arthur Elvin bought the stadium, in 1927, and introduced greyhound racing and speedway to pay the bills. This first decade also saw the Rugby League Cup Final established as an annual pilgrimage for fans of the northern-based sport.

Giantkillers and Bridesmaids

Before the war, Southern League sides had enjoyed great success in the F.A. Cup, with Tottenham Hotspur lifting the trophy in 1901. After the hostilities ceased, the Football League virtually doubled in size and the Southern League was promoted en masse. This was the point when non-league successes became a rarity. One result stood out, therefore, at Crystal Palace, London, in January 1924, when five times winners of the Cup, Blackburn Rovers, lost by a single goal, in the first round, to Corinthians, the great amateur club, who had never competed in a league. Blackburn were enjoying their best season in the First Division since the war, and were to win the Cup, for a record-equalling sixth time, just four years later.

In 1930, Hull City commemorated their 21st league season (all of which had been spent in the Second Division) by dropping into the Third Division North for the first time, on goal average. Paradoxically, it was also the season when they almost reached the F.A. Cup Final. A 3-1 victory over the eventual Second Division Champions, Blackpool, in the fourth round, was followed by a 2-1 success, at Maine Road, against Manchester City, before Newcastle United were forced to a replay, where they succumbed to the only goal, at Hull. The semi-final pitted the Tigers against the mighty Arsenal, about to embark on a period of dominance in English football. At half-time, Hull were, astonishingly, two goals up, thanks to Howieson catching the keeper off his line, and an Eddie Hapgood own goal. They held out until ten minutes from time, when David Jack pulled one back for the Gunners. An equaliser soon followed, and Jack ended the brave Hull resistance in the replay. Hull have never since been so close to the final.

Southampton remain the only club to have reached the final twice whilst playing non-league football. This was achieved at the beginning of the 20th century. When they finally joined the Football League, in 1920, they quickly established themselves as a Second Division club, and reached the semi-finals twice in three years, a commendable achievement. As if to prove their mantle as a perennial underdog, when they won the Cup for the first time in 1976, it was as a Second Division side.

Hughie Gallacher

Hughie Gallacher was a centre forward in the legendary Scottish team known as the 'Wembley Wizards', after they beat England 5-1 in 1928. He was only 5 feet 5 inches tall, but compensated for this with a remarkable turn of speed and exquisite ball control. In international football, he scored a Scottish record, 22 goals in 19 games. He won the Scottish Cup, with Airdrieonians, and the League Championship, with Newcastle United, in 1927. Giantkillings by Hull and Southampton put paid to his F.A. Cup ambitions in the twenties, but he finally reached the semi-finals, in 1932, with Chelsea, where despite his goal, it was his old club, Newcastle, who emerged victorious and went on to win the trophy.

Bolton Wanderers goalkeeper Dick Pym (left) and teammate David Jack (right) turn away as the police try to push back the huge crowd that spilled onto the Wembley pitch before the match

Bolton Wanderers v West Ham United

F.A. Cup Final, Saturday 28th April 1923

The 'White Horse' Final

Preview

Neither side had previously won a major trophy, and this was their first meeting. Bolton were appearing in their third final, having lost 4-1 to Notts County at Goodison Park, Liverpool, in 1894, and 1-0 to Manchester City at Crystal Palace, London, in 1904. They had knocked out the holders, Huddersfield Town, in the last 16. West Ham had never previously progressed beyond the last 16, but had become the third Second Division side in four years, to reach the final. The other two had lost.

Bolton finished 13th in the First Division, their lowest position since the war. West Ham were in only their fourth season in the league, but were challenging for promotion to the First Division, for the first time.

Semi–Finals, Saturday 24th March 1923

Bolton Wanderers	**1:0**	**Sheffield Utd**	*(Old Trafford, Manchester)*
Jack			
Derby County	**2:5**	**West Ham Utd**	*(Stamford Bridge, London)*
Henderson o.g.		Brown 2, Moore 2	
Moore		Ruffell	

The Match

It is remarkable that this game took place on the day, as an estimated 200,000 people invaded the stadium, and swarmed all over the pitch. The match kicked off 45 minutes late, when the police finally drove the crowds back to the touchlines. One police horse, in particular, had more success than most, probably because of its colouring, and the game subsequently became known as 'The White Horse Final'. Bolton scored within three minutes, when David Jack intercepted a clearance from Young, and smashed an unstoppable shot past Hufton. They increased their lead in the 54th minute, when Vizard's cross was volleyed against the underside of the bar, by J.R. Smith. The referee ruled that it had crossed the line before rebounding back into play.

Bolton Wanderers	**2:0**	**West Ham United**
Jack,		
J.R. Smith		

Bolton Wanderers:
Pym, Haworth, Finney, Nuttall, Seddon, Jennings, Butler, Jack, J.R. Smith, J. Smith (Captain), Vizard
Charles Foweraker (Manager)

West Ham United:
Hufton, Henderson, Young, Bishop, Kay (Captain), Tresadern, Richards, W. Brown, Watson, W. Moore, Ruffell
Syd King (Manager)

Referee: D. Asson (West Bromwich)
Attendance: 126,047

Bolton were to win the F.A. Cup twice more in the 1920s. West Ham clinched promotion, as runners-up, the following week, on goal average, ahead of Leicester City, despite losing their last match, at home, to Notts County, who clinched promotion by winning the Second Division Championship. But West Ham had to wait another 41 years before they finally got their hands on the F.A. Cup, although they did win the Football League War Cup, at Wembley, in 1940.

Wembley Greats

***David Jack** Bolton Wanderers, Arsenal and England*
David Jack was one of three brothers to play for Bolton, and had a knack for scoring winning goals. When he scored Wembley's first ever goal, he knocked over several spectators, such was the closeness of the crowd behind the net. He had also netted the only goal of the semi-final, and returned three years later, to secure Bolton's second F.A. Cup win, with the goal which beat Manchester City. Although he missed out on their third triumph of the decade, Jack became the first player transferred for a five-figure fee, when he joined Arsenal in 1928 for £10,890. He went on to appear in two more finals, picking up a third winners medal, in 1930, the year he also captained England against Scotland at Wembley, and scored in the 5-2 victory.

Action from the F.A. Cup Final
between Aston Villa and Newcastle United

Aston Villa v Newcastle United
F.A. Cup Final, Saturday 26th April 1924

Magpies' Late Strikes

Preview

Aston Villa had won the F.A. Cup a record six times, including a 2-0 win over Newcastle, in the 1905 final, at Crystal Palace, London. Their sixth win had been in 1920, beating Huddersfield Town 1-0, at Stamford Bridge, London.

The 1905 final was Newcastle's first, in a run of five finals in seven years, which only brought one win, in 1910, when they beat Barnsley 2-0, in a replay at Goodison Park, Liverpool. They lost the Cup the following year, 1-0 to Bradford City, in another replayed final, at Old Trafford, Manchester. Villa finished 6th in the First Division, while Newcastle finished 9th, their lowest position since the war.

Semi–Finals, Saturday 29th March 1924

Aston Villa York 2, Kirton	3:0	**Burnley**	(Bramall Lane, Sheffield)
Manchester City	0:2	**Newcastle Utd** Harris 2	(St. Andrews, Birmingham)

The Match

Villa had beaten Newcastle, 6-1, just five days earlier, and had most of the play, without being able to score. But with seven minutes left, Newcastle broke away, and a McDonald shot was saved by Jackson, only for Neil Harris to score from the rebound. Within three minutes, the issue was beyond doubt, when Stan Seymour struck a brilliant shot past Jackson from another breakaway move.

Aston Villa	0:2	**Newcastle United** Harris Seymour

Aston Villa:
Jackson, Smart, Mort, Moss (Captain), Milne, Blackburn, York, Kirton, Capewell, Walker, Dorrell
George Ramsay (Manager)

Newcastle United:
Bradley, Hampson, Hudspeth (Captain), Mooney, Spencer, Gibson, Low, Cowan, Harris, McDonald, Seymour
Frank Watt (Manager)

Referee:	*W. Russell (Swindon)*
Attendance:	*91,695*

Newcastle were League Champions three years later and won the Cup again in 1932, but it was another 33 years before Villa won the F.A. Cup for a record seventh time.

FINAL TIE

Of the Football Association
English Cup Competition
APRIL 25th, 1925

STADIUM

British Empire Exhibition
Wembley

Official Programme – 6d.

Fleetway Press Ltd. 3-9, Dane Street High Holborn, London, W.C.1. Printed and Published by

Cardiff City v Sheffield United

F.A. Cup Final, Saturday 25th April 1925

Welsh Challenge Blunted

Preview

In only their fifth season in the League, Cardiff had become the first Welsh club to reach the F.A. Cup Final. United had won the Cup three times previously, the last occasion being in 1915, with a 3-0 victory over Chelsea, in the final at Old Trafford, Manchester.

Cardiff finished 11th in the First Division, after finishing runners-up, on goal average, to Huddersfield Town the previous season. United finished 14th.

Semi–Finals, Saturday 28th March 1925

Blackburn Rovers McKay	1:3	**Cardiff City** Rollo o.g., Gill Beadles	*(Meadow Lane, Nottingham)*
Sheffield United Parker o.g. Tunstall	2:0	**Southampton**	*(Stamford Bridge, London)*

The Match

The only goal came after half an hour. A long pass from Pantling was missed by Cardiff defender, Wake, and fell to Fred Tunstall, who controlled it, and stabbed it past Farquharson. The occasion and expectancy proved to be too much for Cardiff to handle. They failed to take their opportunities to level and Sheffield United were victorious in a subdued final.

Cardiff City	0:1	**Sheffield United** Tunstall	

Cardiff City:
Farquharson, Nelson, Blair, Wake, Keenor (Captain), Hardy, W. Davies, Gill, Nicholson, Beadles, Evans
Fred Stewart (Manager)

Sheffield United:
Sutcliffe, Cook, Milton, Pantling, King, Green, Mercer, Boyle, H. Johnson, Gillespie (Captain), Tunstall
John Nicholson (Manager)

Referee: G. Watson (Nottingham)
Attendance: 91,763

Cardiff returned two years later, to win the F.A. Cup, but United had reached their peak, and were relegated to the Second Division, in 1934. This did not stop them reaching Wembley, though, in 1936.

FINAL TIE

Of The Football Association Challenge Cup Competition

APRIL 24th 1926
STADIUM
WEMBLEY

Official Programme 6d

PRINTED & PUBLISHE

Bolton Wanderers v Manchester City

F.A. Cup Final, Saturday 24th April 1926

Jack In The Box (Again)

Preview

Bolton had won the F.A. Cup, for the first time, in 1923. City had also won the Cup once, in 1904, when ironically they beat Bolton, 1-0, at Crystal Palace, London. In an earlier round, they had thrashed Huddersfield Town, who were heading for a record third successive League Championship, 4-0.

Bolton finished 8th in the First Division, but City were battling against relegation to the Second Division, and had not beaten Bolton for three seasons.

Semi–Finals, Saturday 27th March 1926

Bolton Wanderers	3:0	**Swansea Town**	(White Hart Lane, London)
Baggett			
J. Smith 2			
Manchester City	3:0	**Manchester United**	(Bramall Lane, Sheffield)
Browell 2			
Roberts			

The Match

Only Greenhalgh of Bolton Wanderers had not played in the 1923 final and there were no signs of nerves as they dominated the early stages. Manchester City had their chances though and Bolton keeper, Dick Pym performed heroics, before Wembley's first Lancashire derby was settled, 13 minutes from time. The man who had scored Wembley's first goal, David Jack, drilled a Vizard cross into the net.

Bolton Wanderers	1:0	**Manchester City**
Jack		

Bolton Wanderers:
Pym, Haworth, Greenhalgh, Nuttall, Seddon, Jennings, Butler, Jack, J.R. Smith, J. Smith (Captain), Vizard
Charles Foweraker (Manager)

Manchester City:
Goodchild, Cookson, McCloy, Pringle, Cowan, McMullan (Captain), Austin, Browell, Roberts, Johnson, Hicks
Peter Hodge (Manager)

Referee: I. Baker (Crewe)
Attendance: 91,447

Bolton returned again, for their third F.A. Cup win, in 1929. City missed a penalty, in their last match, the following week, at Newcastle United, and were relegated. But it took them just two years to return to the top flight, as Second Division Champions, and they returned to Wembley in 1933.

Wembley Greats

Joe Smith *Bolton Wanderers and Manager of Blackpool*

Joe Smith had been capped by England, either side of the Great War, scoring once, and had the honour of becoming the first captain to lift the F.A. Cup at Wembley Stadium, although he couldn't get to the Royal Box to receive the trophy, because of the crowd. Three years later, he climbed the steps, at a more dignified occasion, as once again he led Bolton to glory. After a distinguished playing career, Smith moved into management, and led Blackpool through the most successful period in the seaside club's history. Taking over in 1935, he quickly proved a success by taking them into the First Division, and not only did he keep them there until his retirement in 1958, but he also built a great team, with many skilful players. Grounds were packed wherever Blackpool played. His biggest achievement was signing a 32-year-old Stan Matthews, from Stoke City, in 1947. Three F.A. Cup Finals followed, with 1953 providing Blackpool with their first major trophy, when Stan Mortensen's hat-trick, and Matthews' inspirational wing play overturned Smith's old club, Bolton, in a never-to-be-forgotten Final.

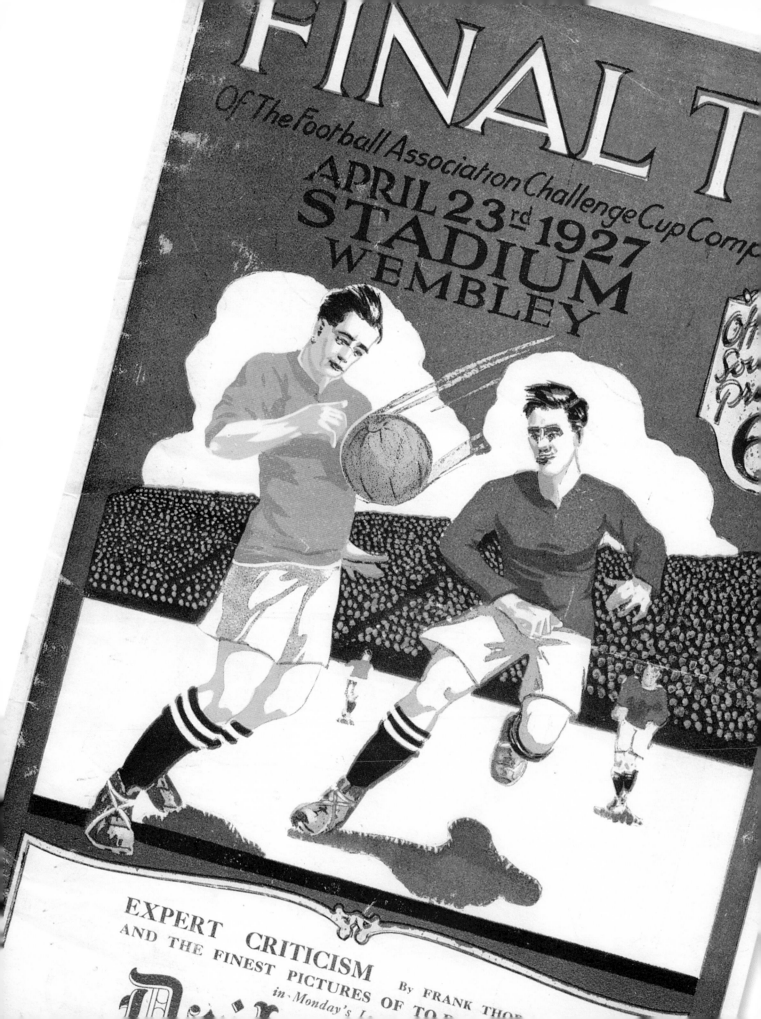

Arsenal v Cardiff City

F.A. Cup Final, Saturday 23rd April 1927

The Pride Of Wales

Preview

Neither side had previously won a major trophy. Arsenal were appearing in their first final, while Cardiff had reached their second final in three years, and were once again attempting to take the F.A. Cup out of England for the first time, having lost the 1925 final. They had already knocked out the holders, Bolton Wanderers, in the last 16.

Arsenal finished 11th in the First Division, after finishing runners-up to Huddersfield Town the previous season. Cardiff finished 14th.

Semi–Finals, Saturday 26th March 1927

Arsenal	2:1	**Southampton**	*(Stamford Bridge, London)*
Hulme, Buchan		*Rawlings*	
Cardiff City	3:0	**Reading**	*(Molineux, Wolverhampton)*
Ferguson 2			
Wake			

The Match

The only goal of a defensive game was scored with only 15 minutes remaining, and was a personal disaster for the Arsenal keeper, Lewis. From a pass by Davies, a seemingly harmless-looking shot from Hugh Ferguson squirmed out of the grasp of Lewis, and ended up in the net. A sad end to Arsenal's first final.

Arsenal	0:1	**Cardiff City**
		Ferguson

Arsenal:
D. Lewis, Parker, A. Kennedy, Baker, Butler, John, Hulme, Buchan (Captain), Brain, Blyth, Hoar
Herbert Chapman (Manager)

Cardiff City:
Farquharson, Nelson, Watson, Keenor (Captain), Sloan, Hardy, Curtis, Irving, Ferguson, L. Davies, McLachlan
Fred Stewart (Manager)

Referee: W. Bunnell (Preston)
Attendance: 91,206

Arsenal reached the semi-finals again the following year, and only had to wait a further two years to win the F.A. Cup for the first time. Cardiff finished bottom of the Third Division South just seven years later, and had to apply for re-election to the Football League. They have yet to emulate those glory years of the 1920s.

FINAL TIE
of the
FOOTBALL ASSOCIATION CHALLENGE
CUP COMPETITION

April
21st
1928

WEMBLEY · STADIUM

EXPERT CRITICISM
By FRANK THOROGOOD
and the finest pictures of to-day's Cup-Tie
in Monday's

Daily News & Westminster

PRODUCED & PUBLISHED BY FRED. E. BLOWER & CO., 132 HIGH ST., WATFORD

Blackburn Rovers v Huddersfield Town

F.A. Cup Final, Saturday 21st April 1928

Rovers' Return To Glory

Preview

Blackburn were aiming to equal Aston Villa's record, of six F.A. Cup wins, but their last had been in 1891, when they beat Notts County 3-1 at Kennington Oval, London. In the semi-finals, they had beaten the previous year's finalists. Huddersfield had won the Cup only once, in 1922, when they beat Preston North End 1-0 at Stamford Bridge, London, and they had just come through a gruelling semi-final.

Blackburn finished 12th in the First Division, while Huddersfield were battling with Everton in an attempt to regain the League Championship for the fourth time in five years, having completed the first hat-trick of League Championships two years earlier.

Semi–Finals, Saturday 24th March 1928

Arsenal	0:1	**Blackburn Rovers** Roscamp	(Filbert Street, Leicester)	
Huddersfield Town Jackson Brown	2:2	**Sheffield United** Johnson 2	(Old Trafford, Manchester)	
Huddersfield Town	0:0 (AET)	**Sheffield United**	(Goodison Park, Liverpool)	Replay (Monday 26th March 1928)
Huddersfield Town Jackson	1:0	**Sheffield United**	(Maine Road, Manchester)	2nd Replay (Monday 2nd April 1928)

The Match

Wembley's first Roses match got off to a sensational start, with Blackburn scoring in the first minute. Healless knocked the ball across, Puddefoot barged into the keeper, Mercer, as he came to collect the ball, and Jack Roscamp touched it over the line. Huddersfield fought back, but found themselves two down before half-time, as Tom McLean struck a great shot from just inside the penalty area. Huddersfield did score in the second half, however, when a fine passing move left Alex Jackson to prod it past Crawford as the keeper came out, and they pushed men forward in search of an equaliser. But they were caught on the break in the dying minutes, as Roscamp took a pass from Thornewell, and rifled home his second past Mercer.

Blackburn Rovers Roscamp 2 McLean	3:1	**Huddersfield Town** Jackson

Blackburn Rovers:
Crawford, Hutton, Jones, Healless (Captain), Rankin, Campbell, Thornewell, Puddefoot, Roscamp, McLean, Rigby
Bob Crompton (Manager)

Huddersfield Town:
Mercer, Goodall, Barkas, Redfern, Wilson, Steele, Jackson, Kelly, Brown, Stephenson (Captain), Smith
Jack Chaplin (Manager)

Referee: *T. Bryan (Willenhall)*
Attendance: *92,041*

This was Blackburn's only highlight, in a very long barren spell. Their next final was 32 years later, but they did reach the Football League War Cup Final in 1940. Huddersfield's long season finally caught up with them, and they finished League runners-up, for the second year in succession. They reached the semi-finals again the following year, and the final again the year after, but were beginning a steady decline from heights they have not re-attained since.

Wembley Greats

Alex Jackson Huddersfield Town and Scotland
Alex Jackson, a right winger with immaculate timing, who was adept at charging into the middle to notch vital goals, never won an F.A. Cup winners medal, although he did score in the 1928 final, and in three successive semi-finals. Three weeks earlier, he had been the tallest member of the Scotland forward line (5 feet 7 inches) which thrashed England, 5-1, at Wembley, to inflict on the hosts their heaviest defeat for 47 years. Jackson notched a hat-trick, and immortalised himself as one of the 'Wembley Wizards'. He went on to win 17 caps for his country, scoring 8 goals. Huddersfield had signed him in 1925 from Aberdeen, and they completed an historic League Championship hat-trick in his first season with them.

Bolton Wanderers F.A. Cup Winners of 1929:
(back row left to right) Charles Foweraker (Manager), Fred Kean, Bob Haworth, Dick Pym, Alex Finney, Harry Nuttall, Hauson (Trainer).
(front row left to right) Billy Butler, Jimmy McClelland, Jimmy Seddon, Harry Blackmore, George Gibson, Willie Cook.

Bolton Wanderers v Portsmouth

F.A. Cup Final, Saturday 27th April 1929

Wanderers Return Yet Again

Preview

Bolton were becoming regular visitors after their two earlier F.A. Cup wins, in the 1920s. They had knocked out the holders, Blackburn Rovers, in the quarter-finals, and the previous year's other finalists in the semi-finals. Portsmouth, by comparison, had never previously been beyond the last 32 in the competition.

Bolton finished 14th in the First Division, their lowest position since the war, while Portsmouth, who had only been a First Division club for two years, narrowly escaped relegation again, by finishing 20th for the second year in succession.

Semi–Finals, Saturday 23rd March 1929

Aston Villa	0:1	*Portsmouth* Smith (penalty)	(Highbury, London)
Bolton Wanderers Blackmore Butler, Gibson	3:1	*Huddersfield Town* Jackson	(Anfield, Liverpool)

The Match

Bolton's experience allowed them to control the game, but it was not until 11 minutes from the end that they scored. A run from Billy Butler ended in the winger shooting past Gilfillan and defender Mackie on the line. Butler laid on the second, in the last minute, crossing for Harold Blackmore to blast it past the helpless keeper.

Bolton Wanderers Butler Blackmore	2:0	*Portsmouth*

Bolton Wanderers:
Pym, Haworth, Finney, Kean, Seddon (Captain), Nuttall, Butler, McClelland, Blackmore, Gibson, Cook, Charles Foweraker (Manager)

Portsmouth:
Gilfillan, Mackie, Bell, Nichol, McIlwaine (Captain), Thackeray, Forward, J. Smith, Weddle, Watson, Cook, Jack Tinn (Manager)

Referee: A. Josephs (South Shields)
Attendance: 92,576

Bolton were not to return for a further 24 years, but Portsmouth managed to establish themselves as a First Division side, and reached another final, in 1934.

Arsenal v Huddersfield Town

F.A. Cup Final, Saturday 26th April 1930

Gunners Off The Mark

Preview

Having turned Huddersfield into a great side in the 1920s, manager, Herbert Chapman was about to transform Arsenal from a team without a major honour to their name, into a team which would dominate the 1930s. Both sides had lost recent finals. Huddersfield had knocked out the League Champions in the Semi-Finals.
Arsenal finished 14th in the First Division, while Huddersfield finished 10th.

Semi–Finals, Saturday 22nd March 1930

Arsenal	2:2	**Hull City**	(Elland Road, Leeds)
Jack		Howieson	
Bastin		Hapgood o.g.	
Huddersfield Town	2:1	**Sheffield Wednesday**	(Old Trafford, Manchester)
Jackson 2		Hooper	
Arsenal	1:0	**Hull City**	(Villa Park, Birmingham) Replay (Wednesday 26th March 1930)
Jack			

The Match

Arsenal took the lead, after 16 minutes. Alex James took a quick free kick after being fouled, and played the ball out to Bastin on the wing. James moved into the middle, and met Bastin's centre with the outside of his right foot, to set the Gunners on their way to victory. Arsenal sat back in the second half, and rode their luck, as their keeper, Preedy, made several errors. As so often happens though, the dominant side were caught on the break. With two minutes remaining, a long clearance from James, sent Jack Lambert clean through, to put the ball past Turner. Arsenal had at last won a major trophy.

Arsenal	2:0	**Huddersfield Town**
James, Lambert		

Arsenal:
Preedy, Parker (Captain), Hapgood, Baker, Seddon, John, Hulme, Jack, Lambert, James, Bastin
Herbert Chapman (Manager)

Huddersfield:
Turner, Goodall, Spence, Naylor, Wilson (Captain), Campbell, Jackson, Kelly, Davies, Raw, Smith
Clern Stephenson (Manager)

Referee: *T. Crew (Leicester)*
Attendance: *92,448*

Arsenal became the first London club to win the League Championship the following year, and were back at Wembley in 1932. Huddersfield finished as League runners-up, to Arsenal, in 1934, and reached another F.A. Cup Final four years later.

Wembley Greats

Herbert Chapman *Arsenal Manager*

Herbert Chapman was years ahead of his time. As a player, he made no great impression, but as a manager, he was a pioneer, a man of ideas, and a manager who brought unprecedented success to two clubs, which had never seen the like before. After cutting his teeth at Northampton Town and Leeds City, he moved to Huddersfield in 1920. They won the F.A. Cup two years later, and Chapman's signings and team building took the Yorkshire club to the very top. In 1924, they pipped Cardiff City to the League Championship, and retained it the following year. With Huddersfield heading for the hat-trick, Chapman stunned them by moving on to Arsenal, a club without a major honour. Recognising the potential in north London, he made big signings in Charlie Buchan and David Jack, and began to mould an even greater side than the one he'd left behind. Chapman's methods made the rest of the country seem amateurish in their preparations. Apart from his tactical success in making his formations more flexible to combat the new offside law, he was constantly innovating and experimenting, and the team benefited hugely from personal attention to detail in training routines and medical treatment. Arsenal's F.A. Cup win, in 1930, ironically against a declining Huddersfield, was the first triumph of a new era. The following year, they took the League Championship to the south for the first time. His untimely death in 1934 came as Arsenal were midway through emulating Huddersfield's achievement, of three successive titles, but this unique man had made his mark on the game's history, and Arsenal would not be the club they are today but for Herbert Chapman.

*An aerial shot of the action at Wembley Stadium during the
1932 F.A. Cup Final between Arsenal and Newcastle United.*

Chapter Two
1931 - 40

Storm clouds were well and truly gathering throughout the decade, as Adolf Hitler became German Chancellor in 1933 and his policies began to alarm the watching world. Britain was still in a depressed state, with unemployment reaching two million. The new monarch, King Edward VIII, abdicated his throne to marry an American divorcée, leaving his younger brother, now King George VI, to lead the country into inevitable confrontation with the Nazis.

Once again, football provided a welcome boost to morale. Arsenal were the most successful team, winning the League Championship five times, in eight years, setting new standards with Herbert Chapman's modern approach. The British nations were still isolated internationally and Italy won both the decade's World Cups. In 1939, the hostilities forced the suspension of the Football League, and the next seven years were to signify the end of so many promising young lives and careers.

Wembley's second decade saw few innovations, but the stadium was now regarded as the rightful home of the F.A. Cup Final. Traditions were becoming firmly established, and television and radio were now broadcasting the games to a wider audience.

Giantkillers and Bridesmaids

Although Arsenal dominated the 1930s, there was one day, in January 1933, when little Walsall, from the Third Division North, humbled them in the F.A. Cup Third Round. There were many at the time who resented Arsenal's rise to prominence above the more traditional powers from the north and midlands, and Walsall's 2-0 victory was a very popular result. Arsenal were guilty of complacency, and even though they fielded three debutants because of a 'flu epidemic, they still had seven internationals in the side, and rested the experienced Joe Hulme. A valuable lesson was learned, and Arsenal went on to win three successive League Championships, followed by a second F.A. Cup in 1936.

Millwall's F.A. Cup run in 1937 saw them beat Chelsea 3-0, and high-flying Derby County 2-1, before a 2-0 success against the eventual League Champions, Manchester City, made them the first Third Division side to reach the Semi-Finals. They had twice appeared in the last four, as a Southern League club, at the turn of the century, but this time they were even closer to the Final, when Dave Mangnall gave them the lead against Sunderland, after ten minutes. Eventually, the Wearsiders overcame the Lions, and went on to lift the trophy. Millwall had earned widespread respect, however, and confidently lifted the Third Division South Championship the following year.

Grimsby Town spent most of the 1930s in the First Division, and made two serious assaults on the F.A. Cup during that period. Unfortunately, their Semi-Final appearances were blighted by misfortune, and they have not risen to such heady heights since. In 1936, they were pitted against the all-conquering Arsenal, who could only manage to breach the Grimsby defence on one occasion, with the Mariners having a goal disallowed. Three years later, it was title-chasing Wolverhampton Wanderers, who stood in Grimsby's way on the road to Wembley. Who knows what the outcome would have been had Moulson, Grimsby's keeper, not been carried off with a head injury after 20 minutes, with the score goalless. Wolves seized the initiative and were two goals up by half-time against the ten men. The final score was 5-0, and Grimsby's all too brief flirtation with glory was over.

Tommy Lawton

When the Second World War broke out, 19-year-old Tommy Lawton was already a big star. He had been Burnley's youngest ever first team player, at 16, and was snapped up by Everton within a year of his league debut, to learn from the ageing Dixie Dean. He was a willing pupil, and in each of the two seasons before all fixtures were suspended, Lawton was the Football League's top scorer. In 1938-39, Everton won the last pre-war League Championship and Lawton was called up by England, scoring in each of his first six internationals. The only disappointment was defeat in the F.A. Cup Sixth Round, to Wolves. Sadly it was to be the closest he ever came to a Cup Final appearance. Wembley was still to see the best of this fine centre forward however. During the war, no one scored more at Wembley than Lawton. With Stan Matthews providing the crosses, and Lawton powerfully heading them in, England had one of its most successful periods, albeit unofficial. Chelsea signed him in 1945, but two years later, aged 28, he caused a sensation by dropping down two divisions to join Notts County, for a record transfer fee of £20,000 plus another player. The incentive for him, in the age of the maximum wage, was the promise of a part-time job as well. Not surprisingly, his England career soon came to an end, but with 22 goals from 23 peacetime internationals, it was surely premature. County won the Third Division South Championship in 1950, with Lawton the division's top scorer once more. Brentford and Arsenal had the benefit of his later years in football.

Birmingham v West Bromwich Albion

F.A. Cup Final, Saturday 25th April 1931

Wembley's First 'Double'

Preview

Birmingham had never been beyond the last 16 of the competition before, but West Brom had strong cup traditions. They were appearing in their seventh final, and had won the Cup twice. Their last win however had been in 1892, when they beat Aston Villa 3-0, at Kennington Oval, London. Birmingham finished 19th in the First Division, their lowest position since promotion ten years earlier, and perilously close to the relegation zone. West Brom were on the verge of returning to the First Division, after four seasons in the Second, but they had to stay ahead of Tottenham Hotspur, to finish runners-up, to Everton. The last Second Division team to win the Cup had been Barnsley in 1912, when they ironically beat West Brom.

Semi–Finals, Saturday 14th March 1931

Birmingham Curtis 2	2:0	**Sunderland**	*(Elland Road, Leeds)*
Everton	0:1	**West Brom** Glidden	*(Old Trafford, Manchester)*

The Match

In very wet conditions, the Second Division side took a 26th minute lead, when Billy Richardson got on to the end of a cross from Carter, shot, and fell. Barkas blocked it, but Richardson managed to scramble it over the line. In the 57th minute, their local rivals drew level, as a long ball from Cringan, was picked up by Joe Bradford, to shoot past Pearson. Within a minute, West Brom were back in front, when Richardson collected Cringan's attempted back pass to score his second.

Birmingham Bradford	1:2	**West Bromwich Albion** W.G. Richardson 2

Birmingham:
Hibbs, Liddell, Barkas (Captain), Cringan, Morall, Leslie, Briggs, Crosbie, Bradford, Gregg, Curtis
Leslie Knighton (Manager)

West Bromwich Albion:
Pearson, Shaw, Trentham, Magee, W. Richardson, Edwards, Glidden (Captain), Carter, W.G. Richardson, Sandford, Wood
Fred Everiss (Manager)

Referee: *A. Kingscott (Long Eaton)*
Attendance: *92,406*

It was 25 years before Birmingham reached the final again, and they have yet to win the trophy. West Brom clinched promotion the following week, to complete a memorable season. They returned to Wembley in 1935, but both clubs had been relegated by the end of the decade.

Newcastle United's Jack Allen (left) fires the controversial equalizing goal past Arsenal goalkeeper Frank Moss (right, hidden)

Arsenal v Newcastle United

F.A. Cup Final, Saturday 23rd April 1932

Over The Line

Preview

Arsenal were attempting to regain the F.A. Cup for the second time in three years, having won it, for the first time, in 1930. Newcastle had last won the Cup in 1924, and had slumped since their League Championship win of 1927.

Arsenal had won the League Championship for the first time the previous year, and were chasing Everton in an attempt to retain it. Newcastle finished 11th in the First Division.

Semi–Finals, Saturday 12th March 1932

Arsenal *Bastin*	1:0	**Manchester City**	*(Villa Park, Birmingham)*
Chelsea *Gallacher*	1:2	**Newcastle United** *Allen, Lang*	*(Leeds Road, Huddersfield)*

The Match

The favourites took the lead after 15 minutes. A Hulme cross was misjudged by the Newcastle defence, and Bob John took the easiest of opportunities to score. The 38th minute brought one of the most controversial goals ever scored in an F.A. Cup Final. Davidson's pass down the wing seemed to be too long for Richardson, who crossed the ball, after it had clearly gone over the goal line. As Jack Allen put the ball in the net, the Arsenal players stood motionless, waiting for the referee to give a goal kick. To their amazement, he gave a goal. With 13 minutes left, a Roberts miskick was picked up by Allen. With defenders converging on him, he moved out to the left, and drove a low shot into the corner, past Moss, to give Newcastle the Cup.

Arsenal *John*	1:2	**Newcastle United** *Allen 2*

Arsenal:
Moss, Parker (Captain), Hapgood, Jones, Roberts, Male, Hulme, Jack, Lambert, Bastin, John
Herbert Chapman (Manager)

Newcastle United:
McInroy, Nelson (Captain), Fairhurst, McKenzie, Davidson, Weaver, Boyd, Richardson, Allen, McMenemy, Lang
Andy Cunningham (Manager)

Referee:	*W. Harper (Stourbridge)*
Attendance:	*92,298*

Arsenal had to concede defeat in the title race, the following week and finished runners-up. But they found ample consolation in winning the next three League Championships, so emulating Huddersfield Town's feat of the 1920s. Following this, they returned to win the F.A. Cup again in 1936. Newcastle were relegated to the Second Division two years later, and it was 19 years before they won the Cup again.

FINAL TIE

of the
Football Association Challenge Cup Competition

OFFICIAL
SOUVENIR
PROGRAMME
6D.

EMPIRE STADIUM · WEMBLEY
APRIL 29th 1933

| BEST PICTURES | EXPERT CRITICISM OF TO-DAY'S CUP TIE BY CHARLES BUCHAN (the famous International and ex-Arsenal Captain) | ON MONDAY |

News Chronicle

Everton v Manchester City

F.A. Cup Final, Saturday 29th April 1933

Everton Complete The Set

Preview

Everton were appearing in their fifth final, but had won it only once. Their solitary success had been in 1906, when they beat Newcastle United, 1-0, at Crystal Palace, London. The following year, they lost the final 2-1 to Sheffield Wednesday, at Crystal Palace. City's only F.A. Cup win had been two years before Everton's, but they had previously appeared at Wembley, in 1926.

Everton had had an eventful three years; relegated in 1930, straight back, as Second Division Champions, in 1931, and then League Champions in their first season back. Their defence of the title, though, saw them drop to 11th in the First Division. City finished 16th, their lowest position since promotion in 1928.

Semi-Finals, Saturday 18th March 1933

Derby County	*2:3*	***Manchester City***	*(Leeds Road, Huddersfield)*
Fabian		*Toseland, Tilson*	
Crooks		*McMullan*	
Everton	*2:1*	***West Ham United***	*(Molineux, Wolverhampton)*
Dunn, Critchley		*V. Watson*	

The Match

Everton took the lead five minutes before half-time, when Britton tried a speculative lob into the middle, from 25 yards out, near the touchline. Langford misjudged its flight, and came out too far. He got a touch, but it left Jimmy Stein with an easy tap-in. Seven minutes into the second half, Britton tried the same lofted pass, from a similar position. This time, Dixie Dean charged Langford, and the ball ended up in the net. Geldard's corner was headed in by Jimmy Dunn with eight minutes left, for the biggest winning margin in an F.A. Cup Final since 1915.

Everton	*3:0*	***Manchester City***
Stein, Dean		
Dunn		

Everton:
Sagar, Cook, Cresswell, Britton, White, Thomson, Geldard, Dunn, Dean (Captain), Johnson, Stein
Tom McIntosh (Manager)

Manchester City:
Langford, Cann, Dale, Busby, Cowan (Captain), Bray, Toseland, Marshall, Herd, McMullan, Brook
Wilf Wild (Manager)

Referee:	*E. Wood (Sheffield)*
Attendance:	*92,950*

City returned the following year to win the F.A. Cup, but it was to be another 33 years before Everton lifted the trophy again.

OFFICIAL
PROGRAMME
6D.

FINAL TIE
OF THE FOOTBALL ASSOCIATION
CHALLENGE CUP
COMPETITION

EMPIRE
STADIUM
WEMBLEY

USERS OF BOVR?
ARE MILLIONS
STRONG

Manchester City v Portsmouth

F.A. Cup Final, Saturday 28th April 1934

City Back To Their Best

Preview

City were back, to make amends for their performance in the previous year's final. Portsmouth's only previous final, had been in 1929.

City finished 5th in the First Division, a big improvement on the previous two seasons. Portsmouth finished 10th.

Semi–Finals, Saturday 17th March 1934

Aston Villa	1:6	**Manchester City**	*(Leeds Road, Huddersfield)*
Astley		Toseland, Tilson 4	
		Herd	
Leicester City	1:4	**Portsmouth**	*(St. Andrews, Birmingham)*
Lochhead		Weddle 3	
		Rutherford	

The Match

In the 27th minute, Weddle sent Sep Rutherford away down the left. He cut inside, and fired past Swift to give Portsmouth the lead. They held it until 16 minutes from the end, when Allen, the Portsmouth captain, went off injured. City seized their chance. Brook set off on a mazy run, passed to Fred Tilson, and the striker, who had netted four times in the semi-final, shot past Gilfillan for the equaliser. With the game heading for extra time, Herd's pass enabled Tilson to score again with four minutes left.

Manchester City	2:1	**Portsmouth**	
Tilson 2		Rutherford	

Manchester City:
Swift, Barnett, Dale, Busby, Cowan (Captain), Bray, Toseland, Marshall, Tilson, Herd, Brook
Wilf Wild (Manager)

Portsmouth:
Gilfillan, Mackie, W. Smith, Nichol, Allen (Captain), Thackeray, Worrall, J. Smith, Weddle, Easson, Rutherford
Jack Tinn (Manager)

Referee: S. Rous (Watford)
Attendance: 93,258

City won the League Championship three years later, but, incredibly, they were relegated the season after. It was to be 21 years before they returned to Wembley. Portsmouth's league form continued to be unimpressive, but they won the F.A. Cup for the first time, in 1939.

FINAL TIE

OF THE
FOOTBALL
ASSOCIATION
CHALLENGE CUP
COMPETITION

AT THE

EMPIRE STADIUM

WEMBLEY

SATURDAY · APRIL 27th · 1935

Their Majesties'
Silver Jubilee Year

OFFICIAL PROGRAMME SIXPENCE

Sheffield Wednesday v West Brom

F.A. Cup Final, Saturday 27th April 1935

Wednesday Edge Thriller

Preview

Wednesday had won the Cup twice before. The last occasion had been in 1907, when they beat Everton 2-1 at Crystal Palace, London. They had eliminated Arsenal, who were heading for their third successive League Championship, in the quarter-final. West Brom had won the F.A. Cup at Wembley in 1931, and were fielding nine of the same side. Wednesday finished 3rd in the First Division, for the fourth time in five years. West Brom finished 9th, their lowest position, since returning to the First Division in 1931.

Semi–Finals, Saturday 16th March 1935

Bolton Wanderers	1:1	**West Bromwich A**	(Elland Road, Leeds)	
Walton		*W.G. Richardson*		
Burnley	0:3	**Sheffield Wednesday**	(Villa Park, Birmingham)	
		Rimmer		
		Palethorpe 2		
Bolton Wanderers	0:2	**West Bromwich A**	(Victoria Ground, Stoke)	Replay (Wednesday 20th March 1935)
		W.G. Richardson		
		Sandford (penalty)		

The Match

This fast and flowing game sprung to life in only the second minute. Hooper's cross enabled Jack Palethorpe to control it, before placing it past Pearson to give Wednesday the lead. Twenty minutes later, West Brom drew level, when Carter sent Wally Boyes away on a brilliant run, ending with a powerful shot into the net. At the same point, in the second half, Mark Hooper cut in from the wing, to receive a ball from Starling and beat Pearson via the post with a swerving shot which barely crossed the line. West Brom came fighting back, and five minutes later were level again, from Boyes' throw-in to   Ted Sandford, whose shot from the edge of the box, spun off Millership's head, which took it into the angle of the goal. Wednesday settled it with three minutes remaining. Ellis Rimmer ran on to Sharp's long ball and headed it over the advancing keeper, into the net, thus becoming the first player to score in all six rounds of the Cup. Rimmer scored again in the dying seconds from a rebound after Pearson had saved Hooper's effort, as Wednesday became the first to score four in an F.A. Cup Final since Bury in 1903.

Sheffield Wednesday	4:2	**West Bromwich Albion**
Palethorpe		*Boyes*
Hooper		*Sandford*
Rimmer 2		

Sheffield Wednesday:
Brown, Nibloe, Catlin, Sharp, Millership, Burrows, Hooper, Surtees, Palethorpe, Starling (Captain), Rimmer
Billy Walker (Manager)

West Bromwich Albion:
Pearson, Shaw, Trentham, Murphy, W. Richardson, Edwards, Glidden (Captain), Carter, W.G. Richardson, Sandford, Boyes
Fred Everiss (Manager)

Referee: A. Fogg (Bolton)
Attendance: 93,204

Wednesday were relegated two years later, and did not return to Wembley until 1966. West Brom were relegated three years later, but were back to win the Cup in 1954.

Arsenal v Sheffield United

F.A. Cup Final, Saturday 25th April 1936

Arsenal Made To Work For Prize

Preview

Arsenal were appearing in their fourth final in ten years, but had won the Cup only once. United had last won the Cup in 1925, their fourth win in the competition.

After winning the League Championship for the previous three years, Arsenal finished a lowly 6th in the First Division. United had been in the Second Division for two years, and had an outside chance of winning promotion.

Semi–Finals, Saturday 21st March 1936

Arsenal Bastin	1:0	**Grimsby Town**	(Leeds Road, Huddersfield)
Fulham Arnold	1:2	**Sheffield United** Bird, Pickering	(Molineux, Wolverhampton)

The Match

In a game of several missed chances, the only goal came in the 74th minute. Bastin's pass to Ted Drake, enabled the prolific striker, with his knee strapped up because he was recovering from an operation on the cartilage, to get past Johnson, for the first time in the match, and score with a well struck shot, Dodds, almost immediately, hit the bar at the other end, but Arsenal held on for victory.

Arsenal Drake	1:0	**Sheffield United**

Arsenal:
A. Wilson, Male, Hapgood, Crayston, Roberts, Copping, Hulme, Bowden, Drake, James (Captain), Bastin
George Allison (Manager)

Sheffield United:
Smith, Hooper (Captain), Wilkinson, Jackson, T. Johnson, McPherson, Barton, Barclay, Dodds, Pickering, Williams
Ted Davison (Manager)

Referee: H. Nattrass (Seaham)
Attendance: 93,384

Arsenal won another League Championship two years later and then the war interrupted things. They made two visits to Wembley during the war, and their third F.A. Cup win came in 1950. United's promotion hopes ended four days later. They took another three years to win promotion back to the First Division, but they did not appear at Wembley again until the F.A. Cup Semi-Final of 1993.

Wembley Greats

Ted Drake Arsenal

Ted Drake joined Arsenal in 1933 from Southampton, and became one of their greatest ever goalscorers. He was the Football League's top marksman in 1934-35, as the Gunners secured their third successive title, and he also scored on his England debut, against the World Champions, Italy, at Highbury. The following season saw Drake become the only player in history to score seven goals in a top flight match. Remarkably, this was achieved away from home, at Aston Villa. Drake, whose knee was strapped up because of a troublesome injury, only had eight shots on goal, the other being pushed onto the crossbar by the goalkeeper! He eventually had surgery on the knee, but returned in time to score the Cup Final winner. The war denied him a chance to set more official records, but he scored six goals in five internationals, and netted eight times at Wembley during the war, with two hat-tricks for the Royal Air Force, and a brace against Charlton, in the Football League South Cup Final of 1943. He moved into management with Reading in 1947, and consistently high finishes in the Third Division South earned him a move to Chelsea, where he made one last outstanding achievement. In 1955, Chelsea were unexpectedly crowned League Champions for the first time in their history, and Ted Drake became the first man to win the title as both player and boss.

Sunderland captain Raich Carter receives the F.A. Cup from the Queen after his team's 3-1 victory over Preston North End

Preston North End v Sunderland

F.A. Cup Final, Saturday 1st May 1937

Six-Times Champs Finally Lift Cup

Preview

Preston had won the F.A. Cup once before, way back in 1889, beating Wolverhampton Wanderers 3-0 in the final at Kennington Oval, London. They also won the first League Championship that year. Since then, their achievements had been modest. Their last final had been in 1922, when they lost 1-0 to Huddersfield Town, at Stamford Bridge, London. Sunderland's only final had been in 1913, when they lost 1-0 to Aston Villa, at Crystal Palace, London. Sunderland won the League Championship that year, and just failed to emulate Preston's earlier 'double'.

Preston finished 14th in the First Division, their lowest position since promotion in 1934. Sunderland, as defending League Champions, finished 8th.

Semi–Finals, Saturday 10th April 1937

Millwall	1:2	**Sunderland**	*(Leeds Road, Huddersfield)*
Mangnall		Gurney	
		Gallacher	
Preston North End	4:1	**West Bromwich A.**	*(Highbury, London)*
F. O'Donnell 2		Robbins	
Dougal 2			

The Match

In the 38th minute, Frank O'Donnell took a pass from Dougal, and blasted it past Mapson to give Preston the lead, making him only the second player to score in all six rounds of the Cup. Sunderland came back strongly in the second half. From a 52nd minute corner by Burbanks, Carter headed it on, for Bobby Gurney to score. With 17 minutes left, it was Gurney's header which laid on Sunderland's second, for Raich Carter to shoot past Burns, and five minutes later Eddie Burbanks scored the third, when he ran on to meet Gallacher's pass with a powerful drive.

Preston North End	1:3	**Sunderland**
F. O'Donnell		Gurney, Carter
		Burbanks

Preston North End:
Burns, Gallimore, A. Beattie, Shankly, Tremelling (Captain), Milne, Dougal, Beresford, F. O'Donnell, Fagan, H. O'Donnell
Tommy Muirhead (Manager)

Sunderland:
Mapson, Gorman, Hall, Thomson, Johnson, McNab, Duns, Carter (Captain), Gurney, Gallacher, Burbanks
Johnny Cochrane (Manager)

Referee: R. Rudd (Kenton)
Attendance: 93,495

Preston returned the following year, to win the F.A. Cup, and Sunderland nearly joined them in a repeat Final, but lost in the Semi-Finals. They were not to win it again for 36 years.

Wembley Greats

Raich Carter *Sunderland, Derby County and England*

At the age of 23, Sunderland's captain, Horatio Carter was the inspiration behind a team which shook off mid-table mediocrity in order to bring major trophies back to Roker Park. His incisive passing and positional play enabled him to control games from midfield, and his cool confidence also made him a regular goalscorer. He won his first England cap, aged 20, against Scotland at Wembley, but only made five more international appearances before the war. Nevertheless, he had already become a Sunderland legend after their League Championship win, followed by the long awaited Cup triumph, in which Carter was such a pivotal figure. His pass led to the equaliser in the semi-final, as did his header in the final, before Carter himself put the Roker men into a lead they would add to before the end. During the war, he finally established himself in the England side, and netted seven times in five Wembley visits. He had also formed a deadly partnership with the Irish international Peter Doherty whilst guesting for Derby County, and they both joined the Rams when the hostilities ended. This was the swansong of Carter's career. In 1946, Derby won the first post-war F.A. Cup at Wembley, with Doherty scoring and Carter picking up his second winner's medal. He also joined Tommy Lawton and Stan Matthews as the only players to win England caps both before and after the war. Two more honours followed. As player-manager of Hull City, Carter took them to the Third Division North Championship in 1949, and four years later, at 39, he was in the Cork Athletic side which won the F.A. of Ireland Cup.

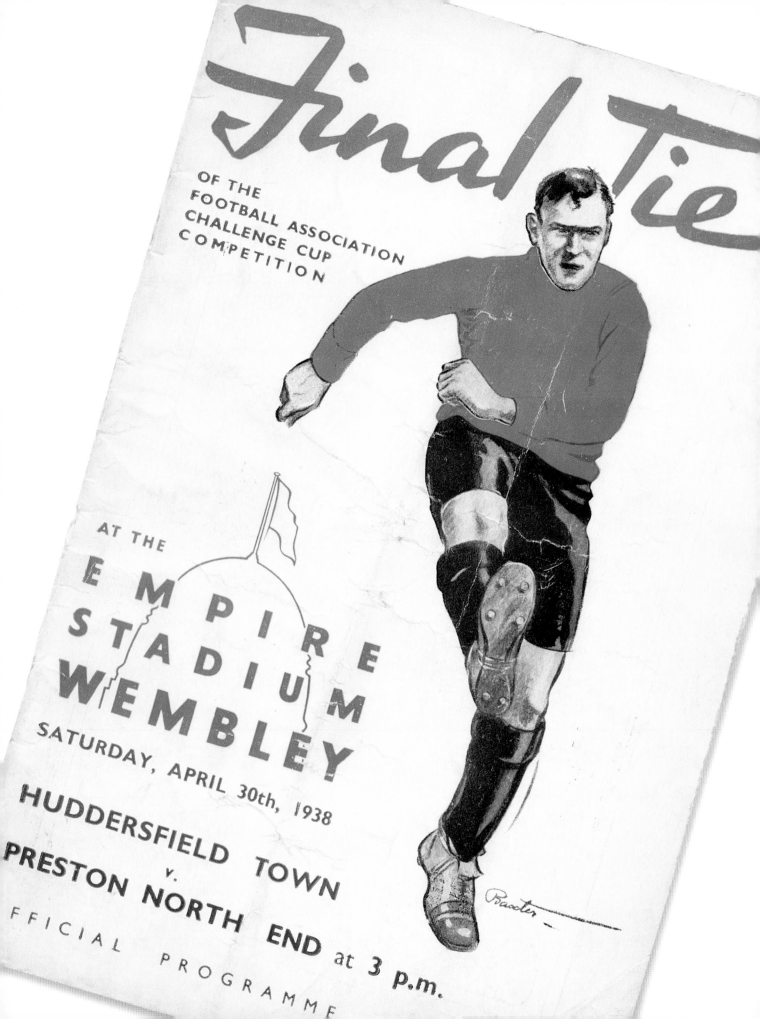

Final Tie

OF THE FOOTBALL ASSOCIATION CHALLENGE CUP COMPETITION

AT THE

EMPIRE STADIUM WEMBLEY

SATURDAY, APRIL 30th, 1938

HUDDERSFIELD TOWN
v.
PRESTON NORTH END at 3 p.m.

OFFICIAL PROGRAMME

Huddersfield Town v Preston North End

F.A. Cup Final, Saturday 30th April 1938

Last Gasp Penalty Drama

Preview

Huddersfield were back for their third Wembley Final, having lost in 1928 and 1930. They had beaten the holders in the semi-finals, and were looking for their second F.A. Cup win, against the team they had beaten in the 1922 final. On that occasion, they had won with a penalty, given for a foul, apparently committed outside the area. Preston were in their second successive final, having lost the previous year, and had knocked out Arsenal, who were heading for their fifth League Championship in eight years, in the last 16.

Huddersfield were now a shadow of their former glories, and were battling against relegation to the Second Division. Preston were having their best season since promotion in 1934, and still had an outside chance of winning the League Championship, for the first time since 1890.

Semi–Finals, Saturday 26th March 1938

Aston Villa Shell	*1:2*	**Preston North End** O'Donnell, Mutch	*(Bramall Lane, Sheffield)*
Huddersfield Town Beasley, Wienand McFadyen	*3:1*	**Sunderland** Burbanks	*(Ewood Park, Blackburn)*

The Match

A boring match, which seemed to be heading for a replay when, in the very last minute of extra time, George Mutch was tripped on the edge of the Huddersfield penalty area by Young. Mutch took the penalty himself, and beat Hesford, as the ball went in off the bar. As in 1922, the penalty award was disputed, but this time the luck had gone Preston's way.

Huddersfield Town	*0:1*	**Preston North End**
	(AET)	Mutch (penalty)

Huddersfield:
Hesford, Craig, Mountford, Willingham, Young (Captain), Boot, Hulme, Isaac, McFadyen, Barclay, Beasley
Clern Stephenson (Manager)

Preston North End:
Holdcroft, Gallimore, A. Beattie, Shankly, T. Smith (Captain), Batey, Watmough, Mutch, Maxwell, R. Beattie, O'Donnell,
Jim Taylor (Chairman)

Referee: A. Jewell (London)
Attendance: 93,497

In an extraordinary end to the league season the following week, Huddersfield escaped relegation by defeating the defending League Champions, Manchester City, and relegating them in the process. The victory lifted them to 15th, in an incredibly tight finish. They reached the F.A. Cup semi-finals again the following year, but their decline continued after the war, and they were eventually relegated in 1952. They did not appear at Wembley again, until the Autoglass Trophy Final of 1994. Preston's Championship hopes faded just two days later, but they returned to Wembley for the Football League War Cup Final, in 1941. They held on to their First Division status until 1949, returning two years later as Second Division Champions, and they were back at Wembley in 1954.

Portsmouth captain Jimmy Guthrie holds the
F.A. Cup aloft as he is chaired by his teammates

Portsmouth v Wolverhampton Wanderers

F.A. Cup Final, Saturday 29th April 1939

Young Wolves Tamed

Preview

Portsmouth were hoping to take the F.A. Cup to the South Coast for the first time. They had lost their two previous finals, in 1929 and 1934. In the quarter-finals, they had knocked out the holders, Preston North End, and in the semi-finals they had eliminated the previous year's other finalists. Wolves had won the Cup twice before, the last occasion being in 1908, when they beat Newcastle United 3-1, in the final, at Crystal Palace, London. Their last of five previous finals had been in 1921, when they went down 1-0 to Tottenham Hotspur at Stamford Bridge, London.

Portsmouth were a struggling First Division side, and finished 17th. Wolves finished as League runners-up, for the second year in succession to Everton, despite beating them 7-0 in a league game, and knocking them out of the Cup in the quarter-finals.

Semi–Finals, Saturday 25th March 1939

Grimsby Town	0:5	**Wolves**	*(Old Trafford, Manchester)*
		Westcott 4	
		Galley (penalty)	
Huddersfield Town	1:2	**Portsmouth**	*(Highbury, London)*
	Barclay	Barlow, Anderson	

The Match

The burden of being overwhelming favourites made Wolves look nervous, and Portsmouth took the lead on the half-hour. Bert Barlow, signed from Wolves only two months earlier, took a pass from Anderson and struck a great shot past Scott into the corner. Jock Anderson scored the second, just before half-time. Collecting Worrall's high cross, and going past Cullis, he shot. Scott got his hands to the ball but only succeeded in pushing it into the top of the net. Any hopes Wolves had of recovering were dashed only a minute into the second half. Scott initially saved from Barlow, but the ball squirmed out of his grasp. He managed to recover, and stopped it, with one hand, on the line. Unfortunately for him, Cliff Parker ran in and knocked the ball in before the keeper could get his other hand on it. Wolves struck back when Westcott put Dickie Dorsett through to score, but they were never really in the game, and Parker completed the scoring with his second, a header from another Worrall cross.

Portsmouth	4:1	**Wolves**	
Barlow		Dorsett	
Anderson, Parker 2			

Portsmouth:
Walker, Morgan, Rochford, Guthrie (Captain), Rowe, Wharton, Worrall, McAlinden, Anderson, Barlow, Parker
Jack Tinn (Manager)

Wolverhampton Wanderers:
Scott, Morris, Taylor, Galley, Cullis (Captain), Gardiner, Burton, McIntosh, Westcott, Dorsett, Maguire
Frank Buckley (Manager)

Referee: T. Thompson (Leamington-on-Tyne)
Attendance: 99,370

Britain was at war five months later, and Portsmouth could not defend the F.A. Cup for seven years, but they reached the London War Cup Final, at Wembley, in 1942, and won two successive League Championships at the end of the 1940s. Wolves were to win the F.A. Cup ten years later.

Wembley's Other Finals

Although the F.A. Cup was suspended in 1939, Wembley still managed to host a big final, in the spring of each war year. West Ham United won the first Football League War Cup Final, in June 1940, beating Blackburn Rovers by a single goal. The following year saw Tom Finney's Wembley debut, in a 1-1 draw with Arsenal. His Preston side won the replay at Blackburn. The hardships of the conflict forced the Football League to regionalise more, and Wembley consequently staged the London War Cup Final, in 1942, with Brentford beating Portsmouth. Three Football League South Cup Finals followed, notable for Reg Lewis grabbing four goals for Arsenal in 1943 against Charlton Athletic, who returned the following year to win the trophy against Chelsea, who also returned, to beat Millwall in 1945, despite a line-up which included eight guest players.

Fans during the 1949 F.A. Cup Final between
Leicester City and Wolverhampton Wanderers

Chapter Three

The Second World War was a long and painful conflict, with millions of people losing their lives. In 1941, the Japanese bombed the Hawaiian port of Pearl Harbor, and the United States joined the allied forces. Eventually, Hitler was defeated after British and American troops drove the Nazis back across Europe, and the Japanese surrendered after atomic bombs were dropped on their cities. The peace process began and new countries were created as agreements were drawn up to lessen the chances of future hostility.

Official football competitions began again in 1945 with the F.A. Cup (the Football League restarted the following year), and record attendances, that still stand, showed how much they had been missed. Unfortunately, it was overcrowding which led to 33 people being crushed to death at an F.A. Cup sixth round tie, at Bolton in 1946. Arsenal were still successful after the war, but they were no longer the dominant force, and England rejoined FIFA only to be humiliated by the U.S.A. at the World Cup in Brazil.

Wembley's role during the war had given the nation a huge boost, by staging prestige internationals and wartime Cup Finals, as well as providing a home to refugees and raising money for charities. Arthur Elvin was knighted in 1946, and the stadium went from strength to strength. It became world famous two years later when hosting the main events in the Olympic Games, again providing a welcome relief from the hardships of the time. The decade ended with more and more events raising their profile simply by being staged at Wembley.

Giantkillers and Bridesmaids

The late 1940s were significant for First Division clubs falling to non-league sides in successive years in the F.A. Cup. In January 1948, Colchester United of the Southern League defeated First Division Huddersfield Town by a solitary goal. Perhaps more significantly, they then beat Second Division Bradford Park Avenue 3-2 in the fourth round, to become the first non-league side to reach the last 16 of the F.A. Cup, since the expansion of the Football League in 1920. It took a Blackpool side heading for the Final to beat them in the fifth round, by 5-0, but Colchester's achievement was not forgotten, and when, two years later, the Football League was expanded again, Colchester were admitted to the Third Division South. They would hit the Cup headlines again in 1971, with an even bigger scalp.

Unfortunately for Colchester, their heroics were soon overshadowed by the remarkable achievement of Yeovil Town, just 12 months later. They had already beaten Second Division Bury 3-1 in the third round, and were then drawn at home to Sunderland, who were to finish 8th in the First Division. Yeovil were lying sixth from bottom in the Southern League, their goalkeeper, Dyke, was making only his second appearance, and their winger, Hargreaves, pulled a muscle in the first ten minutes, making him a passenger for the rest of the game. It seemed only a matter of time before the class of Sunderland engulfed them. Yet it was Yeovil who took the lead, through player-manager Alec Stock, their only man with Football League experience. Sunderland drew level, when ex-England international Jack Robinson netted from close range. The game went into extra time, a temporary post-war ruling, designed to keep replays to a minimum. Unbelievably Yeovil regained their lead, when a misplaced overhead kick, by England's Len Shackleton, unwittingly put his defence under pressure, from where Eric Bryant hit the winner. This small Somerset club had reached the fifth round, where normality returned. The holders, Manchester United, beat them 8-0 in front of 81,565. Yeovil have continued to defeat Football League opposition regularly over the years, but this was undoubtedly the highlight, and no other non-league team has beaten top flight opposition so late in the competition since. Alec Stock went on to win Wembley's first Football League Cup Final as manager of Third Division Queens Park Rangers in 1967, and took Second Division Fulham to their first F.A. Cup Final in 1975.

Chelsea fans could have been forgiven for thinking that they were on their way to Wembley, as half-time approached, with their side two goals to the good, both Roy Bentley efforts, in the 1950 semi-final against Arsenal. Freddie Cox then stunned them by scoring direct from a corner, with the last kick of the half. Chelsea held out until five minutes from the end, when Leslie Compton headed in the equaliser, from his brother's corner. Arsenal won the replay, with a single goal in extra time. Two years later, Chelsea reached the semi-finals again, only to meet Arsenal again. Once more, it ended in a draw, before the Gunners won comfortably in the replay. Chelsea would have to wait another 15 years to reach the final.

Len Shackleton

Len Shackleton was undoubtedly a ball-playing genius, and his sense of humour earned him the nickname 'Clown Prince'. Having been released by Arsenal as a youngster, he spent the war years with his local club Bradford Park Avenue, and was selected for England in a Victory International, against Scotland at Hampden Park. It was not a happy debut, as Shackleton gave away the free kick from which the Scots scored the only goal, but after making his Football League bow aged 24, the following season he was soon snapped up by Newcastle United. In his first game, he made all the headlines, scoring six times in a 13-0 demolition of Newport County, the biggest ever victory in the top two divisions. Newcastle were in the Second Division at the time, and reached the F.A. Cup semi-finals, although they were well beaten by Charlton Athletic on the day. They were promoted the following season, although Shackleton had been sold to their closest rivals, Sunderland, for a record fee of £20,050, before the end of it. His crowd-pulling skills earned him an England recall, but sometimes he was a bit too casual, as in 1948, when his attempts at ball juggling at Yeovil were wholly inappropriate and led to his team's embarrassing downfall. He did, however, score with a superb chip against the World Champions, West Germany, at Wembley in 1954. Strangely enough, he never played for England again, but this was typical of the selection process at the time, with their belief that he was 'too clever'. Sunderland were inconsistent in the 1950s, but reached the F.A. Cup semi-finals in successive years. Despite Shackleton's efforts, they lost them both, and he ended his career without a major honour to his name.

THE FOOTBALL ASSOCIATION

Final Tie

at the

EMPIRE STADIUM
WEMBLEY
Managing Director A. J. ELVIN

CHARLTON ATHLETIC
v
DERBY COUNTY

SATURDAY APRIL 27TH 1946

Charlton Athletic v Derby County

F.A. Cup Final, Saturday 27th April 1946

Rams In Charge

Preview

Charlton had never been beyond the last 16 of the competition before, but had won the Football League South Cup, in 1944, at Wembley. Derby were appearing in their fourth final, but had never won the Cup. Their last final had resulted in a miserable 6-0 defeat, by Bury, at Crystal Palace, London, in 1903.

The Football League was not to resume again, until the following season. Both teams had had top First Division sides at the beginning of the war in 1939.

Semi–Finals, Saturday 23rd March 1946

Birmingham Mulraney	1:1	**Derby County** Carter	**(Hillsborough, Sheffield)**	
Bolton Wanderers	0:2	**Charlton Athletic** Duffy 2	**(Villa Park, Birmingham)**	
Birmingham	0:4 (AET)	**Derby County** Doherty 2 Stamps 2	**(Maine Road, Manchester)**	Replay (Wednesday 27th March 1946)

The Match

The first post-war F.A. Cup Final was dominated by Derby, yet they needed extra time to win it. They almost won it with five minutes remaining when Bert Turner diverted Duncan's shot into his own net. Turner made amends within a minute. His free kick from outside the area was deflected by Doherty past Woodley for the equaliser. Having had victory snatched from their grasp, Derby responded with three more goals in extra time. Within a minute of the restart, Peter Doherty slotted home the rebound, after Bartram had parried a Stamps shot. Doherty then laid on the third, for Jack Stamps to finish. In the first minute of the second extra period, Doherty again supplied Stamps with a pass, and the striker netted his second.

Charlton Athletic H. Turner	1:4 (AET)	**Derby County** H. Turner o.g. Doherty, Stamps 2

Charlton Athletic:
Bartram, Phipps, Shreeve, H. Turner, Oakes, Johnson, Fell, Brown, A. Turner, Welsh (Captain), Duffy
Jimmy Seed (Manager)

Derby County:
Woodley, Nicholas (Captain), Howe, Bullions, Leuty, Musson, Harrison, Carter, Stamps, Doherty, Duncan
Stuart McMillan (Manager)

Referee:	E. Smith (Whitehaven)
Attendance:	98,000

Charlton were back the following year, to win the Cup, but Derby's glory days were not to return for a quarter of a century. They came back to Wembley, to win the F.A. Charity Shield in 1975.

Burnley v Charlton Athletic

F.A. Cup Final, Saturday 26th April 1947

Duffy Ends Stalemate

Preview

Burnley had won the F.A. Cup once, in 1914, beating Liverpool 1-0 in the final at Crystal Palace, London. This time, in the semi-finals, they had beaten the same opponents, who were about to win the first post-war League Championship. Charlton had never won the Cup, but had lost the previous year's final, in extra time, and were appearing in their fourth Wembley final in five years.

The first post-war league season had been extended, due to a very severe winter. Burnley were well placed in the Second Division promotion race, whilst Charlton had struggled, after three consecutive top four placings before the war.

Semi–Finals, Saturday 29th March 1947

Burnley	*0:0*	*Liverpool*	*(Ewood Park, Blackburn)*	
	(AET)			
Charlton Athletic	*4:0*	*Newcastle United*	*(Elland Road, Leeds)*	
Dawson				
Welsh 2, Hurst				
Burnley	*1:0*	*Liverpool*	*(Maine Road, Manchester)*	*Replay (Saturday 12th April 1947)*
Harrison				

The Match

Neither side played to its potential in a defensive game. An early Potts effort struck the crossbar, but Burnley were too often hesitant and they were made to pay, with only six minutes of extra time remaining, Charlton had looked the more dangerous, but did not threaten enough until finally, Robinson's cross was headed on by Welsh to Chris Duffy, who fired it past Strong and gave them a long awaited triumph.

Burnley	*0:1*	*Charlton Athletic*	
	(AET)	*Duffy*	

Burnley:
Strong, Woodruff, Mather, Attwell, Brown (Captain), Bray, Chew, Morris, Harrison, Potts, Kippax
Cliff Britton (Manager)

Charlton Athletic:
Bartram, Croker, Shreeve, Johnson, Phipps, Whittaker, Hurst, Dawson, Robinson, Welsh (Captain), Duffy
Jimmy Seed (Manager)

Referee: *J. Wiltshire (Sherborne)*
Attendance: *99,000*

Burnley finished as Second Division runners-up to Manchester City, and spent the next 24 seasons in the First Division. They returned to Wembley in 1962. Charlton finished 19th in the First Division. Their run of Wembley appearances came to an end with this success, and it was to be another 40 years before they were back, for the Full Members Cup Final.

Blackpool v Manchester United

F.A. Cup Final, Saturday 24th April 1948

United Win Attacking Feast

Preview

Blackpool had never been past the quarter-finals before, and had never won a major trophy. United had won the Cup in 1909, beating Bristol City 1-0 in the final at Crystal Palace, London. They had knocked out the holders, Charlton Athletic, in the last 16.

Blackpool finished 9th, in the First Division, while United finished runners-up for the second year in succession, to Arsenal.

Semi–Finals, Saturday 13th March 1948

Blackpool	*3:1*	***Tottenham Hotspur***	*(Villa Park, Birmingham)*
Mortensen 3	*(AET)*	*Duquemin*	
Derby County	*1:3*	***Manchester United***	*(Hillsborough, Sheffield)*
Steel		*Pearson 3*	

The Match

An exciting game, which came to life in the 14th minute. Mortensen bore down on goal, and would have had only the goalkeeper to beat, but was tripped from behind by Chilton. Although he fell into the area, the foul actually took place outside, but the referee gave a penalty, and Eddie Shimwell hit a poor strike, which went straight underneath the diving Crompton. In the 28th minute, United were level. From a Delaney lob into the goalmouth, a misunderstanding between Hayward and Robinson left Jack Rowley with a simple task to equalise. Five minutes later, Matthews played a free kick across to Kelly, who knocked it through for Stan Mortensen to turn and fire past Crompton, to put Blackpool back in front. He had thus scored in every round. United began to take control in the second half, but there were only 21 minutes left when they finally equalised. A quickly taken free kick from Morris was centred to Rowley, whose diving header produced his second for United. With ten minutes remaining, Crompton saved a Mortensen shot, and United went straight upfield, to score again. An Anderson pass found Stan Pearson, whose shot went in off the post. In the 83rd minute, a shot from John Anderson was deflected off the head of Kelly, into the far corner, to complete the scoring.

Blackpool	*2:4*	***Manchester United***
Shimwell (penalty)		*Rowley 2*
Mortensen		*Pearson, Anderson*

Blackpool:
J. Robinson, Shimwell, Crosland, Johnston (Captain), Hayward, Kelly, Matthews, Munro, Mortensen, Dick, Rickett
Joe Smith (Manager)

Manchester United:
Crompton, Carey (Captain), Aston Snr, Anderson, Chilton, Cockburn, Delaney, Morris, Rowley, S. Pearson, Mitten
Matt Busby (Manager)

Referee:	*C. Barrick (Northampton)*
Attendance:	*99,000*

Blackpool reached the final again, in 1951. United were League runners-up yet again the following year, whilst also reaching the F.A. Cup semi-finals again. They rebuilt, and then proceeded to dominate the mid-1950s, returning to Wembley in 1957.

Wembley's Other Finals

Wembley Stadium hosted the final four games in the 1948 Olympic football tournament. After Yugoslavia had beaten Matt Busby's Great Britain side, in the semi-final, they were defeated 3-1 by Sweden in the final. Boris Stankovic had the distinction of being the first man to be sent off, at Wembley, when he gave the Swedes a penalty with a reckless foul. It was to be another 18 years, before the second dismissal (Argentina's Rattin). Sweden were coached by Englishman, George Raynor, who took them to the World Cup Final, in 1958, with two of their Olympic gold medallists, Gunnar Gren and Nils Liedholm, in the side.

In the 25 years after the war, Matt Busby awoke the sleeping giant that was Manchester United, and built four great sides, culminating in their 1968 European Cup triumph at Wembley. As a player, he won the F.A. Cup with Manchester City, and was capped by Scotland, appearing three times at Wembley during the war, but it is as a manager that Busby will be long remembered. The army gave him an opportunity to manage some great players, and he recognised the value of treating players individually. In 1945 he was offered the job at a bomb-ravaged Old Trafford. By 1948, they had won the F.A. Cup, and Busby was also selected to coach the Great Britain Olympic squad, which reached the Semi-Finals at Wembley. After four runners-up finishes in five years, United finally won the League Championship in 1952. This was where Busby's managerial skills came to the fore, as he ruthlessly broke up the title winning squad, and introduced several untried youngsters.

The next few years were fruitless in terms of honours, but by 1956 these 'Busby Babes', as they were termed, had blossomed into a great side, which romped home with the league title, by 11 points. They retained it the following year, and also reached the European Cup Semi-finals, thanks to Busby's insistence that United defied the Football League's recommendation not to enter the competition. He now had a side that could conceivably have conquered Europe, and in January 1958 he was also appointed as Scotland's manager, with the forthcoming World Cup in Sweden to look forward to.

Then tragedy struck, on the afternoon of February 6th, when United's plane crashed at Munich, when returning from a successful European Cup quarter-final in Belgrade. Twenty-four people were killed, including eight of United's squad. Busby was in hospital for months, with a punctured lung. He recovered in time to attend United's second successive F.A. Cup Final, at Wembley, but now had to rebuild quickly. After two games in charge of Scotland, he resigned in order to dedicate himself to United, and his new team won the Cup in 1963, whilst struggling in the league, but two years later, they were League Champions again, and ready for a renewed assault on Europe.

The victory over Benfica at Wembley in 1968, was an emotional moment for Busby, and was a fitting tribute to the players who died at Munich. Busby was deservedly knighted, and with little more to prove, he relinquished control of the team the following year. Manchester United owed him so much, and as the team fell into decline, his successors found it increasingly difficult to deliver trophies, until the 1990s, when Alex Ferguson took United back to the heights they last enjoyed over 25 years earlier.

Leicester v Wolverhampton Wanderers

F.A. Cup Final, Saturday 30th April 1949

Wolves In Command

Preview

Leicester were appearing in their first final, Wolves in their seventh, but they had not won the Cup since 1908, and were hoping to avenge their humiliating defeat of ten years previously. Both sides had come through tough semi-finals, Leicester avenging their previous semi-final defeat, of 1934, by beating the soon-to-be League Champions, and Wolves beating the holders.

Leicester were, ironically, having one of the worst league seasons in their history, and were in danger of being relegated to the Third Division South for the first time. Wolves finished 6th in the First Division which, by contrast, was their lowest position since 1936. Leicester had not beaten them for 24 years.

Semi–Finals, Saturday 26th March 1949

Leicester City *Revie 2* *Chisholm*	3:1	**Portsmouth** *Harris*	*(Highbury, London)*
Manchester United *Mitten*	1:1 *(AET)*	**Wolverhampton W** *Smyth*	*(Hillsborough, Sheffield)*
Manchester United	0:1	**Wolverhampton W** *Smyth*	*(Goodison Park, Liverpool)* *Replay (Saturday 2nd April 1949)*

The Match

Wolves took an expected lead, in the 12th minute. A cross from Hancocks was headed in by Jesse Pye, as he ran in between two defenders. Three minutes before half-time they scored again. Leicester failed to clear a corner properly, a Dunn shot hit a team-mate, and it fell for Pye to score his second. Leicester came out for the second half with plenty of fighting spirit and scored within two minutes. Williams saved at the feet of Chisholm, but the ball ran loose, for Mal Griffiths to score. Springthorpe tried to head it off the line, but only succeeded in heading it against the post, and in. Sammy Smyth clinched Wolves' third F.A. Cup win, however when he scored after a brilliant solo run through the Leicester defence in the 68th minute.

Leicester City *Griffiths*	1:3	**Wolverhampton W** *Pye 2, Smyth*

Leicester City:
Bradley, Jelly, Scott, W. Harrison, Plummer (Captain), J. King, Griffiths, Lee, J. Harrison, Chisholm, Adam
John Duncan (Manager)

Wolverhampton Wanderers:
Williams, Pritchard, Springthorpe, Crook, Shorthouse, Wright (Captain), Hancocks, Smyth, Pye, Dunn, Mullen
Stan Cullis (Manager)

Referee:	*R. Mortimer (Huddersfield)*
Attendance:	*99,500*

Leicester played three games in four days, the following week, and escaped relegation by a point. They won the Second Division Championship twice in the 1950s, and were back at Wembley in 1961. Wolves were League runners-up, to Portsmouth, the following year, and only lost the title on goal average. But by the time they won the F.A. Cup for the fourth time in 1960 they had won the League Championship three times.

Wright

Billy Wright was the first player to win 100 caps for England, and was a model of consistency from the end of the war, right through to his retirement in 1959.

He was captain of England at the age of 24, and led the team out on 90 occasions. His hard tackling and great positional sense made him the rock at the heart of Wolves' defence throughout their most successful period. In 1949, he captained them to the F.A. Cup, and they were League Champions three times in the 1950s, with Wright picking up the Footballer of the Year award in 1952. The respect he earned as a model professional allowed him to retire at the very top, aged 35, having just played his 105th international, and with Wolves having just won their second successive title.

Three years later, he was manager of Arsenal, who were going through a transitional period. Perhaps he was too popular to be ruthless, and after four seasons of mid-table mediocrity, he was sacked. Turning his back on the game to which he had been such a loyal servant, he became a successful and well-respected television broadcaster.

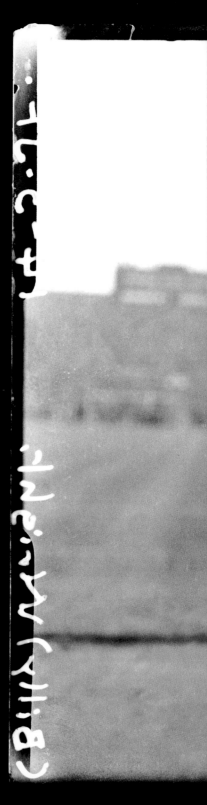

LIVERPOOL
FOOTBALL CLUB

Shareholders'
Celebration
Dinner

Monday, Sept. 25th, 1950

Liverpool F.C.
WEMBLEY 1950
Players' Souvenir Brochure

2/-

Arsenal v Liverpool

F.A. Cup Final, Saturday 29th April 1950

Reg At The Ready

Preview

Arsenal had last won the Cup in 1936, but had won the Football League South Cup at Wembley in 1943. Liverpool were appearing in only their second final, having lost 1-0 to Burnley at Crystal Palace, London, in 1914, and were appearing at Wembley for the first time.

Arsenal finished 6th in the First Division, after winning the League Championship in 1948. Liverpool finished a point behind them, in 8th position. They had won the first post-war League Championship, in 1947.

Semi–Final, Saturday 18th March 1950

Arsenal Cox L. Compton	**2:2**	**Chelsea** Bentley 2	(White Hart Lane, London)

Semi–Final, Saturday 25th March 1950

Everton	**0:2**	**Liverpool** Paisley Liddell	(Maine Road, Manchester)
Arsenal Cox	**1:0** **(AET)**	**Chelsea**	(White Hart Lane, London) Replay (Wednesday 22nd March 1950)

The Match

After 17 minutes, a pass from Logie enabled Reg Lewis, who had scored four on his previous Wembley appearance in 1943, to stride through a lethargic Liverpool defence, to slot the ball past Sidlow for the opening goal. In the 63rd minute, Arsenal scored again, when Cox flicked the ball through for Lewis to get his second. Arsenal won the Cup for the third time, after being two goals down in the Semi-Final.

Arsenal Lewis 2	**2:0**	**Liverpool**

Arsenal:
Swindin, Scott, Barnes, Forbes, L. Compton, Mercer (Captain), Cox, Logie, Goring, R. Lewis, D. Compton
Tom Whittaker (Manager)

Liverpool:
Sidlow, Lambert, Spicer, Taylor (Captain), L. Hughes, W. Jones, Payne, Baron, Stubbins, Fagan, Liddell
George Kay (Manager)

Referee: H. Pearce (Luton)
Attendance: 100,000

Arsenal reached the final again, two years later. Within four years, Liverpool were in the Second Division. After six years of near misses they won promotion, and won the F.A. Cup for the first time in 1965.

Genial Joe Mercer was an inspirational figure, who never gave less than 100%, and confounded his critics on more than one occasion by bouncing back to the very top. His early pre-war years were spent with Everton, and he won his first England cap in the same season that his club won the League Championship. At 25 years old, when war broke out, like so many other players, he could have been forgiven for thinking that the best years of his career were over. The conflict did, however, give him the opportunity to establish himself in a very successful England side, and he even scored at Wembley, against Scotland in 1944.

Later that year he was appointed captain, and with the war coming to an end, there was hope that Mercer could still resume a club career, in his thirties. A knee injury sustained in a Victory International, against Scotland at Hampden Park, almost ruined his plans though, and he needed an operation, in which his cartilage was removed. Everton no longer wanted him, and sold him to Arsenal, who were hoping his experience might halt the post-war slide they seemed set to embark on. Mercer could no longer cover the whole pitch tirelessly, and was switched to a more defensive role. The move revitalised both him and the club. The following season, he captained them to the League Championship, and in 1950 the F.A. Cup, alongside a well-deserved Footballer of the Year award. Another Cup Final followed, and then incredibly, at the age of 39, he led them to yet another league title. Who knows how long he would have continued, if he hadn't broken his leg in 1954, in an accidental collision with a team-mate, which abruptly ended his career.

Mercer was an obvious managerial candidate, but after cutting his teeth at Sheffield United, with relegation in his first season, and then moving on to Aston Villa, who were also relegated within six months, he began to make his mark in his new career. Villa won the Second Division Championship in 1960, and also reached the F.A. Cup semi-finals for the second year in succession. They quickly established themselves again in the top flight, and won the first Football League Cup a year later, reaching the final again in 1963.

Mercer's health then began to deteriorate, and he suffered a stroke. Once again, he was assumed to have retired, but the best was yet to come. Following a year's rest, he was appointed as manager of Second Division Manchester City. He appointed the flamboyant Malcolm Allison as coach to share the workload, and so began one of the most successful managerial partnerships in history, as together they built an attractive, attacking team. They were promoted as Champions in their first season, and two years later they won the League Championship, after pipping their fiercest rivals, Manchester United, who were about to win the European Cup. For a time, City couldn't stop winning trophies, and their fans couldn't believe it, as the title was followed by the F.A. Cup in 1969, and then both the League Cup (Mercer's second) and their first European trophy, the Cup-Winners Cup, in 1970.

After a season when injuries curtailed their ambitions, Mercer moved upstairs, leaving team selection to Allison, before finally retiring. Even then, there was one last job for Joe Mercer. When Sir Alf Ramsey was sacked as England manager in 1974, 59-year-old Joe was drafted in to lead his country to the summer break, before Don Revie's appointment the following season. England had failed to qualify for the World Cup, and Mercer restored the squad's confidence, with his humour and genial manner, and typically, had them playing attractive, attacking football. He died in 1990, and the game mourned the passing of a very popular man.

*Aston Villa's Peter McParland (right) charges Manchester United goalkeeper Ray Wood (left),
causing him to be carried off injured with a fractured cheekbone in the 1957 F.A. Cup Final*

Chapter Four

Queen Elizabeth II succeeded her late father in 1952, as the United Kingdom looked forward to a prosperous and peaceful future. This was threatened when the Egyptian President seized the Suez Canal in 1956, but after a brief bombing raid on the area, and intervention by the United Nations, the crisis was averted. At home, rock 'n' roll music began to influence the youth on both sides of the Atlantic, and more leisure activities became available to the masses.

The 1950s saw the emergence of the 'Busby Babes' at Manchester United, and the lure of European competition, but the Munich air disaster not only cut down this great team in its prime, but also ripped the heart out of the England side. Hungary and Brazil took international football to new levels, whilst the domestic game was still thriving, despite falling attendances. Stan Matthews demonstrated an amazing level of fitness, by playing for England at the age of 42.

Wembley staged some dramatic and memorable matches, which have passed into folklore. 1953, in particular, saw the 'Matthews Final', as Blackpool staged a remarkable recovery to win the F.A. Cup, and England were torn apart by a rampant Hungarian team, destroying once and for all the myth that England were the masters. The stadium looked to the future, and staged its first floodlit games in 1955, although the death of Sir Arthur Elvin, two years later, brought sadness at the passing of the man who had done so much to turn Wembley into a 'Venue of Legends'.

Giantkillers and Bridesmaids

There were no First Division clubs succumbing to non-league sides in this decade, although Worcester City beat a Liverpool side going through a rare spell in the Second Division, in 1959. The 1950s saw three instances of Third Division teams reaching the semi-finals.

In 1954, Port Vale became the first club from the Third Division North to reach the semi-finals. In the Fourth Round, they had won at First Division Cardiff, and then knocked out the holders, Blackpool, in the last 16, a 2-0 victory bringing Stan Matthews and company back down to earth after their heroics of the previous year. Vale's secret was a watertight defence in an era of attacking football. They won the Third Division North Championship by 11 points, conceding only 21 goals, a record for 46 games and 43 less than the next best defence. In the Semi-Final, they met West Bromwich Albion, top of the First Division, and with designs on the elusive 'double'. Incredibly, Vale held a half-time lead, after absorbing the advances of their lofty neighbours, and breaking away to score through Albert Leake. Just when it seemed they could pull off the impossible, West Brom hit back from a deflected cross by Dudley. Ronnie Allen, who had signed from Port Vale, scored the winner from a penalty 20 minutes from time. The following year, York City emulated Port Vale's achievement, and even took the eventual winners, Newcastle United, to a Semi-Final replay, after Alf Bottom's equaliser made the Magpies realise they would have to battle to get through. York also knocked out Blackpool, this time on their own ground, and Tottenham were beaten 3-1 in the fifth round. Newcastle eventually ended their run, with a 2-0 victory in the replay.

In 1958, the two Third Divisions were restructured. They were no longer regionalised, and became the Third and Fourth Divisions. Norwich City found themselves in the Third Division, and the next season saw them reaching the semi-finals after a glorious run. Their first big scalp was Manchester United, less than a year after Munich, but still good enough to finish runners-up to Wolves. In the fifth round, Norwich almost won at Tottenham, but still managed to finish them off in the replay before fanatical home support. After holding, and then beating, Second Division Sheffield United in the Sixth Round, Norwich fans dared to think that Luton Town, from the bottom half of the First Division and also appearing in their first semi-final, would become their next victims. Their support was certainly louder, but Luton struck first, only for Bobby Brennan, an ex-Luton player, to take it to a replay, where Billy Bingham's second half strike finally ended the brave resistance of the Canaries.

For Tottenham Hotspur, the 1960s were to bring huge successes, especially in the F.A. Cup, but in the preceding years reaching the Final had proved frustratingly elusive for them. Villa Park was certainly not their favourite ground in this period, as they were to lose three close Semi-Finals at the home of Aston Villa. In 1948, Len Duquemin took advantage of hesitancy in the Blackpool defence, to put Second Division Spurs ahead, with only a quarter of the game remaining. It was the first goal conceded by Blackpool in the whole competition, and left them staring defeat in the face. Four minutes remained when Stan Mortensen rescued the Seasiders, and he added two more in extra time to end the contest. Five years later, the same teams met again, at the same stage, at the same venue, Spurs having been promoted, and won the Championship in 1951, at the end of the very next season. This eagerly awaited match came alight after seven minutes, when Perry gave Blackpool the lead. It was a lead they held until five minutes into the second half, when Duquemin popped up again to level matters. Spurs were now in command, and peppered the Blackpool goal with a wave of attacks. If they had broken through, the 'Matthews Final' would never have happened. In the very last minute, a poorly hit back pass by Alf Ramsey, destined to become England's greatest manager, let in Jackie Mudie to send Blackpool to Wembley and leave Spurs in despair once again. They returned to Villa Park in 1956, where a second half header from Bobby Johnstone gave Manchester City a 1-0 win, against Tottenham.

Johnny Haynes

Johnny Haynes, one of the greatest ever passers of the ball, spent his entire career with Fulham, and it was this loyalty to the west London side that ended any hopes he might have had of winning medals. His first claim to fame was at the age of 15, when he starred for England in Wembley's first schoolboy international, scoring twice in an 8-2 win against Scotland. Just over two weeks before his 20th birthday, he scored on his full England debut, against Northern Ireland. Fulham were in the Second Division until 1959, but Haynes was still a regular for England, such was the value of his central midfield role. In 1960 he became captain, and led his country in the 1962 World Cup in Chile. His international career ended abruptly two months later, with a car accident, but he stayed at Fulham, becoming the first player to earn £100 a week, after the maximum wage was abolished, and set a club record of 594 league appearances. In the F.A. Cup, Fulham made two semi-final appearances during the period, led in both, but lost, in replays, to Manchester United and Burnley respectively. Each of Haynes' last two seasons with Fulham ended in relegation, as they dropped into the Third Division, although he did win a title with Durban City in South Africa, a small consolation for one of England's greatest players.

Blackpool v Newcastle United

F.A. Cup Final, Saturday 28th April 1951

'Wor Jackie'

Preview

Blackpool were back for a further attempt at winning a major trophy, for the first time after their gallant failure in 1948. Newcastle were back at Wembley for the first time since their 1932 triumph.

Blackpool finished 3rd in the First Division, their highest ever league position, while Newcastle finished a point and a place behind, in only their third season back in the First Division. Blackpool had failed to beat Newcastle throughout that period.

Semi–Finals, Saturday 10th March 1951

Birmingham	0:0	**Blackpool**	*(Maine Road, Manchester)*
Newcastle United	0:0	**Wolves**	*(Hillsborough, Sheffield)*
Birmingham Smith	1:2	**Blackpool** Mortensen, Perry	*(Goodison Park, Liverpool)* Replay (Wednesday 14th March 1951)
Newcastle United Milburn, Mitchell	2:1	**Wolves** Walker	*(Leeds Road, Huddersfield)* Replay (Wednesday 14th March 1951)

The Match

Newcastle broke the deadlock after five minutes of the second half. Robledo's pass beat the offside trap, and Jackie Milburn was totally free to run on and slot the ball past Farm. He scored again five minutes later. Taylor cleverly back-heeled the ball, and Milburn sent a 25-yard bullet flying past the helpless Farm.

Blackpool	0:2	**Newcastle United** Milburn 2

Blackpool:
Farm, Shimwell, Garrett, Johnston (Captain), Hayward, Kelly, Matthews, Mudie, Mortensen, Slater, Perry
Joe Smith (Manager)

Newcastle United:
Fairbrother, Cowell, Corbett, Harvey (Captain), Brennan, Crowe, Walker, Taylor, Milburn, G. Robledo, Mitchell
Stan Seymour (Manager)

Referee:	*W. Ling (Cambridge)*
Attendance:	*100,000*

The 1960 Footballer of the Year, Bill Slater, made his first appearance, at Wembley.
Newcastle retained the F.A. Cup the following year, whilst Blackpool won it the year after.

Wembley's Other Finals

The F.A. Amateur Cup had its heyday during the 1950s. With rising attendances, the final was switched to Wembley in 1949, and two years later a full house of 100,000 saw Pegasus beat Bishop Auckland 2-1 to win the trophy for the first time. Pegasus had only been in existence for three years, and was comprised of players from Oxford and Cambridge Universities, who were older because the war had delayed their educations. They did not play in a league, and did not have a home ground, yet they rose to become Britain's finest amateur side, after beating the seven times winners Bishop Auckland. Pegasus won the cup again in 1953, but the Bishops went on to record a hat-trick of triumphs, before the amateur game went into decline, to be replaced by semi-professionals. The Amateur Cup was last played in 1974, with only 30,500 at the last final.

Milburn

Jackie Milburn was a legend on Tyneside, and was affectionately known as 'Wor Jackie'. Born in Ashington, to a family which also spawned the Charlton brothers, Milburn joined Newcastle during the war, making his league debut in 1946. He was soon playing at centre forward, and gaining a reputation as a fast player with awesome shooting power. The Magpies were promoted to the First Division in 1948, and Milburn broke into the England team.

His highlight came in 1951, when he scored in every round, with both goals in the Final, as Newcastle won the first of three F.A. Cups in five years. Milburn also scored, in 1955, at the time the quickest final goal ever (45 seconds). Although he'd scored ten goals in 12 internationals, he was to lose his England place to Nat Lofthouse the same year.

He only won one more cap, but he'd already fulfilled his dreams, and gave his beloved Newcastle 15 years service, before moving to Linfield, where he ended his career, averaging 50 goals a season, in the Irish League. They won the title in 1959, and gave Milburn a fourth cup winners' medal, by lifting the Irish Cup in 1960.

METROPOLITAN BOROUGH OF ISLINGTON

CIVIC RECEPTION

in honour of the

ARSENAL FOOTBALL CLUB

May 8th, 1952

Islington Town Hall

DAY & MASON

F.A. CUP ANNUAL

1952

35 PICTURES
including
THIS YEAR'S
FINALISTS
All Cup Results
PRICE 1/-

F. A. CUP
EMPIRE STADIUM
Newcastle United

MENU

Tomato Juice Cocktail
Cream St. Germain

Scotch Salmon Mayonnaise Sauce
New Potatoes

Asparagus Melted Butter

Ice Biscuit Magpie

Cheese and Biscuits
Watercress

Coffee

2nd May, 1952

Newcastle United Football Club

CELEBRATION DINNER

to commemorate the winning of the

F.A. CHALLENGE CUP 1952

at the

COUNTY HOTEL
NEWCASTLE UPON TYNE

MONDAY, 19th JANUARY, 1953

Chairman:
Dr. R. RUTHERFORD, M.C.

Newcastle United Football Club

DINNER

To Celebrate the

F.A. CHALLENGE CUP FINAL TIE 1952

at the

SAVOY HOTEL
W.C.2

SATURDAY, 3rd MAY, 1952

Chairman
Dr. R. RUTHERFORD M.C.

Arsenal v Newcastle United

F.A. Cup Final, Saturday 3rd May 1952

Brave Gunners Beaten By George

Preview

Arsenal were attempting to regain the F.A. Cup for the second time in three years, after winning it in 1950. They had beaten the same semi-final opponents as in 1950, at the same venue, and again, after a replay. It was also an opportunity to avenge their controversial defeat by Newcastle in the 1932 final. Newcastle were the holders, and aiming to become the first team to retain the F.A. Cup since Blackburn Rovers (who they had beaten in the semi-final) in 1891. They had already reached a record ninth final.

Arsenal finished 3rd in the First Division, their highest position since winning the League Championship in 1948. Newcastle finished 8th, their lowest position since promotion, also in 1948.

Semi–Final, Saturday 5th April 1952

Arsenal	**1:1**	**Chelsea**	**(White Hart Lane, London)**
Cox		Gray	

Semi–Final, Saturday 29th March 1952

Blackburn Rovers	**0:0**	**Newcastle United**	**(Hillsborough, Sheffield)**
Arsenal	**3:0**	**Chelsea**	**(White Hart Lane, London)** **Replay (Monday 7th April 1952)**
Cox 2, Lishman			
Blackburn Rovers	**1:2**	**Newcastle United**	**(Elland Road, Leeds)** **Replay (Wednesday 2nd April 1952)**
Quigley		G. Robledo	
		Mitchell (penalty)	

The Match

The turning point came after 19 minutes. Arsenal had begun well, when Barnes was injured in a tackle with Milburn. He lasted until the 35th minute, but then went off. Arsenal's ten men fought magnificently against the marauding Newcastle forwards. With five minutes left, Newcastle finally broke through. Mitchell's cross was headed in, off the post, by the Chilean George Robledo. Newcastle had won the Cup, but Arsenal had won overwhelming sympathy from the crowd.

Arsenal	**0:1**	**Newcastle United**	
		G. Robledo	

Arsenal:
Swindin, Barnes, L. Smith, Forbes, Daniel, Mercer (Captain), Cox, Logie, Holton, Lishman, Roper
Tom Whittaker (Manager)

Newcastle United:
Simpson, Cowell, McMichael, Harvey (Captain), Brennan, E. Robledo, Walker, Foulkes, Milburn, G. Robledo, Mitchell
Stan Seymour (Manager)

Referee: A. Ellis (Halifax)
Attendance: 100,000

Arsenal received adequate compensation, in winning their second post-war League Championship the following year. But there then followed a long period of mediocrity, before another great Arsenal side emerged in the late 1960s. Newcastle secured a third F.A. Cup win in five years in 1955.

Blackpool v Bolton Wanderers
F.A. Cup Final, Saturday 2nd May 1953

The Two Stans

Preview

Blackpool had yet to win a major trophy, and were appearing in their second final in three years. Much media attention was centred on Stan Matthews who, at 38, was surely going to get no more chances to win an F.A. Cup winners medal. He had played in Blackpool's two previous Finals in 1948 and 1951. In the quarter-finals, they had knocked out the previous year's finalists, and shortly to be League Champions, Arsenal, on their own ground. Bolton were appearing in their first final, since their third F.A. Cup win of the 1920s.
Blackpool finished 7th in the First Division, whilst Bolton finished a disappointing 14th.

Semi–Final, Saturday 21st March 1953

Blackpool Perry, Mudle	2:1	**Tottenham Hotspur** Duquemin	(Villa Park, Birmingham)
Bolton Wanderers Holden, Moir Lofthouse 2	4:3	**Everton** Parker 2 Farrell	(Maine Road, Manchester)

The Match

Bolton took a second minute lead when Nat Lofthouse took a pass from Holden, and shot from 25 yards. Farm allowed it to slip through his hands into the net. Bolton began to take control, but suffered a blow when Bell went down injured, with a pulled muscle. His team-mates reshuffled, and Bell was moved out to the wing. With ten minutes to go before half-time, Blackpool drew level. Hassall, who had dropped back to defence, deflected a Stan Mortensen shot past Hanson. But within five minutes, Bolton had regained the lead; when Langton centred, Farm hesitated, and Willie Moir nodded in Bolton's second. Blackpool's world fell apart, in the tenth minute of the second half. The injured Eric Bell, of all people, rose to head in Holden's centre. Blackpool were 3-1 down, and no team had ever lost a two-goal lead in an F.A. Cup Final. At this point, Matthews began to take charge of proceedings. Faced with an almost certain third runners-up medal, he began to pressurize the Bolton full back, Banks, and started to put dangerous crosses into the penalty area. From one of these, in the 68th minute, Hanson fumbled, and Mortensen ran in to scramble the ball over the line. Bolton, who had almost lost a four-goal lead in the semi-final, now looked tired and vulnerable. Banks went down with cramp, but was still left to mark Matthews. In the very last minute, from a free kick, on the edge of the penalty area, Mortensen found a gap at the end of the Bolton defensive wall, and blasted in the equaliser to complete his hat-trick. And then, in injury time, Matthews beat Banks, and crossed for Bill Perry to knock in Blackpool's winner, and complete the most remarkable recovery in the history of the F.A. Cup.

Blackpool Mortensen 3 Perry	4:3	**Bolton Wanderers** Lofthouse Moir, Bell

Blackpool:
Farm, Shimwell, Garrett, Fenton, Johnston (Captain), C. Robinson, Matthews, Taylor, Mortensen, Mudie, Perry
Joe Smith (Manager)

Bolton Wanderers:
Hanson, Ball, R. Banks, Wheeler, Barrass, Bell, Holden, Moir (Captain), Lofthouse, Hassall, Langton
Bill Ridding (Manager)

Referee: M. Griffiths (Newport)
Attendance: 100,000

The 'Matthews Final', as it became known, still remains the only occasion when Blackpool won a major trophy. They did not appear at Wembley again until 1991, when they reached the Fourth Division Promotion Play-Off Final. Bolton came back to win the F.A. Cup in 1958.

Matthews

Stanley Matthews is, to many people, the greatest player of all time. He was certainly unique, one of the fastest and most skilful wingers of them all, with an armoury of tricks that very few defenders could handle. His unswerving dedication to his fitness and training meant that he could still play First Division football at the age of 50, and he won his last England cap at 42.

Those feats alone would have ensured his place in the record books, but Matthews was an entertainer, who filled stadiums all over the world throughout his incredibly long career. The defining moment was undoubtedly the 1953 Cup Final, when he finally got his hands on a treasured winner's medal. The circumstances of Blackpool's remarkable recovery that day have gone down in folklore, and only Stan Matthews could possibly have taken the glory away from the only man ever to score a hat-trick in an F.A. Cup Final at Wembley, Stan Mortensen.

Matthews always showed great humility, though, in claiming that it should have been called the 'Mortensen Final', but there could be no denying that Matthews' quest for the Cup had become a national obsession, and the manner of his eventual success could not have been scripted any better. His career began with Stoke City; his debut was in 1932. The following year they were Second Division Champions, and Matthews played for England at 19. He never really established himself on the international stage until the war years, and when Blackpool signed him, in 1947, aged 32, it appeared to be for the final years of his career. The move rejuvenated him, and the players around him thrived on his wing play. They reached Wembley the following season, and Matthews was the first winner of the Footballer of the Year award.

By 1953, he was enjoying his football so much that retirement never crossed his mind. He was back in the England team, and astonishing everyone by maintaining his speed and trickery into his forties.

In 1956, aged 41, he tormented the Brazilians in a 4-2 victory at Wembley, and became the first recipient of the European Footballer of the Year award. In a 23-year international career, he made 54 appearances (plus 29 in wartime), scoring 11 goals (plus two in wartime), although he failed to score in any of his 27 Wembley appearances.

In 1961, he returned to Stoke, and once again helped them to win promotion, scoring the goal which clinched the Second Division title. It was the last of his career. He was 48, and for the second time, was voted Footballer of the Year. Finally, aged 50, he made his very last appearance, the oldest player ever in the top division, and was knighted in the same year. It is difficult to believe that any modern player could be more dedicated to the game of football.

Stan Mortensen
Blackpool & England

Stan Mortensen recovered from crashing a Wellington bomber during the war to become one of England's finest forwards of the next decade. His Wembley debut in 1943, was as a substitute for Wales against England, even though he was an England reserve, such were the limitations of the Welsh squad. England won, 8-3, but Mortensen made it into his home country's team the following year, and netted twice against Scotland in 1945, as well as getting a brace for the Combined Services in a charity match at Wembley.

When he finally got his chance to play league football, after the war, he didn't disappoint. Combining well with Stan Matthews, he was a regular goalscorer for Blackpool and England. He scored in every round of the 1948 F.A. Cup, including the final, but like Matthews, it was 1953, when he was finally rewarded. His firepower rescued the Seasiders and he remained the only player to score a hat-trick in a Wembley F.A. Cup Final.

For England, he scored 23 goals in 25 appearances (or 26 in 28, if you include wartime internationals), a phenomenal record. Six months after winning the Cup, he won his last England cap, scoring in the 6-3 defeat by Hungary. Always a cheerful personality, he stayed in football as his age caught up with him. After spells with Hull and Southport, he played non-league for Bath and Lancaster beyond his 40th birthday and then returned to Blackpool as manager in 1967, just before their inevitable relegation.

He almost took them back to the First Division in his first full season, but despite winning their last seven games, they failed to catch Queen's Park Rangers, who were promoted on goal average. They didn't quite sustain a challenge the next season, but Mortensen was surprisingly sacked, and never returned to the game. Blackpool were promoted the following year, with many of his signings still in the squad.

Preston North End v West Brom
F.A. Cup Final, Saturday 1st May 1954

Baggies' Dramatic Finale

Preview
Preston had won the F.A. Cup at Wembley in 1938, and had appeared in the Football League War Cup Final in 1941. West Brom had won the Cup in 1931, and had lost the 1935 final. The two teams had met in the 1888 final, with West Brom winning 2-1 at Kennington Oval, London.

Preston finished 11th in the First Division, their lowest position since promotion in 1951. The previous season, they had been League runners-up to Arsenal, on goal average. West Brom finished as League runners-up, to Wolverhampton Wanderers. This was their highest league position since 1925.

Semi–Final, Saturday 27th March 1954

Port Vale Leake	1:2	**West Bromwich Albion** Dudley Allen (penalty)	(Villa Park, Birmingham)
Preston North End Wayman Baxter	2:0	**Sheffield Wednesday**	(Maine Road, Manchester)

The Match
In the 21st minute, Lee blocked a Cunningham clearance, chased after it, and crossed it. Ronnie Allen was in the centre to beat Thompson, and give West Brom the lead. Within a minute, Preston were level, Angus Morrison heading in from a Docherty cross. Early in the second half, Preston took the lead. Finney and Foster combined to send Charlie Wayman through. The prolific striker rounded Sanders to join the elite few to have scored in every round. In the 63rd minute, Docherty brought down Barlow, and Allen equalised from the penalty. Two minutes remained, when West Brom snatched the winner. Frank Griffin took a pass from Ryan, cut inside and slammed it past the keeper.

Preston North End Morrison Wayman	2:3	**West Bromwich Albion** Allen 2 (1 penalty) Griffin

Preston North End:
Thompson, Cunningham, Walton, Docherty, Marston, Forbes, Finney (Captain), Foster, Wayman, Baxter, Morrison
Scot Symon (Manager)

West Bromwich Albion:
Sanders, Kennedy, Millard (Captain), Dudley, Dugdale, Barlow, Griffin, Ryan, Allen, Nicholls, Lee
Vic Buckingham (Manager)

Referee:	A. Luty (Leeds)
Attendance:	100,000

Preston dropped out of the First Division, in 1961, but reached the F.A. Cup Final again in 1964. It was another 14 years before West Brom won the Cup again, but there was to be a Football League Cup Final appearance at Wembley the year before (1967).

Tom Finney spent his entire career with Preston North End, but had to wait until he was 24 before making his league debut, because of the war. He had, however, been a member of Preston's Football League War Cup Winners in 1941, when he was only 19, making his first appearance at Wembley in a 1-1 draw with Arsenal, before North End won the replay at Blackburn.

His first of 76 England caps came in 1946, when he replaced the injured Stanley Matthews. Finney had similar qualities to Sir Stanley, beginning as a right winger, but whilst Matthews was a specialist in that position, Finney was more versatile, ending up on the left wing, to accommodate them both in the England team, and later as centre forward.

He scored 30 goals in his England career. There was huge debate at the time as to which was the better player, but they were both world class. Preston were relegated in 1949, but returned as Second Division Champions two years later, and then came agonisingly close to winning a major trophy. Firstly, they lost out to Arsenal in the title race, on goal average, in 1953, and then were narrowly beaten in the following year's F.A. Cup Final, when Finney was unable to inspire his team, as he had on so many previous occasions.

They were League runners-up again in 1958, but Finney retired at the end of the decade, without that elusive winners medal, although he was a veteran of three World Cups. He reappeared, aged 41, in 1963, to captain Irish League Champions, Distillery to a 3-3 draw with mighty Benfica in the European Cup, and was knighted in 1997, to commemorate a lifetime of dedication to his beloved Preston, and the game of football.

Newcastle United's Ron Batty (number 3) heads the ball away from Manchester City's Don Revie (right)

Manchester City v Newcastle United
F.A. Cup Final, Saturday 7th May 1955

'Wor Jackie' Quick Off The Mark

Preview

City had last won the F.A. Cup in 1934. Newcastle had won the Cup four times at Wembley from four visits, and were aiming to regain it for the third time in five years, having won it in 1951 and 1952. Victory would give them a record-equalling sixth Cup win.

City finished 7th in the First Division, their highest position since promotion in 1951. Newcastle finished a place below them.

Semi–Final, Saturday 26th March 1955

Manchester City Clarke	**1:0**	**Sunderland**	*(Villa Park, Birmingham)*
Newcastle United Keeble	**1:1**	**York City** Bottom	*(Hillsborough, Sheffield)*
Newcastle United White, Keeble	**2:0**	**York City**	*(Roker Park, Sunderland)* *Replay (Wednesday 30th March 1955)*

The Match

Newcastle took the lead in the very first minute. White's corner was headed in by Jackie Milburn. In the 18th minute, City lost Meadows with a knee injury, and so, as in 1952, Newcastle had ten men to beat. However, City managed to equalise on the stroke of half-time. Hayes crossed, and Bobby Johnstone beat Simpson with a diving header. Newcastle made their experience and numerical advantage tell in the second half. After 53 minutes, Bobby Mitchell took a pass from White, and then showed great skill in beating Spurdle, taking the ball to the goal line, and then shooting from an acute angle. Trautmann, who was expecting a cross, could not get down quick enough, and the ball went under him. Seven minutes later, Mitchell laid on the third, for George Hannah (who joined City three years later) to shoot past Trautmann.

Manchester City Johnstone	**1:3**	**Newcastle United** Milburn, Mitchell Hannah

Manchester City:
Trautmann, Meadows, Little, K. Barnes, Ewing, Paul (Captain), Spurdle, Hayes, Revie, Johnstone, Fagan
Les McDowall (Manager)

Newcastle United:
Simpson, Cowell, R. Batty, Scoular Captain), Stokoe, Casey, White, Milburn, Keeble, Hannah, Mitchell
Duggie Livingstone (Manager)

Referee: *R. Leafe (Nottingham))*
Attendance: *100,000*

Bert Trautmann, the German goalkeeper, appeared at Wembley for the first time. Twelve months later, he returned as Footballer of the Year. City returned to win the Cup the following year. Newcastle went into decline, and were relegated six years later. It was 1974 when they reached their next Final.

FOOTBALL ASSOCIATI
CUP FINAL

WEST
STANDING
ENCLOSURE

ENTER AT TURNSTILES
(see plan & conditions on back.)

ENTRANCE

G
68

EMPIRE STADIUM, WEMBLEY
The Football Association
Cup Competition

FINAL TIE

SATURDAY, MAY 5th, 1956
KICK-OFF 3 p.m.

Price 3/6
(Including Tax)

Chairman & Managing Director
Wembley Stadium Limited

THIS PORTION TO BE RETAINED
This Ticket is issued on the condition that
it is not re-sold for more than its face value

EMPIRE STADIU
WEMBLEY

BIRMINGHAM CITY
v
MANCHESTER CITY
SATURDAY MAY 5 195

DAILY EXPRESS
COMMUNITY SINGING

Birmingham City v Manchester City

F.A. Cup Final, Saturday 5th May 1956

Brave Bert And The 'Revie Plan'

Preview

Birmingham's only previous final had been in 1931, and they had still to win a major trophy. City had won the Cup for the second time in 1934, and were eager to make amends for their defeat in the previous year's final.

Birmingham finished 6th in the First Division, their highest ever league position. They had only been promoted, on goal average, the previous season but were Second Division Champions, as three clubs finished on the same number of points. City finished 4th a point ahead of Birmingham, their highest position since they won the League Championship in 1937.

Semi–Final, Saturday 17th March 1956

Birmingham City *Kinsey, Astall* *Brown*	*3:0*	**Sunderland**	**(Hillsborough, Sheffield)**
Manchester City *Johnstone*	*1:0*	**Tottenham Hotspur**	**(Villa Park, Birmingham)**

The Match

Manchester City took only three minutes to score. Clarke's cross found Revie, who back-heeled the ball into the path of Joe Hayes, who had time to steady himself before driving it past Merrick. Birmingham recovered from this early blow by equalising in the 15th minute. A Newman throw-in was flicked on by Brown, for Noel Kinsey to blast a shot in off the post. The game then developed into an exciting, end-to-end attacking game. It was Man City who scored next, 20 minutes into the second half. Barnes put Jack Dyson through to score. Within five minutes, they had effectively clinched it. A long kick from Trautmann was touched on by Dyson, and Bobby Johnstone ran on to score the third. With 15 minutes left, Trautmann made a brave save at the feet of Murphy, sustaining an injury which was diagnosed four days later as a broken neck. The heroic German goalkeeper, and Footballer of the Year, completed the match however, without being beaten again.

Birmingham City *Kinsey*	*1:3*	**Manchester City** *Hayes, Dyson* *Johnstone*

Birmingham City:
Merrick, Hall, Green, Newman, Smith, Boyd (Captain), Astall, Kinsey, Brown, Murphy, Govan
Arthur Turner (Manager)

Manchester City:
Trautmann, Leivers, Little, K. Barnes, Ewing, Paul (Captain), Johnstone, Hayes, Revie, Dyson, Clarke
Les McDowall (Manager)

Referee: A. Bond (Fulham)
Attendance: 100,000

Birmingham reached the semi-finals again, the following year, but did not return to Wembley until 1991, when they won the Leyland DAF Trophy. They have yet to better their league position of 1956. Manchester City were relegated seven years later but returned, with a trophy-winning side, in the late 1960s. In 1969, they won the F.A. Cup for the fourth time.

Don Revie made his mark in football as both a player and a manager. His first club was Second Division Leicester City, and he scored twice as they surprisingly defeated Portsmouth to reach Wembley in 1949. Pompey were to finish the season as the League Champions. Revie suffered from severe nosebleeds in the weeks leading up to the final. This was eventually diagnosed as a burst blood vessel, and he was too ill to play at Wembley.

The following season, he moved on to Hull City, and spent only two seasons with the Tigers, before Manchester City took him into the First Division, where Revie was used as a deep-lying centre forward in a similar role to the great Hungarian striker, Hidegkuti. This became known as the 'Revie Plan'. In 1954, he was capped by England, and ended the season with two Wembley appearances, scoring in a 7-2 victory against Scotland, but ending up on the losing side as City lost the F.A. Cup Final to Newcastle. Revie's consolation was the Footballer of the Year award.

City returned the following year and won the F.A. Cup, but then transferred him to Sunderland the following season. In 1958, they suffered their first ever relegation. Leeds United then signed him, only to drop back down to the Second Division themselves in 1960. This was to be a blessing in disguise, however. With Leeds struggling again the following season, Revie took over as player-manager. They only finished 17th, but he retired from playing, and set about a transformation which would result in Leeds becoming one of the most feared clubs in Europe.

In 1964, they were Second Division Champions, and Revie's managerial style and attention to detail, with his tactical and psychological dossiers, were beginning to bear fruit. His team was a highly professional unit, building a team spirit which was to keep them challenging for major honours for the next ten years. They were at Wembley the following year, narrowly losing to Liverpool in extra time, and also ran Manchester United close in the Championship race, missing out only on goal average. In 1968, they beat Arsenal at Wembley, to win the Football League Cup, and also lifted the European Fairs Cup.

The League Championship followed the next season, with the loss of only two games. Leeds were uncompromising, but also highly skilled, and the same core team stayed fiercely loyal. Their weakness seemed to be that they often fell at the final hurdle, finishing runners-up more times than winners, but they were not the most popular side, and that in itself often inspired their opponents. Nevertheless, they won the Fairs Cup again, the F.A. Cup in 1972, and the League Championship again, after a record breaking start to the season, of 29 games unbeaten.

In 1974, Revie became manager of England, but his style didn't quite work without the daily contact of his players, and with the team heading for World Cup elimination, in 1977 he defected to the United Arab Emirates. The manner of his departure was slammed by the Football Association, and he never managed again in England.

Aston Villa's captain Johnny Dixon
holds aloft the F.A. Cup after their
2-1 win over Manchester United

Aston Villa v Manchester United

F.A. Cup Final, Saturday 4th May 1957

McParland The Villain

Preview

For the second year in succession, a team from Birmingham met a team from Manchester in the final. Villa's last final had been in 1924, and they were attempting to win the Cup for a record seventh time. United had won the Cup in 1948 for the second time, and had defeated the previous year's finalists in the semi-final.

Villa finished 10th in the First Division. United had convincingly retained the League Championship for a second year, with a team which was now on the verge of the first League and F.A. Cup 'double' since 1897, when it was achieved by Villa. They had also become the first English club to enter the European Cup, reaching the semi-finals, where they lost to the holders, and eventual winners, Real Madrid.

Semi–Final, Saturday 23rd March 1957

Aston Villa McParland 2	2:2	**West Bromwich Albion** Whitehouse 2	**(Molineux, Wolverhampton)**	
Birmingham City	0:2	**Manchester United** Berry Charlton	**(Hillsborough, Sheffield)**	
Aston Villa Myerscough	1:0	**West Bromwich Albion**	**(St. Andrews, Birmingham)**	**Replay (Thursday 28th March 1957)**

The Match

The whole pattern of the game was decided in the sixth minute, when United's keeper, Wood was stretchered off, with a fractured cheekbone, after being charged by McParland. United reorganised, and Blanchflower went in goal. They had such a powerful side, though, that they still gave their opponents a hard game. Wood came back in the 33rd minute, but played out on the wing. In the 68th minute, Villa at last broke through. Peter McParland, who was being booed almost every time he touched the ball, headed in from Dixon's cross. Five minutes later, McParland added a second, with the rebound from a Dixon shot which had hit the bar. United pulled one back, with seven minutes remaining, when Tommy Taylor headed in an Edwards corner. Wood went back into goal, so United could reorganise, back to full strength, in a desperate attempt to snatch an equaliser. But it was not to be, and Villa secured the most unpopular of their record seven F.A. Cup wins.

Aston Villa McParland 2	2:1	**Manchester United** Taylor

Aston Villa:
Sims, Lynn, Aldis, Crowther, Dugdale, Saward, Smith, Sewell, Myerscough, Dixon (Captain), McParland
Eric Houghton (Manager)

Manchester United:
Wood, Foulkes, Byrne (Captain), Colman, Blanchflower, Edwards, Berry, Whelan, T. Taylor, Charlton, Pegg
Matt Busby (Manager)

Referee: F. Coultas (Hull)
Attendance: 100,000

Villa were relegated two years later, but returned as Second Division Champions the following year. They were, however, a Third Division club, when they next appeared at Wembley, in the 1971 Football League Cup Final. For United, everything paled into insignificance when six of the Wembley team were killed in the Munich air disaster, the following February (Byrne, Colman, Edwards, Whelan, Taylor and Pegg), whilst the careers of Blanchflower and Berry were ended. Incredibly, on a wave of emotion, United reached the F.A. Cup Final again.

THE FOOTBALL ASSOCIATION CHALLENGE CUP COMPETITION

FINAL TIE

BOLTON WANDERERS
v
MANCHESTER UNITED

SATURDAY, MAY 3rd, 1958   KICK-OFF 3 pm

EMPIRE ST

WEM

OFFICIAL PROGRAMME

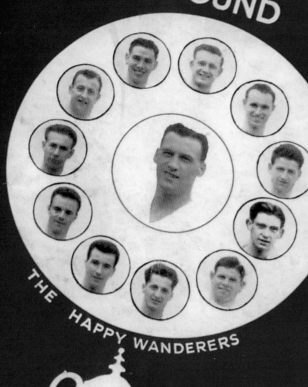

WEMBL
BOUND

THE HAPPY WANDERERS

F.A CUP FINAL SOUVENIR

1958

2/6

Bolton Wanderers v Manchester United

F.A. Cup Final, Saturday 3rd May 1958

Lofthouse Ends United Revival

Preview

It had been 29 years since Bolton had last won the F.A. Cup, and in 1953 they had had victory snatched from their grasp. In the quarter-finals they had knocked out Wolverhampton Wanderers, who were heading for the League Championship. United had picked themselves up from their unfortunate defeat in the previous year's final, and had been contenders in all three competitions until the Munich air disaster, which decimated the team. But with overwhelming national sympathy, they had reached the final again, with a rebuilt side.
Bolton finished a disappointing 15th in the First Division.
United had started out chasing a hat-trick of League Championship, but finished 9th, their lowest position for 20 years. The pre-Munich side had also taken them to the European Cup semi-finals, for the second year in succession. Milan proved too much for them, after the tragedy.

Semi–Final, Saturday 22nd March 1958

Blackburn Rovers Dobing	1:2	**Bolton Wanderers** Gubbins 2	(Maine Road, Manchester)	
Fulham Stevens, Hill	2:2	**Manchester United** Charlton 2	(Villa Park, Birmingham)	
Fulham Stevens, Chamberlain Dwight	3:5	**Manchester United** Dawson 3 Brennan, Charlton	(Highbury, London)	Replay (Wednesday 26th March 1958)

The Match

Bolton took the lead in the third minute. A cross from Edwards fell to Nat Lofthouse, who beat Gregg from close range. The result was never really in doubt, and Bolton scored a second, in the 55th minute, in controversial circumstances. A shot from Stevens was saved by Gregg, but as he collected the ball, Lofthouse came charging in, and forced the ball over the line for his second. Gregg was knocked out in the collision, but the goal stood.

Bolton Wanderers Lofthouse 2	2:0	**Manchester United**

Bolton Wanderers:
Hopkinson, Hartle, T. Banks, Hennin, Higgins, Edwards, Birch, Stevens, Lofthouse (Captain), Parry, Holden
Bill Ridding (Manager)

Manchester United:
Gregg, Foulkes (Captain), Greaves, Goodwin, Cope, Crowther, Dawson, E. Taylor, Charlton, Viollet, Webster
Matt Busby (Manager)

Referee:	*J. Sherlock (Sheffield)*
Attendance:	*100,000*

Bolton were relegated six years later, and did not return to Wembley until 1986, for the Freight Rover Trophy Final. Then, in 1995, they reached the final of another major trophy, the Coca-Cola Cup.
United were rebuilt once more by Matt Busby, after amazingly finishing League runners-up the following year. They won the F.A Cup five years after Munich, as yet another great side emerged.

Nat Lofthouse, like Tom Finney, devoted his entire footballing career to his home town team, and even equalled Tom Finney's England scoring record, of 30 goals. Lofthouse only played in 33 internationals, but was one of his country's most formidable centre forwards. Bolton Wanderers signed him during the war, and when he finally made his league debut, at the age of 21, he had honed his natural goalscoring ability, and become a powerful two-footed striker.

In the air, he was fearless, and more than a match for any defender. In 1950, he marked his international debut with two goals against Yugoslavia, but it was in Austria, two years later, when Lofthouse really came of age. He scored twice in a 3-2 win, including the winner when he ran from the halfway line, and tucked the ball home a split second before the advancing keeper knocked him unconscious. After being carried off, he returned for the last five minutes, and even hit the bar, with a late strike.

From then on, he was known as the 'Lion of Vienna'. The following season, he scored in every round of the F.A. Cup, and was voted Footballer of the Year. His goal in the Wembley final gave Bolton the best possible start, but his England team-mates, Matthews and Mortensen, denied him a winners medal in the most dramatic climax. Five years later, Lofthouse captained his club to a deserved F.A. Cup triumph, despite, once again, public support being against them.

Lofthouse scored both goals, the second of which would not be allowed in today's game, and sadly, he is remembered for that goal more than any other. After a brief international

recall, he retired from the game, but came back to Bolton in 1968, succeeding his long-time manager, Bill Ridding. He stayed two years, but the club had fallen on hard times in the Second Division. Another spell followed in 1971, as they were about to drop into the Third Division for the first time, but Lofthouse wisely moved upstairs, eventually becoming club president, and remaining a hero in Bolton, for evermore.

LONDON SOCIETY OF ASSOCIATION REF
President: VICTOR RAE, Esq., A.C.C.S.
Hon. General Secretary
Chairman: A. E. D. SMITH,
Capt. G. H. ALLEN.   37, Castelnau
                                                  Barnes

ANNUAL
"EVE-OF-THE-FINAL RA
To Honour the Officials of the F.A. Challenge Cup
AT
THE ASSEMBLY ROOM, ST. PANCRAS TOWN
LONDON, N.W.1
FRIDAY, 1st MAY, 1959
KICK-OFF 7.30 p.m.

t, Officers, Council and members of the Lon
sociation Referees extend a hearty welcome to
rs, and trust they will retain happy and last
memories of the occasion

Social Committee:—
G. BERRY   W. POTTS (Hon. Secretary)
                  F. L. WARBURTON   F. J. WINT

LUTON TOWN F.C.
WEMBLEY 1959

Luton Town v Nottingham Forest

F.A. Cup Final, Saturday 2nd May 1959

Broken Leg Fails To Stop Forest

Preview

Neither side had appeared at Wembley before. Luton had never won a major trophy, and had not been beyond the F.A. Cup quarter-finals before. Forest had won the Cup way back in 1898, when they beat Derby County 3-1 in the final at Crystal Palace, London. In the quarter-finals, they had knocked out the holders, Bolton Wanderers. Luton finished a lowly 17th in only their fourth season in the First Division. Forest finished 13th in their second season after promotion.

Semi–Final, Saturday 14th March 1959

Aston Villa	0:1	**Nottingham Forest**	(Hillsborough, Sheffield)
		Quigley	
Luton Town	1:1	**Norwich City**	(White Hart Lane, London)
Brown		Brennan	
Luton Town	1:0	**Norwich City**	(St. Andrews, Birmingham) Replay (Wednesday 18th March 1959)
Bingham			

The Match

Forest took the lead, in the tenth minute. A low cross from Imlach was blasted into the corner by Roy Dwight. Four minutes later, a cross from Gray was headed in by Tommy Wilson, and Forest threatened to destroy Luton. But after 32 minutes, Dwight was carried off with a broken leg, after a tackle with McNally. Despite the numerical advantage, Luton were unable to rescue the game. In the 62nd minute, a cross from Hawkes passed through the middle, for Dave Pacey to score for Luton, but Forest held on for victory.

Luton Town	1:2	**Nottingham Forest**
Pacey		Dwight
		Wilson

Luton Town:
Baynham, McNally, Hawkes, Groves, Owen (Captain), Pacey, Bingham, Brown, Morton, Cummins, Gregory
Thomas Hodgson (Chairman)

Nottingham Forest:
Thomson, Whare, McDonald, Whitefoot, McKinlay, Burkitt (Captain), Dwight, Quigley, T. Wilson, W. Gray, Imlach
Billy Walker (Manager)

Referee:	J. Clough (Bolton)
Attendance:	100,000

Luton were relegated the following season, and dropped right through the divisions, in six years. They eventually fought their way back. It took Forest 19 years to win another major trophy, but that was to be the beginning of the greatest period in their history, although it was 1991 before they reached an F.A. Cup Final again.

Blackburn Rovers v Wolverhampton W

F.A. Cup Final, Saturday 7th May 1960

Another Broken Leg Ruins Final

Preview

It had been 32 years since Blackburn had won the F.A. Cup, but they were attempting to equal Aston Villa's record of seven wins. They had knocked out Burnley, who went on to win the League Championship, in the quarter-finals. Wolves had last won the Cup in 1949, and had knocked out the previous year's finalists, Luton Town, in the last 16. Blackburn finished 17th in only their second season back in the First Division, just three points clear of relegation. Wolves had been chasing a hat-trick of League Championships, but were pipped by a point, and finished runners-up to Burnley, despite beating them 6-1 in March. They also reached the European Cup quarter-finals, before Barcelona comfortably beat them.

Semi–Final, Saturday 26th March 1960

Aston Villa	0:1	*Wolverhampton W.*	(The Hawthorns, West Bromwich)
		Deeley	
Blackburn Rovers	2:1	*Sheffield Wednesday*	(Maine Road, Manchester)
Dougan 2		Fantham	

The Match

Four minutes before half-time, Stobart crossed, and Mick McGrath diverted it past Leyland, for an own goal. Two minutes later, Whelan broke his leg in a collision with Deeley. For Blackburn, with ten men and a goal down, things went from bad to worse. Norman Deeley scored from Horne's cross midway through the second half, and, two minutes from time, Deeley netted the rebound when Stobart hit the post. Wolves had their consolation for losing the League title.

Blackburn Rovers	0:3	*Wolverhampton W.*
		McGrath o.g.
		Deeley 2

Blackburn Rovers:
Leyland, Bray, Whelan, Clayton (Captain), Woods, McGrath, Bimpson, Dobing, Dougan, Douglas, McLeod
Dally Duncan (Manager)

Wolves:
Finlayson, Showell, Harris, Clamp, Slater (Captain), Flowers, Deeley, Stobart, Murray, Broadbent, Horne
Stan Cullis (Manager)

Referee: K. Howley (Middlesbrough)
Attendance: 100,000

Blackburn stayed in the First Division for a further six years, but they had to wait until 1987 before appearing at Wembley again, when they won the Full Members Cup. Wolves became England's first representatives in the European Cup Winners Cup the following season, and reached the Semi-Finals, before falling to Rangers. It was to be 14 years before they reached another Wembley final, when they won the Football League Cup.

(left to right) Manchester United's Pat Crerand, Albert Quixall and David Herd, who scored two of United's goals, all celebrate winning the F.A. Cup in 1963

Chapter Five

1961 - 70

The swinging sixties brought a fashion revolution and huge changes in social behaviour, as discipline crumbled under youthful rebellion. From Liverpool, the Beatles conquered the world with their music, and mass hysteria followed them, wherever they appeared.

Football was suffering from the onset of defensive tactics, as players were able to earn much more, because of the abolition of the maximum wage, and failure became more costly. Liverpool and Manchester United dominated the middle of the decade, smaller clubs found they could no longer compete on an equal footing. Several British clubs were conquering Europe though, and England managed to find ultimate success in the World Cup.

Wembley Stadium acquired a new roof in 1963 and now all spectators were covered. Three years later, the World Cup Final gave Wembley its greatest ever moment. This was followed, in 1968, by Manchester United's emotional European Cup triumph, coming ten years after the Munich air disaster. The Football League Cup Final hit the big time, by relocating to Wembley, and Henry Cooper almost defeated Cassius Clay, who went on to achieve a greatness which went far beyond the sport of boxing.

Giantkillers and Bridesmaids

The 1960s saw fewer shocks than in previous decades, as the big clubs achieved more consistency, but in 1964 a couple of exceptions proved that the F.A. Cup could still bite back. At the beginning of the decade, few had heard of Headington United, but thanks to the efforts of Arthur Turner, who took Birmingham City to Wembley in 1956, they came from nowhere to hit the headlines. Eighteen months after he was appointed manager they changed their name to Oxford United and won the Southern League Championship twice in succession. The timing of this was perfect as they were then voted into the Football League to take up the space left by Accrington Stanley's resignation. They struggled at first but in 1964, in their second season, they amazed everyone by becoming the first Fourth Division side to reach the F.A. Cup sixth round, the quarter-finals. Captained by Ron Atkinson, later to manage four winning teams at Wembley they defeated six times winners Blackburn Rovers 3-1 in the Fifth Round. The Lancashire club were enjoying their most successful First Division season since 1930. The run ended in the quarter-final, when Second Division Preston North End came to Oxford and won 2-1, but the little club from the university city had shown that there was more to the place than academic study. They were promoted to the Third Division the following year, reaching the Second Division in 1968, where they faced Blackburn in the league. Preston's reward for beating Oxford was an all-Second Division semi-final against Swansea Town. The Welshmen had produced a huge shock themselves in the sixth round, just as Preston were ending Oxford's historic run, by going to Liverpool and winning. The Reds would finish the season as League Champions, but they were two down to the struggling Second Division side at half-time at Anfield. Despite a second half barrage of attacks, Swansea held out, only conceding once, and went through to the semi-final. Liverpool would win the F.A. Cup the following year, but suffered further embarrassment in 1970, when another lowly Second Division side, Watford, dumped them out of the Cup at the same stage. Preston also put an end to Swansea's heroics, but had to fight back from being a goal down at half-time. A penalty and then a speculative 30-yard lob from Singleton, which sailed over everyone into the net, gave Preston a 2-1 victory. At Wembley, they would become the underdogs themselves, and very nearly beat West Ham. Swansea escaped relegation to the Third Division by a point, but they were only delaying the inevitable. They finished bottom the following year, and by 1967 they were in the Fourth Division, making the win at Anfield look even more remarkable.

A number of clubs made return visits to the semi-finals, once they got a taste for the excitement and drama. Manchester United, for example, reached the last four in five consecutive years, winning only once, and Everton and West Bromwich Albion threatened to repeat their Final of 1968, when they both reached the following year's semi-finals, but both failed narrowly to book their return visit to Wembley. Leeds United possibly felt the most aggrieved, even though they'd already appeared in the 1965 final. Two years later, they met a Chelsea side which had fallen at the semi-final stage in each of the previous two years. Chelsea took a first half lead, from a Tony Hateley header, but Leeds came back strongly after the interval, only to have two goals disallowed in the last ten minutes – the first for offside, and the second, in the last minute, when substitute Peter Lorimer's shot flew into the top corner, from a free kick, only for the referee to order it to be retaken, because the Chelsea defensive wall had been less than ten yards from the ball when the kick was taken. Chelsea hung on for a few more seconds. The following year, Leeds met Everton in the semi-final, and again lost by a single goal scored just before half-time, this time a penalty from Johnny Morrissey. Everton's tight defence resisted all Leeds' second half efforts to respond. Leeds had more success in the 1970s in the F.A. Cup, but also acquired more hard luck tales to tell.

George Best

George Best had a range of skills on the football field that most other players could only dream of. Body swerves and perfect balance made it incredibly difficult to get the ball off him, and for sheer cheek and invention, he had no equal. Even now, some of the goals he scored are simply breathtaking. Best's good looks meant that he became the first football superstar, but his pop star lifestyle eventually became too much for him, and he drifted in and out of the game at a succession of lesser clubs. Manchester United got ten fantastic years out of him, however. He made his league debut, aged 17, four months after United's 1963 F.A. Cup success. The following season they were League Champions, again in 1967, and then came United's, and Best's, biggest triumph. They faced Benfica in the European Cup Final at Wembley, and it was Best who unlocked the Portuguese defence, at the beginning of extra time, with a typical run which took him around the keeper, to send United on their way to a historic victory. He was already Footballer of the Year, after finishing the season as the Football League's joint top scorer, and after this performance he was also voted European Footballer of the Year. Yet for all his success, he made only three appearances at Wembley, the other two for Northern Ireland, and the F.A. Cup proved strangely elusive for him. In each of the three years after United's 1963 victory, they reached the semi-finals, losing to West Ham United, Leeds United and Everton respectively. They took Leeds to a replay, before Billy Bremner's winner ended United's hopes. Five years later, they met Leeds again, and a marathon struggle without goals finally ended in a second replay, when Bremner again popped up to net the winner. Best had scored six goals, in the fifth round, at Northampton, on his return from a month's suspension, but this fourth semi-final was to be the closest he ever got to the showpiece of the English game.

Page 97

A SOUVENIR OF THE
F.A. CUP FINAL 1961
WEMBLEY STADIUM · SATURDAY MAY 6

Best wishes

WITH THE COMPLIMENTS OF THE
DAILY EXPRESS

WEMBLEY 1961
Success City!

LEICESTER CITY FOOTBALL CLUB

BANQUET

to celebrate the occasion of the
appearance of the Club
in the Final of the
Football Association Cup

SATURDAY, 6th MAY, 1961

THE DORCHESTER
Park Lane, London

THE DORCHESTER

LEICESTER CITY FOOTBALL CLUB

Menu

Le Filet de Sole Walewska

L'Entrecôte Sauté Marchand de Vin
Les Haricots Verts au Beurre
Les Pommes Mousseline

L'Ananas Tout Paris
Les Biscuits Perlés

Le Café

Saturday, 6th May, 1961

SEMPER EADEM

EMPIRE WEMBL...

LEICESTER CITY
v
TOTTENHAM HOTSPUR
SATURDAY MAY 6 1961

DAILY EXPRESS
COMMUNITY SING...

SP...
19...

The Official Publication
of the Spurs' Players

PRICE 2'6

Leicester City v Tottenham Hotspur

F.A. Cup Final, Saturday 6th May 1961

The Elusive 'Double'

Preview

Leicester had lost their only previous final, in 1949. They had never won a major trophy, and had fought their way through a difficult semi-final. Tottenham had won the Cup twice before, but their last victory had been in 1921, with a 1-0 win against Wolverhampton Wanderers at Stamford Bridge, London. This was their first Wembley appearance. Leicester finished 6th in the First Division, their highest position since 1929. Tottenham won the League Championship for the second time in their history, and were aiming to become the first team to win the 'double' since Aston Villa in 1897.

Semi–Finals, Saturday 18th March 1961

Burnley 	0:3	**Tottenham Hotspur** Smith 2, Jones	*(Villa Park, Birmingham)*	
Leicester City	0:0	**Sheffield United**	*(Elland Road, Leeds)*	
Leicester City	0:0 *(AET)*	**Sheffield United**	*(City Ground, Nottingham)*	*Replay (Thursday 23rd March 1961)*
Leicester City Walsh, Leek	2:0	**Sheffield United**	*(St. Andrews, Birmingham)*	*2nd Replay (Monday 27th March 1961)*

The Match

Yet again, the Wembley 'hoodoo' determined the course of an F.A. Cup Final. After 18 minutes, Chalmers picked up a leg injury in a tackle with Allen, and was reduced to being a passenger on the wing, for the rest of the game. Leicester had begun strongly, but Tottenham eventually overcame them. In the 66th minute, Bobby Smith took a pass from Dyson, turned brilliantly past King, and hit an unstoppable rising shot past the keeper. Nine minutes later, Terry Dyson ran in unmarked, to meet Smith's centre with a powerful header past the diving Banks, and the 'double' was won.

Leicester City	0:2	**Tottenham Hotspur** Smith, Dyson

Leicester City:
Banks, Chalmers, Norman, McLintock, I. King, Appleton, Riley, J. Walsh (Captain), McIlmoyle, Keyworth, Cheesebrough
Matt Gillies (Manager)

Tottenham Hotspur:
Brown, Baker, Henry, Blanchflower (Captain), Norman, Mackay, Jones, White, Smith, L. Allen, Dyson
Bill Nicholson (Manager)

Referee: J. Kelly (Chorley)
Attendance: 100,000

Because of Tottenham's qualification for the European Cup, Leicester took their place in the European Cup Winners Cup, but lost in the last 16 to the eventual winners, Atletico Madrid. They reached the F.A. Cup Final again, though, in 1963. Tottenham went on to retain the F.A. Cup the following year.

Bill Nicholson's loyalty to Tottenham Hotspur Football Club has become a virtual lifetime's devotion, and he is now approaching 70 years service to the club. It all began in 1936, when he made the trip from his native Scarborough for a trial with Spurs. He made his league debut in the final season before the war, and then had to wait until the late 1940s to establish himself in the Second Division side, as a right half. Nicholson missed out on playing at Wembley, Blackpool twice denying Spurs in F.A. Cup semi-finals, but under Arthur Rowe's guidance, the push and run side won the Second Division Championship in 1950, and then surprised all by lifting the League Championship the following year.

England called on Nicholson for an international, against Portugal at Goodison Park, and he made the most explosive introduction, by scoring after 19 seconds with a thunderous shot. Alas, it was his only cap, because Billy Wright played in the same position. When Nicholson retired, he became a coach, taking over as manager in 1958. A succession of big signings, allied to tactical awareness, turned Tottenham into the best side in the country, and they began the 1960-61 season by winning their first 11 league games, a record which still stands.

They won the Championship with a brand of attacking football which earned them many admirers, and they were so much in command that the F.A. Cup Final was an anti-climax, even though they had become the first team to win the elusive 'double' since 1897. Nicholson's captain, Danny Blanchflower, won his second Footballer of the Year award.

They retained the F.A. Cup, the following year, and then became the first British club to win a European trophy, when they blitzed the holders, Atletico Madrid, 5-1, to lift the Cup Winners Cup. After a little rebuilding, Nicholson's Spurs captured their third F.A. Cup of the decade in 1967. He retired in 1974, after two League Cup victories gave him an unbeaten Wembley record from five finals, and Spurs also picked up another European trophy, the UEFA Cup, in 1972. This hard-working man, who avoided publicity, eventually became president of the club he had served for so long, and the club's address is now on Bill Nicholson Way.

Burnley v Tottenham Hotspur

F.A. Cup Final, Saturday 5th May 1962

Spurs Still Too Strong

Preview

Burnley had lost to a late winner, in extra time, in their only previous Wembley appearance in 1947. They had a good F.A. Cup record in more recent years, and had lost to Tottenham in the previous year's semi-final, but they had won the Cup only once, in 1914. Tottenham were the holders.

Burnley finished as League runners-up to Ipswich Town, having won the Championship in 1960. Tottenham finished a point and a place below them, in their defence of the title. They had also reached the European Cup semi-finals, before losing to the holders, and eventual winners, Benfica.

Semi–Finals, Saturday 31st March 1962

Burnley Connelly	1:1	**Fulham** Leggat	(Villa Park, Birmingham)	
Manchester United Herd	1:3	**Tottenham Hotspur** Greaves, Jones Medwin	(Hillsborough, Sheffield)	
Burnley Robson 2	2:1	**Fulham** Langley	(Filbert Street, Leicester)	Replay (Monday 9th April 1962)

The Match

Tottenham took a third minute lead. Smith's header sent Jimmy Greaves through. Finding himself surrounded by defenders, Greaves suddenly stopped and checked back, before brilliantly turning and shooting past Blacklaw. Burnley equalised five minutes after the interval. From a cross by Harris, Jimmy Robson beat Brown at the near post. But within a minute, White crossed and Bobby Smith turned and fired Tottenham back in front. With ten minutes left, it was all over. Medwin's shot was handled on the line by Cummings. Danny Blanchflower sent Blacklaw the wrong way from the penalty, and Tottenham had won the Cup for the fourth time.

Burnley Robson	1:3	**Tottenham Hotspur** Greaves, Smith Blanchflower (penalty)

Burnley:
Blacklaw, Angus, Elder, Adamson (Captain), Cummings, Miller, Connelly, McIlroy, Pointer, Robson, Harris
Harry Potts (Manager)

Tottenham Hotspur:
Brown, Baker, Henry, Blanchflower (Captain), Norman, Mackay, Medwin, White, Smith, Greaves, Jones
Bill Nicholson (Manager)

Referee: J. Finney (Hereford)
Attendance: 100,000

Burnley gained their revenge by knocking Tottenham out of the F.A. Cup in their first defence the following year, with an emphatic 3-0 away win. They gradually fell into decline, however, and were relegated in 1971. For their next visit to Wembley, in the 1988 Sherpa Van Trophy Final, they were a Fourth Division club. Tottenham became Britain's first winners of a European trophy the following year, when they thrashed the holders, Atletico Madrid, 5-1, in the final of the European Cup Winners Cup in Rotterdam. They also finished as League runners-up to Everton. They returned to win the F.A. Cup again in 1967.

Jimmy Greaves

Tottenham Hotspur & England

Greaves

Jimmy Greaves was one of the deadliest strikers of all time. From his arrival in Chelsea's first team, at 17 in 1957, to his premature retirement, aged 31 in 1971, he continued to score goals at a phenomenal rate. He made his first appearance at Wembley whilst still 17, scoring twice for the England Under-23 side, eventually netting a record 13 goals in 12 games. Also in his first season, he scored for a London select team, in the first European Fairs Cup Final against Barcelona.

He had scored 100 league goals before his 21st birthday, and was also scoring regularly for England, including a hat-trick against Scotland, in the 9-3 rout at Wembley. Chelsea were struggling, however. So the ambitious Greaves signed for Italian giants, Milan, in 1961. Despite nine goals in his first ten games, he failed to settle, and with the maximum wage being abolished, he returned to England, to sign for his boyhood favourites, Tottenham Hotspur, to spearhead their bid to defend the 'double'.

Milan went on to win the European Cup the following season, but Greaves' decision proved sound enough. He scored a hat-trick on his debut, and was an instant hit, scoring within three minutes of the F.A. Cup Final, as Spurs retained the trophy. In his first full season at White Hart Lane, he was the Football League's top scorer, and netted twice in the Cup Winners Cup Final, as Spurs became the first British club to find success on the continent.

Greaves' goals were always from inside the area, and he had brilliant ball control, with ice cool finishing. He was the First Division's top scorer for three consecutive seasons (six in all). With England, it was the same story: 44 goals from 57 internationals, spoiled only by his missing the 1966 World Cup Final, after Geoff Hurst capitalised on Greaves' shin injury to carve his own place in history.

Greaves won another F.A. Cup winner's medal in 1967 with Tottenham, and topped the Football League charts again, two years later, but his blistering pace then began to fade, and he was transferred to West Ham United in a swap deal, which took Martin Peters to Spurs. Typically, he scored twice on his debut, but decided to finish whilst still at the top. A popular figure, with a great sense of humour, he went on to star as a television pundit.

The Reds 2'6 at Wembley

MANCHESTER

OFFICIAL SOUVEN

THE FOOTBALL ASSOCIATION CHALLENGE CUP COMPETITION

THE FOOTBALL ASSOCIATION CENTENARY YEAR

1863 — 1963

FINAL TIE

LEICESTER CITY

v

MANCHESTER UNITED

OFFICIAL PROGRAMME

WEN

EMPI

SATURDAY, M

LEIC CIT Wen 196

WEMBLEY 1963

THE OFFICIAL PUBLICATION OF THE LEICESTER CITY PLAYERS

2'6

FOOTBALL CUP FINAL

LEICESTER CITY v MANCHESTER UNITED

SATURDAY MAY 25 1963

DAILY EXPRESS COMMUNITY

Leicester City v Manchester United

F.A. Cup Final, Saturday 25th May 1963

Red Devils Rise Again

Preview

Leicester were appearing in their third final, and their second in three years. They had yet to win the Cup. United had also lost their previous two finals, in 1957 and 1958, but had won the Cup twice. They had reached the semi-finals a year earlier.

Leicester finished 4th in the First Division, their highest position since 1929. United were still rebuilding after Munich, and finished 19th, narrowly escaping relegation in their worst league season since promotion in 1938. They had not beaten Leicester in the 1960s.

Semi–Finals, Saturday 27th April 1963

Leicester City	*1:0*	**Liverpool**	(Hillsborough, Sheffield)
Stringfellow			
Manchester United	*1:0*	**Southampton**	(Villa Park, Birmingham)
Law			

The Match

After 29 minutes of a final, delayed three weeks because of the severe winter, Crerand's pass came to Denis Law, who turned sharply and shot past Banks. In the 57th minute, Charlton's shot was saved by Banks, but David Herd netted the rebound. Leicester pulled a goal back, with Ken Keyworth's diving header from a McLintock cross ten minutes from time. Five minutes later Banks dropped a cross from Giles, and Herd scored again. The new United had won their first trophy.

Leicester	*1:3*	**Manchester United**
Keyworth		Law,
		Herd 2

Leicester City:
Banks, Sjoberg, Norman, McLintock, King, Appleton (Captain), Riley, Cross, Keyworth, Gibson, Stringfellow
Matt Gillies (Manager)

Manchester United:
Gaskell, Dunne, Cantwell (Captain), Crerand, Foulkes, Setters, Giles, Quixall, Herd, Law, Charlton
Matt Busby (Manager)

Referee: K. Aston (Ilford)
Attendance: 100,000

Leicester won their first major trophy, the Football League Cup, the following year, and reached another F.A. Cup Final in 1969. United reached the semi-finals in each of the next three years, losing them all. They were League runners-up to Liverpool the following year, and knocked the holders, Tottenham Hotspur, out of the European Cup Winners Cup, before losing a 4-1 first leg lead to Sporting Lisbon, the eventual winners, in the quarter-finals. But they were League Champions twice, in three years (1965 and 1967), and won the European Cup on an emotional night in 1968. Their next F.A. Cup Final would not be for a further eight years, however.

wembley
The FA Cup Finals
1923-2000

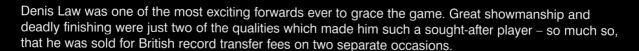

Denis Law was one of the most exciting forwards ever to grace the game. Great showmanship and deadly finishing were just two of the qualities which made him such a sought-after player – so much so, that he was sold for British record transfer fees on two separate occasions.

His first club was Huddersfield Town, and after Matt Busby had failed to sign him for Manchester United, he gave him his first Scotland cap, at the age of 18 instead. Manchester City signed him in 1960, and his inspirational quick-witted sharpness made him the first player to be transferred for a six-figure fee, when he signed for Torino after just over a season at Maine Road.

Busby brought him back to Manchester the following year, for a record £115,000, and Law fitted perfectly into the new United side. After scoring the first goal to set them on their way to their 1963 F.A. Cup win, he was the star of a Rest of the World side which narrowly lost to England in the F.A. Centenary match at Wembley. In 1964, he was voted European Footballer of the Year, the only Scottish player ever to win the award.

He loved scoring against England, and got the first goal in 1967 when Scotland inflicted on them their first defeat since winning the World Cup. United won two League Championships, with Law hitting the back of the net regularly, although a knee injury forced him to miss the 1968 European Cup Final at Wembley. His last season was spent back at Manchester City, and proved quite eventful, with City appearing in the League Cup Final, at Wembley, although losing to Wolves, and then Law's final touch in league football was an impudent back-heel at, of all places, Old Trafford.

In the ultimate irony, it effectively relegated Manchester United to the Second Division. No player could have signed off in a more dramatic fashion, and Law was distraught, taking no pleasure whatsoever from his final goal. This wasn't quite the end, as the 34-year-old still fulfilled one of his last ambitions by appearing in that summer's World Cup, and ended his international career with a record 30 goals from 55 games.

His F.A. Cup tally of 41 was also a record until Ian Rush overtook him in 1996. Law could always point to the six he scored at Luton in 1961, however, that were expunged from the records because the game was abandoned. If those had been allowed to stand, he would still hold the record.

Charlton

Bobby Charlton, one of the all-time greats, was a hugely popular ambassador for the English game. He was a perfect sportsman, who reached the very pinnacle of his career, and was deservedly knighted, in 1994. Charlton was born in Ashington, with brother, Jack, to a footballing family, which had already produced Jackie Milburn. His powerful shooting, speed and ball control were spotted at an early age, and he signed for Manchester United, aged 15, having already scored twice for England Schoolboys at Wembley.

United helped him to develop his all-round skills, and finally blooded him at 19. He ended the season at the F.A. Cup Final, which they lost to Aston Villa. Charlton was gaining valuable experience with the 'Busby Babes', and they had just reached the European Cup quarter-finals in 1958, when tragedy struck. Eight of the squad were killed in the Munich air disaster. Charlton was thrown clear, with just cuts and severe shock. It took him several weeks to come to terms with the deaths of so many young friends and team-mates, and he almost quit the game, but he returned a more mature person, and vowed to help make United great again.

Two months after the crash, he made a spectacular scoring debut for England against Scotland at Hampden Park, and played in his second F.A. Cup Final, which United also lost. After winning the F.A. Cup in 1963, Charlton gained renewed confidence, and England built their World Cup winning team around him. His versatility and, of course, his thunderbolt shooting made him feared throughout the world. He was Footballer of the Year in 1966, and his goals against Portugal took England into the World Cup Final, where both Charlton brothers won priceless winner's medals.

Bobby then picked up the European Footballer of the Year award. Although he had also won three League Championship medals with United, he still had one very important honour to achieve. In 1968, United finally made it to the European Cup Final, and Bobby Charlton gave his all, both physically and mentally. Captaining the side at Wembley, he gave them the lead, and then scored again, in extra time, to clinch the trophy. For Charlton and his manager, Matt Busby, it was a fitting tribute to the players who gave their lives, ten years earlier.

In his years in football, Charlton won his 106th and last England cap at the 1970 World Cup, having scored a record 49 international goals. He made 50 Wembley appearances, scoring 27 goals, also a record.

His last season was spent as player-manager of Preston North End, but it ended in relegation to the Third Division, and Charlton dropped out of the game, later returning to his beloved Manchester United to join the club's board, from where he still inspires future generations of footballers.

Preston North End v West Ham Utd

F.A. Cup Final, Saturday 2nd May 1964

Hammer Blow For Underdogs

Preview

Preston had last won the Cup in 1938, and had surrendered a 2-1 lead in the closing stages of the 1954 final. West Ham had never won the Cup, and their only final had been back in 1923. They had however, won the Football League War Cup at Wembley in 1940. In the semi-finals, they had beaten the holders.

Preston had been in the Second Division for three years, and finished 3rd. West Ham finished 14th in the First Division, and also reached the Football League Cup Semi-Finals, where they lost to the eventual winners, Leicester City.

Semi–Finals, Saturday 14th March 1964

Manchester United Law	1:3	**West Ham United** Boyce 2 Hurst	**(Hillsborough, Sheffield)**
Preston North End Dawson (penalty) Singleton	2:1	**Swansea Town** McLaughlin	**(Villa Park, Birmingham)**

The Match

The Second Division side took a surprise lead, in the ninth minute. Standen saved from Dawson, but Doug Holden knocked the ball into the net. A minute later, John Sissons played a one-two with Byrne, and drove home the equaliser. Five minutes before the interval, Alex Dawson headed in from a Wilson corner, and West Ham were rocking. In the 52nd minute, they equalised again. Kelly stopped Brown's header, but Geoff Hurst headed the rebound back in. Kelly managed to push it onto the bar, but it hit him on the way out, and went over the line. West Ham scored a dramatic winner, in injury time. Brabrook's cross found the head of Ronnie Boyce at the far post, and the gallant underdogs were beaten.

Preston North End Holden Dawson	2:3	**West Ham United** Sissons, Hurst Boyce	

Preston North End:
Kelly, Ross, J. Smith, Lawton (Captain), Singleton, Kendall, Wilson, Ashworth, Dawson, Spavin, Holden
Jimmy Milne (Manager)

West Ham United:
Standen, Bond, Burkett, Bovington, K. Brown, R. Moore (Captain), Brabrook, Boyce, Byrne, Hurst, Sissons
Ron Greenwood (Manager)

Referee:	*A. Holland (Barnsley)*
Attendance:	*100,000*

Preston did not appear at Wembley again for another 30 years, when they reached the Third Division Promotion Play-Off Final. They had dropped into the lower divisions in 1970. West Ham received little praise for their victory, but went on to win the European Cup Winners Cup at Wembley the following year.

Whatever else Geoff Hurst does with his life, he will surely always be remembered for what he achieved on the afternoon of 30th July 1966.

He is still the only man ever to have scored a hat-trick in a World Cup Final. This fact is made even more startling when you consider the likes of Pele, Muller, Maradona, Zidane and Ronaldo, each of whom couldn't quite match the achievement of the 24-year-old West Ham striker winning just his eighth cap. Hurst didn't even begin as a forward. He spent two years as an unremarkable, but hard-working, reserve wing half, destined to play in the shadow of Bobby Moore.

When Ron Greenwood became West Ham's manager, in 1961, he decided to channel Hurst's dedication into a new striking role. It meant he would co-ordinate with the midfield to lay passes off, before drifting into unmarked positions, and then reappearing when least expected, often at the near post, to strike with deadly accuracy.

West Ham won the F.A. Cup in 1964, and it was Hurst's header which brought them level for the second time. Cup Winners Cup success followed in 1965, but it was the following year when Geoff Hurst became a household name. Alf Ramsey called him into the England squad, and he made his international debut against West Germany, in a friendly at Wembley. He scored against Scotland at Hampden Park, but lost his place to the great goalscorer Jimmy Greaves, for the start of the World Cup. Hurst seemed to have missed his chance. Then, Greaves picked up a shin injury, and Hurst got back in, for the quarter-final against Argentina. His near-post headed winner, from Martin Peters' cross, so typical of his West Ham scoring, took England into the semi-finals, where Portugal were beaten 2-1.

The country expected the experienced Greaves, who had scored 43 goals in 54 internationals, to return for the final. Alf Ramsey made the biggest decision of his life, and decided to pin his faith on Hurst, who had scored twice in seven games. As history records, his decision paid dividends, and Hurst's quick thinking, timing and shooting power gave his country a day it will always remember with affection. His second goal, in extra time is the easily the most debated in football, did the ball fully cross the line? We'll probably never know, but the goal was given and England certainly deserved their victory.

From then on, Geoff Hurst was a superstar, winning 49 England caps, and scoring 24 international goals, but he remained a model of sportsmanship, and stayed loyal to West Ham for another six years, before ending his career at Stoke City and West Bromwich Albion.

He tried management at Telford United and Chelsea, but it wasn't for him. Hurst was, nevertheless, a great ambassador for English football, and received a knighthood in 1998.

Moore

Bobby Moore captained England to their greatest ever triumph, the 1966 World Cup, with an assured style which inspired confidence in all around him. His positional sense and anticipation were so good that he rarely had to tackle, but when he did, his timing was usually immaculate.

Moore was an obvious leader from an early age, and after graduating through England youth and Under-23 internationals, Alf Ramsey appointed him England's youngest ever captain, in 1963, aged 22.

The following year, he led West Ham to their first major trophy, the F.A. Cup, and picked up the Footballer of the Year award. Bobby Moore climbing the Wembley steps to receive a prize became an annual event, as the Hammers lifted the Cup Winners Cup in 1965, and Moore set his sights on completing a unique hat-trick, with the World Cup, the following year.

During the tournament, he barely put a foot wrong, and led his country to a magnificent triumph. The World Cup made him famous throughout the world, and he even became the B.B.C.'s Sports Personality of the Year. When England defended the World Cup in 1970, Moore further enhanced his reputation, with a fine performance against Pele, as England almost resisted the unstoppable Brazilians.

He was to win no further honours with West Ham, but remained the consummate professional, even saving a penalty in a League Cup semi-final in 1972, when their keeper was injured. England failed to qualify for the 1974 World Cup, but Moore set a new record of 108 caps, before finally leaving West Ham to drop down into the Second Division with Fulham.

Strangely enough, they reached the F.A. Cup Final in his first season with the Cottagers, where they came up against West Ham, the ultimate irony for Moore, after nine barren seasons with the Hammers. His last Wembley appearance ended in a 2-0 defeat.

He left Fulham in 1976 and captained Team America, against England, in the American Bicentennial Tournament, before returning to manage Oxford City and Southend United. The news of his tragically early death, at 51, from cancer, shocked the football world, and was greeted with great sadness.

Leeds United v Liverpool
F.A. Cup Final, Saturday 1st May 1965

Reds Kop The Cup At Last

Preview

Leeds had never been beyond the quarter-finals before, and had yet to win a major trophy. In the semi-finals, they had beaten the team who were to pip them to the League Championship. Liverpool were appearing in their third final, but had still to win the F.A. Cup. In the semi-finals, they had beaten the Football League Cup winners. Their only previous Wembley appearance had been back in 1950.

Leeds had only won the Second Division Championship the previous year, but surprised all by finishing League runners-up to Manchester United, on goal average. Liverpool finished 7th in their defence of the League Championship, and reached the European Cup Semi-Finals, where they lost a 3-1 first leg lead to the holders, and eventual winners, Internazionale.

Semi–Finals, Saturday 27th March 1965

Chelsea	0:2	**Liverpool** *Thompson* *Stevenson (penalty)*	*(Villa Park, Birmingham)*
Leeds United	0:0	**Manchester United**	*(Hillsborough, Sheffield)*
Leeds United *Bremner*	1:0	**Manchester United**	*(City Ground, Nottingham)* **Replay (Wednesday 31st March 1965)**

The Match

After a bruising 90 minutes, the game was three minutes into extra time, when Byrne (who broke his collar bone in the ninth minute) crossed, for Roger Hunt to break the deadlock with a low header. With Storrie hobbling on the wing, Leeds looked beaten, but eight minutes later, from Charlton's header, the unmarked Billy Bremner volleyed the equaliser past Lawrence. With nine minutes left, Callaghan crossed, and with Sprake tempted out of his goal, Ian St. John dived to head the winner past Reaney on the line.

Leeds United *Bremner*	**1:2** *(AET)*	**Liverpool** *Hunt, St. John*

Leeds United:
Sprake, Reaney, Bell, Bremner, Charlton, Hunter, Giles, Storrie, Peacock, Collins (Captain), Johanneson
Don Revie (Manager)

Liverpool:
Lawrence, Lawler, Byrne, Strong, Yeats, Stevenson, Callaghan, Hunt, St. John, Smith, P. Thompson
Bill Shankly (Manager)

Referee:	*W. Clements (West Bromwich)*
Attendance:	*100,000*

Leeds were League runners-up again the following year, as Liverpool regained the Championship, for the second time in three years. Leeds also reached the European Fairs Cup semi-finals, and finally won a major trophy, the Football League Cup, in 1968, before reaching another F.A. Cup Final in 1970. Liverpool reached the European Cup Winners Cup Final the following year, but lost to a Ron Yeats own goal in extra time, to Borussia Dortmund at Hampden Park, Glasgow. They were to reach the F.A. Cup Final next in 1971.

Wembley's Other Finals

Wembley staged its first European Cup Winners Cup Final in 1965, and West Ham United hit top form, to beat Munich 1860 2-0. Alan Sealey scored both goals in a highly entertaining, attacking game, to give the Hammers their first European trophy, and the acclaim they had been denied when winning the F.A. Cup the previous year. Munich 1860 were Bundesliga Champions in 1966, before their near neighbours, Bayern Munich, became the dominant force. Wembley's first European final had been in 1963, when Milan denied Benfica a hat-trick of European Cup triumphs, with a 2-1 victory. Benfica also lost the 1968 final at Wembley, when Manchester United overcame them in extra time. Three years later, Ajax Amsterdam won the first of their three successive European Cup wins, at Wembley. Liverpool were the next to lift the trophy in front of the twin towers in 1978, when Kenny Dalglish's goal defeated Bruges, as the Reds became the first British club to win it twice. Barcelona secured a long overdue European Cup victory, at Wembley in 1992, and Parma were the last to win European silverware at the stadium, the following year, in the Cup Winners Cup.

Everton's two-goal hero Mike Trebilcock (centre) is crowned with the F.A. Cup by teammates Brian Harris (left) and Brian Labone (right) after their fantastic 3-2 victory over Sheffield Wednesday

Everton v Sheffield Wednesday

F.A. Cup Final, Saturday 14th May 1966

Fightback Keeps Cup On Merseyside

Preview

It had been over 30 years since either side had last won the F.A. Cup. Everton had won it for the second time in 1933, and Wednesday, for the third time, two years later.

Everton had won the League Championship three years earlier, but only finished 11th in the First Division, their lowest position for six years. Wednesday finished 17th, their lowest position since promotion in 1959.

Semi–Finals, Saturday 23rd April 1966

Chelsea	0:2	**Sheffield Wednesday** Pugh, McCalliog	(Villa Park, Birmingham)
Everton Harvey	1:0	**Manchester United**	(Burden Park, Bolton)

The Match

After four minutes, Everton conceded their first goal in the competition, when Ford centred, and Jim McCalliog's shot was deflected, by Wilson, past West. In the 57th minute, West saved Fantham's shot, but David Ford scored Wednesday's second, with the rebound, and they appeared to have clinched their fourth Cup win. Mike Trebilcock had other ideas though, and a minute later, took a pass from Temple and fired a shot past Springett to reduce the arrears. Then in the 63rd minute, a defensive header from Ellis fell to the eager Trebilcock, to wipe out Wednesday's lead. With ten minutes left, a long ball from Harvey was met by Young, who failed to control it, leaving Derek Temple to run on and score the winner, thus completing an amazing recovery.

Everton	3:2	**Sheffield Wednesday**
Trebilcock 2		McCalliog
Temple		Ford

Everton:
West, Wright, R. Wilson, Gabriel, Labone (Captain), Harris, Scott, Trebilcock, Young, Harvey, Temple
Harry Catterick (Manager)

Sheffield Wednesday:
Springett, Smith, Megson (Captain), Eustace, Ellis, Young, Pugh, Fantham, McCalliog, Ford, Quinn
Alan Brown (Manager)

Referee:	*J. Taylor (Wolverhampton)*
Attendance:	*100,000*

Everton disappointingly went out of the European Cup Winners Cup in the last 16, to Real Zaragoza. But they reached the F.A. Cup Final again in 1968. Wednesday were relegated in 1970. They reappeared at Wembley for the Football League Centenary Tournament in 1988, and then won the Rumbelows Cup, in 1991, before reaching both domestic finals two years later.

Wembley's Other Finals

Everton's great victory was inevitably overshadowed by the greatest show on Earth, the World Cup, which came to Wembley two months later. England had not really been expected to win, which made the ultimate triumph so much more enjoyable. The final, against West Germany, had everything, and could not have been scripted any better. Apprehension after conceding an early goal, admiration for Hurst's equaliser from Moore's quick thinking, joy when it looked as if Peters' goal would be the winner, but then despair at the last gasp equaliser. Alf Ramsey purveyed a quiet confidence throughout, and the players responded magnificently to his words. Hurst's controversial second put England back in the driving seat, and his third, at the end, was the signal for unbridled euphoria, and the game was still recalled with affection several decades later.

Chelsea v Tottenham Hotspur
F.A. Cup Final, Saturday 20th May 1967

Spurs The Pride Of London

Preview

Chelsea had only appeared in one previous final, losing 3-0 to Sheffield United at Old Trafford, Manchester, in 1915. After two successive semi-final defeats, they had now made it to Wembley for the first time since their two wartime appearances. In the quarter-finals, they had beaten the previous year's finalists, Sheffield Wednesday. Tottenham had already won the F.A. Cup twice, in the 1960s, and four times in all. Chelsea finished 9th in the First Division, their lowest position since promotion in 1963. Tottenham finished 3rd, behind the runners-up Nottingham Forest on goal average, their highest position since 1963.

Semi–Finals, Saturday 29th April 1967

Chelsea	1:0	**Leeds United**	*(Villa Park, Birmingham)*
Hateley			
Nottingham Forest	0:2	**Tottenham Hotspur**	*(Hillsborough, Sheffield)*
		Greaves, Saul	

The Match

In the last minute of the first half, Mullery's shot from outside the box hit Ron Harris, and fell to Jimmy Robertson, who fired Tottenham in front. Tottenham were always in control, and in the 68th minute, from a pass by Robertson, Frank Saul turned swiftly to beat the startled Bonetti. Chelsea pulled one back, with four minutes left. Boyle crossed, and Jennings rushed out, when he should have stayed, leaving Bobby Tambling to head the ball in. The scoreline flattered Chelsea, as Tottenham's tactics, of slowing things down, had effectively controlled the game, in the first all-London F.A. Cup Final.

Chelsea	1:2	**Tottenham Hotspur**
Tambling		Robertson
		Saul

Chelsea:
Bonetti, A. Harris, McCreadie, Hollins, Hinton, R. Harris (Captain), Cooke, Baldwin, Hateley, Tambling, Boyle, Kirkup (Sub)
Tommy Docherty (Manager)

Tottenham Hotspur:
Jennings, Kinnear, Knowles, Mullery, England, Mackay (Captain), Robertson, Greaves, Gilzean, Venables, Saul, Jones (Sub)
Bill Nicholson (Manager)

Referee: K. Dagnall (Bolton)
Attendance: 100,000

Chelsea's F.A. Cup form finally had its reward in 1970, when they lifted the trophy for the first time, after drawing at Wembley. Tottenham went out in the last 16 of the European Cup Winners Cup, to Lyon, on away goals, despite scoring four in the home leg. In 1971, they won the Football League Cup for the first time, but it would be a further ten years before they reached the F.A. Cup Final again.

Wembley's Other Finals

The Football League Cup Final was switched to Wembley in 1967, and a dramatic game saw Third Division Queens Park Rangers overcome a two goal deficit to beat the holders, West Bromwich Albion, 3-2. Swindon Town, also from the Third Division, emulated Rangers' feat, by winning it two years later, after defeating Arsenal on a mud bath of a pitch. With qualification for the U.E.F.A. Cup for the winners, the competition grew in importance, and was dominated in the late 1970s by Nottingham Forest, and then Liverpool, who won it four years in succession in the early 1980s. It went under a succession of names, thanks to different sponsors, and lost some credibility as the big clubs preferred to concentrate on the Premier League, using the League Cup to try out fringe players. The final could always be relied upon, however, to produce great drama and thrills.

Jennings

Pat Jennings was one of the greatest goalkeepers of all time. Razor sharp reflexes, huge hands and an unassuming manner made him a very popular and reliable custodian. English clubs first noticed the 17-year-old Newry Town goalkeeper in 1963, when he came to England for the European Youth Tournament and helped Northern Ireland reach the final at Wembley. They were beaten 4-0 by a strong England side, but Jennings had done enough for Watford to make him an offer. Jennings became a regular and Watford were suddenly challenging for promotion, just missing out by two points. It was clear that they could not hold on to such a prospect.

He was to become a permanent fixture for his country for more than two decades. Tottenham Hotspur signed him at the end of that season, as cover for Bill Brown. By 1966-67 he was the first choice keeper, winning his first major honour at the F.A. Cup Final. One of Jennings' strengths was in his long kicks from his area, and this was never better illustrated than in the 1967 F.A. Charity Shield, against Manchester United at Old Trafford, when the Irish goalkeeper stunned the League Champions, by scoring a goal. His huge clearance reached United's penalty area, where their keeper, Alex Stepney, misjudged the bounce and it went over his head, into the net.

In the early 1970s, Spurs began to pick up major trophies again, beginning with the Football League Cup in 1971, the first of four consecutive clean sheets for Jennings at Wembley. The following year, Spurs won the UEFA Cup, and Jennings kept out England's forwards in a famous 1-0 win for Northern Ireland. He was now at his peak and 1973 saw another League Cup win for Tottenham, with Jennings winning the Footballer of the Year award. In one memorable performance, he saved two penalties at Anfield against Liverpool, who went on to win the League Championship.

Another UEFA Cup Final followed in 1974, although this time Spurs were beaten. His fellow professionals voted Jennings their Player of the Year in 1976, but Spurs were relegated the following year and new manager Keith Burkinshaw decided to offload his keeper to their greatest rivals, Arsenal, believing him to be past his best. He was wrong. In his first season with the Gunners, Jennings was back at Wembley, in another F.A. Cup Final. They lost, but it was to be the first of three successive finals, with Jennings helping them to a sensational last minute victory against Manchester United in 1979. The following season was exhausting for the Gunners, and after reaching two cup finals, it all became too much, as they lost both – the F.A. Cup to Second Division West Ham, and the Cup Winners Cup to Valencia, on penalties. Jennings did have the minor satisfaction of saving the first kick of the penalty shootout, however, from the great Argentinian World Cup winner, Mario Kempes.

At club level he had scaled most of the heights, but in 1982, aged 37, he played in his first World Cup, and it was not to be his last. He conceded only one goal in the first three games, as Northern Ireland shocked the world by defeating host nation Spain 1-0, to win their group. They finally fell to France, when victory would have put them into the semi-finals. Two years later, Jennings was released by Arsenal, and never played a league game again, but he returned to Tottenham, and played reserve football, whilst still playing for his country.

He continued to defy logic, and at the age of 40, kept four consecutive clean sheets, all away from home, in Turkey, Romania, at Wembley against England, to take the Irish through to their second successive World Cup, and in France. This impressed Everton so much that they signed him up as cover for the F.A. Cup Final in 1986. It all came to an end, fittingly, at the World Cup in Mexico, where a goalkeeper, winning a world record 119th cap on his 41st birthday, performed heroics against the multi-talented Brazilians, despite not having played league football for over 18 months. Pat Jennings retired on the highest stage, at the end of a glittering career.

THE ALBION

EMPIRE STADIUM · WEMBLEY

The Football Association — CUP COMPETITION

Final Tie
Saturday, May 18, 1968
KICK - OFF 3 p.m.

YOU ARE ADVISED TO TAKE UP YOUR POSITION BY 2.30 P.M.

J.S. Leitch   CHAIRMAN
                WEMBLEY STADIUM LTD.

WEST ENCLOSURE   10/-

ENTER	ENTRANCE
G	65
TURNSTILE	

STANDING

TO BE RETAINED   (See Plan & Conditions on back)

PARK HOTEL

West Bromwich Albion

LUNCHEON

Menu

Melon au Porto

Saumon Froid Parisien
Salade Française
Pommes Nouvelle

Timbale de Fruits Rivier
Biscuit Glacé Praliné

Café

Saturday, 18th May, 1968

Everton v West Brom

F.A. Cup Final, Saturday 18th May 1968

Baggies End Stalemate

Preview

Everton were attempting to regain the F.A. Cup after winning it for the third time in 1966 in a dramatic fightback. In the semi-finals, they had beaten the Football League Cup winners. West Brom had last won the Cup in 1954 and had suffered the humiliation of losing the previous year's Football League Cup Final to a Third Division club, after taking a two goal lead.

Everton finished 5th in the First Division, and had won 6-2 at West Brom two months earlier. West Brom finished 8th.

Semi–Finals, Saturday 27th March 1968

Birmingham City	0:2	*West Bromwich Albion*	*(Villa Park, Birmingham)*
		Astle, Brown	
Everton	1:0	*Leeds United*	*(Old Trafford, Manchester)*
Morrissey (penalty)			

The Match

Up until extra time, Everton were the better side, but both teams found it hard to break through the other's defence on a heavy pitch. The winning goal was scored in the third minute of extra time. Jeff Astle's first shot, from Fraser's pass, rebounded to him off Harvey, but his second flew into the corner, giving West no chance, and giving West Brom the F.A. Cup for the fifth time. Astle had scored in every round.

Everton	0:1	*West Bromwich Albion*
	(AET)	*Astle*

Everton:
West, Wright, R. Wilson, Kendall, Labone (Captain), Harvey, Husband, Ball, Royle, Hurst, Morrissey, Kenyon (Sub)
Harry Catterick (Manager)

West Bromwich Albion:
Osborne, Fraser, Williams (Captain), Brown, Talbut, Kaye, Lovett, Collard, Astle, Hope, Clark, Clarke (Sub)
Alan Ashman (Manager)

Referee: L. Callaghan (Merthyr Tydfil)
Attendance: 100,000

Both sides reached the Semi-Finals again the following year. Everton were League Champions in 1970, but did not return to Wembley until the 1977 Football League Cup Final, eventually winning the F.A. Cup in 1984. West Brom reached the European Cup Winners Cup quarter-finals the following year, losing at home to the Scottish Cup holders, Dunfermline Athletic. But they made their third Wembley appearance in four years at the 1970 Football League Cup Final.

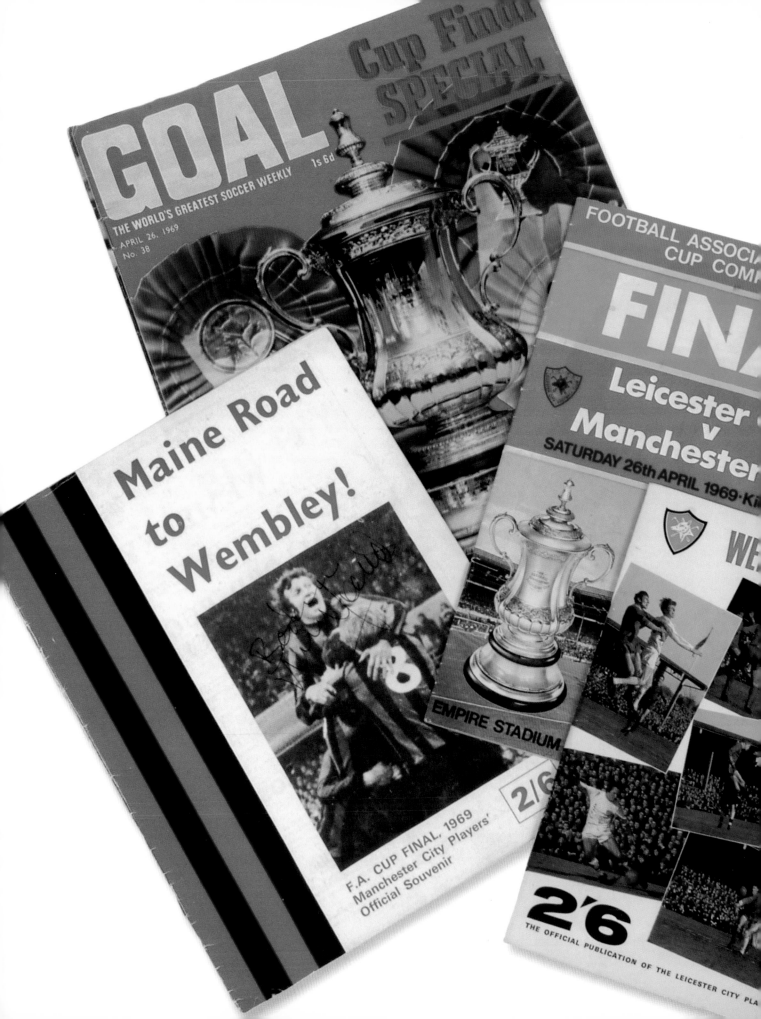

Leicester City v Manchester City

F.A. Cup Final, Saturday 26th April 1969

Mercer's Men On Top

Preview

Leicester had reached their third final of the decade, and their fourth overall, but had still to win the Cup. They had lost to the other Manchester club, United, on their previous visit in 1963. In the semi-finals, they had beaten the holders. City had last won the Cup in 1956, and had beaten the previous year's finalists in the semi-finals.

Leicester were facing a relegation battle after 12 years in the top flight. City had only been in the First Division for three years, but were the reigning League Champions. They finished a miserable 13th however in their defence of the title, and in their first European venture, the Turkish Champions Fenerbahce surprisingly knocked them out in the first round of the European Cup.

Semi–Final, Saturday 22nd March 1969

Everton	0:1	**Manchester City**	*(Villa Park, Birmingham)*
		Booth	

Semi–Final, Saturday 29th March 1969

Leicester City	1:0	West Bromwich Albion	*(Hillsborough, Sheffield)*
Clarke			

The Match

A fast, open game with chances at both ends. Yet there was only one goal, which came in the 24th minute. Summerbee's low cross was hammered into the back of the net by Neil Young to give Manchester City the F.A. Cup, for the fourth time. The competition had been a glorious distraction for Leicester, from their league troubles, and they played their part in an entertaining final, though still ultimately ending up with a third set of runners-up medals.

Leicester City	0:1	**Manchester City**	
		Young	

Leicester City:
Shilton, Rodrigues, Nish (Captain), Roberts, Woollett, Cross, Fern, Gibson, Lochhead, Clarke, Glover, Manley (Sub)
Frank O'Farrell (Manager)

Manchester City:
Dowd, Book (Captain), Pardoe, Doyle, Booth, Oakes, Summerbee, Bell, Lee, Young, Coleman, Connor (Sub)
Joe Mercer (Manager)

Referee: G. McCabe (Sheffield)
Attendance: 100,000

Leicester were left with five league games, and were relegated three weeks later, when they fell one point short of safety. They bounced back by winning the Second Division Championship two years later, but it was 1992 before they returned to Wembley, for the Second Division Promotion Play-Off Final, and a further five years before they reached another major final, in the Coca-Cola Cup. City's trophy winning habit picked up speed the following year, as they won both the Football League Cup and the European Cup Winners Cup, for the first time, but they would not reach the F.A. Cup Final again until 1981.

Peter Shilton was an exceptional goalkeeper, who learned from the great Gordon Banks, and went on to become England's most capped player, with 125 appearances. Only Tony Adams played more games at Wembley, which first saw Shilton keeping a clean sheet for England Schoolboys in 1965. Leicester City then signed him as understudy to Banks, their World Cup winning keeper. Shilton was incredibly dedicated to his training, and impressed manager Matt Gillies so much that he sold Banks to Stoke City, when Shilton was only 17.

In 1969, he played in the F.A. Cup Final, for the only time in his long career, as Leicester lost, by the only goal to Manchester City. A miserable First Division season then ended with relegation. Although he had dropped down a division, Shilton won his first England cap in 1970, and Leicester won the Second Division Championship that season. Two years later, at Wembley, he was blamed for allowing Poland to score on the break, in a match England had to win to qualify for the World Cup. Domarski's shot went under his body, catching him cold after he'd been redundant for most of the game. England went out, Sir Alf Ramsey was sacked and Shilton lost his place in the England team to Ray Clemence.

Leicester almost made it to the F.A. Cup Final that season, before losing in a replay to Liverpool, but Shilton then moved on to Stoke for £325,000, a then world record fee for a goalkeeper. After three seasons, Stoke were relegated, and Shilton once again found himself in the Second Division. It was then that Brian Clough, who had just taken Nottingham Forest in the opposite direction, rescued him. Shilton was the final piece in a side which was to take the First Division by storm. Forest were League Champions at the end of the season, and went on an unbeaten league run which set a new record of 42 games.

Shilton was the players' choice as Player of the Year. More success followed. Forest knocked holders Liverpool out of the European Cup, with Shilton keeping a clean sheet in both legs. They retained the Football League Cup at Wembley (Shilton had been cup-tied the previous year), and won the European Cup at the first attempt. Another European Cup followed in 1980, with Shilton majestically keeping Hamburg's forwards (including Kevin Keegan) at bay in the final. All this success inevitably brought Shilton back into the England side, and after alternating with him for two years, he eventually replaced Clemence at the 1982 World Cup, where only one goal went past him in five games. Shilton's positional sense and narrowing of angles had taken him ahead of the agile Clemence.

He moved on to Southampton after the World Cup, and played in two more F.A. Cup semi-finals, losing both in extra time to each of the Merseyside giants. In his second World Cup in 1986, he had conceded only one goal in the previous four games, when he came up against Diego Maradona, in the quarter-final. The first was handled, and the second, sheer brilliance. England were out. The following year, Shilton signed for Derby County and in 1988 won his 100th cap, against Holland in the European Championship, but was beaten three times, by Marco Van Basten, to end English interest in the competition.

His international career finally came to an end after his third World Cup, in 1990, when England narrowly lost the semi-final to West Germany, on penalties, which had never been Shilton's speciality. Although he had now reached 40, he continued to play league football. He suffered a third relegation the following year, but in 1992, he became player-manager of Second Division Plymouth Argyle. In his second season, they reached the play-offs, but he left the following year, as Argyle were slipping towards the Third Division. After appearing in the First Division play-offs, for Bolton Wanderers, aged 45, he went on to become the first player to make 1000 Football League appearances, when keeping a clean sheet for Leyton Orient, three days before Christmas 1996. At the age of 46, he finally hung up his gloves.

CHELSEA.....0   LEEDS.....1
                       CHARLTON

Action from the F.A. Cup Final with Leeds United leading 1-0, the game eventually finished 2-2 after extra time and Chelsea won the replay 2-1 again after extra time

Chelsea v Leeds United

F.A. Cup Final, Saturday 11th April 1970

Chelsea Hang On

Preview

Chelsea had a good F.A. Cup record in recent years, but had yet to win the trophy. They had lost in the final in 1967. Leeds had also still to win the F.A. Cup, having lost the 1965 final in extra time. They had fought their way through a gruelling semi-final, against the same opponents, as in 1965. On their last visit, in 1968, they had won the Football League Cup. Chelsea finished 3rd in the First Division, and knocked Leeds out of the Football League Cup, but Leeds, who were reigning League Champions, finished two points above them, as runners-up to Everton. They had also reached the European Cup semi-finals at the first attempt, but had lost the first leg, at home to Celtic, the Scottish League Champions.

Semi–Finals, Saturday 14th March 1970

Chelsea *Webb, Osgood* *Houseman 2, Hutchinson*	5:1	**Watford** *Garbett*	*(White Hart Lane, London)*
Leeds United	0:0	**Manchester United**	*(Hillsborough, Sheffield)*
Leeds United	0:0 *(AET)*	**Manchester United**	*(Villa Park, Birmingham)* Replay (Monday 23rd March 1970)
Leeds United *Bremner*	1:0	**Manchester United**	*(Burnden Park, Bolton)* 2nd Replay (Thursday 26th March 1970)

The Match

The pitch was in a poor state. It was heavily sanded, and caused uneven bounces. It probably brought about the first goal, in the 21st minute. From Gray's corner, Jack Charlton outjumped Bonetti, and his header went over the line, underneath McCreadie's foot, as he misjudged the bounce. Perhaps it was only fair that Chelsea's equaliser, 20 minutes later, could possibly also be attributed to the pitch. Hutchinson headed it down for Peter Houseman, whose low shot should have been collected easily by Sprake, but the goalkeeper also misjudged the bounce and allowed it to pass through his arms and under his body. With six minutes left, Clarke headed against the post from Giles' cross, and Mick Jones drove home the rebound, for what seemed to be the winner. But just two minutes later, from a Hollins cross, Ian Hutchinson beat Charlton, to head Chelsea level again. There were no further goals in extra time.

Chelsea *Houseman, Hutchinson*	2:2 *(AET)*	**Leeds United** *Charlton, Jones*

Chelsea:
Bonetti, Webb, McCreadie, Hollins, Dempsey, R. Harris (Captain), Baldwin, Houseman, Osgood, Hutchinson, Cooke, Hinton (Sub)
Dave Sexton (Manager)

Leeds United:
Sprake, Madeley, Cooper, Bremner (Captain), Charlton, Hunter, Lorimer, Clarke, Jones, Giles, E. Gray, Bates (Sub)
Don Revie (Manager)

Referee:	*E. Jennings (Stourbridge)*
Attendance:	*100,000*

Chelsea *Osgood, Webb*	2:1 *(AET)*	**Leeds United** *Jones*	*(Old Trafford, Manchester)*	Replay (Wednesday 29th April 1970)

Leeds lost the replay, after taking the lead once again. Chelsea's resilience finally overcame them in extra time, in what had become the longest ever F.A. Cup Final. Leeds continued their multiple assaults on major prizes. The following year, they were League runners-up again, this time to Arsenal, but they were rewarded with their second European Fairs Cup win.

Wembley's Other Finals

With the decline of amateur football in this country, a competition was formed for the new semi-professional clubs, with the first Final at Wembley in 1970. The F.A. Trophy has seen many dramatic finals over the years, with Scarborough scoring injury time winners in successive years in the 70s. In the 1990s, it became a stepping stone to qualification for the Football League, with Wycombe Wanderers, Colchester United, Macclesfield Town and Cheltenham Town all lifting the Trophy, before moving on to bigger things within a year or two. It was also the decade of Geoff Chapple, who won an unbelievable five F.A. Trophies in seven years, as manager of first Woking and then Kingstonian. Its sister competition, the F.A. Vase, carried on from where the F.A. Amateur Cup left off, in 1974, and provided the much sought-after prize of a Wembley final for the smaller clubs.

wembley
The FA Cup Finals
1923-2000

Chapter Six
1971 - 80

Britain elected Margaret Thatcher as Prime Minister at the end of a decade, which saw three-day weeks, because of a power crisis and a Minister for Drought, because of a water shortage. The Olympic Games were severely hit by terrorism and politics. Nine Israeli athletes were killed in Munich and the United States boycotted the 1980 Games.

Football had its own problems. 66 people were killed in a horrific crush at Ibrox Stadium, Glasgow. Hooliganism drove many fans away from the game. To add to the depression, England suffered a miserable decade, failing to qualify for the World Cup. Meanwhile, European success diminished, until Liverpool emerged to dominate both at home and abroad, beginning a run of six successive European Cup wins by English clubs.

This decade saw the end of the F.A. Amateur Cup Final, which had drawn 100,000 crowds in the 1950's. The first popular music concerts took place at the stadium. In 1973, there were two historic matches at Wembley, Second Division Sunderland's remarkable Cup win, and England's unexpected elimination from the World Cup, by Poland.

Giantkillers and Bridesmaids

After the scarcity of giantkillings in the previous decade, the underdogs fought back in the 1970's. Three Second Division teams in eight years won the trophy itself and dozens of non-league clubs hit the headlines each year. The 1976 competition saw Fourth Division, Bradford City reach the quarter-finals and Crystal Palace, from the Third Division, in the semi-finals, after remarkable away victories at Leeds United, Chelsea and Sunderland.

When Fourth Division, Colchester United were drawn at home to Leeds United in the 1971 fifth round, there were few who thought that the ageing Essex side, six of whom were under 30, stood any chance against the league leaders, packed with internationals and chasing three major trophies. After 18 minutes, 34-year-old Ray Crawford gave them the lead, with a header from a free kick. With the crowd still buzzing, Crawford scored again, decisively slotting the ball in, from a prone position. Leeds were shell-shocked, but surely they had enough armoury to recover. This was a team that was feared throughout the land, and had been for six years. They had been finalists, the previous year. Unbelievably, Dave Simmons beat a hesitant Gary Sprake, in Leeds' goal, to head the minnows into a three-goal lead, after ten minutes of the second half. Colchester couldn't possibly have prepared themselves for being in such a position and with 15 minutes left, Leeds had pulled it back to 3-2, but the exhausted heroes somehow kept them out to become only the second Fourth Division side to reach the quarter-finals. They were well beaten, 5-0, in the sixth round, at Everton, and missed promotion by two points, but no one could take away the memories from the day they beat one of the strongest sides in Europe. The following year, Leeds won the F.A. Cup, reaching the final again, in 1973. Three finals in four years, plus a humbling defeat at tiny Layer Road. In 1978, Blyth Spartans were the closest that any non-league team has ever been to the quarter-finals. Wrexham, soon to win the Third Division Championship, were a goal down, in the last minute, at home to the Northern League side, on a bone hard pitch, when Dixie McNeil grabbed the equaliser to force a replay, which Wrexham won, 2-1 at Newcastle.

Hereford United travelled to Newcastle in January 1972, and audaciously took the lead on two minutes, before forcing a replay with a 2-2 draw. Snow and ice caused six postponements and it was February before the replay could take place, heightening the nervous apprehension of their opponents. Eight minutes from the end, Malcolm Macdonald headed the Magpies in front and Tyneside breathed a huge sigh of relief. Hereford were not ready to lie down however and four minutes later, Ronnie Radford unleashed an absolute screamer from 30 yards, which flew past McFaul. Into extra time, and Hereford seized the moment. After 103 minutes, Ricky George scored the winner and the Edgar Street pitch was invaded by hundreds of celebrating fans. Newcastle's humiliation was complete, but Hereford's ambitions did not end there. Four days later, they held West Ham to a goalless draw and it took a Geoff Hurst hat-trick to beat them in the replay. At the end of the season, Hereford were elected into the Football League. Another Southern League success story was written by Wimbledon, in 1975, when they became the first non-league club to beat a First Division side away from home, since 1920, after defeating Burnley, at Turf Moor. Mick Mahon's second-half goal proved decisive, with Dickie Guy performing heroics in goal. The fourth round took them to Elland Road, home of the defending League Champions, Leeds United, with memories of Colchester still fresh in their minds. Again, Guy proved impossible to beat, and he even saved a late penalty from hot-shot Peter Lorimer. Eventually the Dons fell to a single goal in the replay, at Crystal Palace. It was deflected in, off Dave Bassett, who only 11 years later would take the same club into the First Division, as manager. They were elected to the Football League in 1977, and this incredible rags-to-riches story ended in 1988, when Wimbledon won the F.A. Cup, whilst Burnley had dropped to the Fourth Division.

Stoke City had the misfortune to draw Arsenal in the semi-finals, in both 1971 and 1972. They had never appeared in the Final and found themselves two goals up at half-time, in the first of them. Both goals had come about from Arsenal defensive errors. Back came the Gunners and Peter Storey, a defender not renowned for scoring, struck from the edge of the box. It was all they could manage until injury time, when John Mahoney stopped a goalbound header from Frank McLintock, with his hands and a penalty was awarded. Storey stepped up and sent Gordon Banks the wrong way. Arsenal won the replay, 2-0, and went on to win the 'double'. Twelve months later, Stoke met Arsenal again. Armstrong put the holders ahead, but their goalkeeper, Bob Wilson then picked up a knee injury. With no substitute keeper, he bravely carried on, until Simpson's own goal brought Stoke back level. Centre forward, John Radford took over and kept out the Stoke forwards to force another replay. Radford was to finish them off four days later, as he netted the winner, in a 2-1 victory for Arsenal.

But for Wolfgang Weber's last-minute equaliser in 1966, Martin Peters would be immortalised as the man whose goal won England the World Cup. As one of the West Ham trio that won winner's medals that day, Peters' acclaim was overshadowed by that of captain, Bobby Moore and hat-trick man, Geoff Hurst. He had joined West Ham in 1959, but missed out on the Hammers' F.A. Cup win in 1964, and despite five subsequent Wembley triumphs, never made it to an F.A. Cup Final. Peters did however, star in West Ham's Cup Winners Cup win, in 1965, before winning the first of his 67 international caps, two months before the World Cup. His goal in the final was only his second for his country. Sir Alf Ramsey described him as being 'ten years ahead of his time' because of his elegant running off the ball and ghosting undetected into goalscoring positions. Tottenham signed him in March 1970, as part of a record £200,000 swap deal, which took Jimmy Greaves to West Ham. They won the League Cup and the U.E.F.A. Cup, with Peters then captaining them to a second League Cup in 1973. Despite such success, the F.A. Cup eluded them, and two quarter-finals was all they could manage.

Page 135

Arsenal v Liverpool
F.A. Cup Final, Saturday 8th May 1971

Arsenal's Double

Preview

It had been 21 years since Arsenal had beaten Liverpool to win the F.A. Cup for the third time. Since then, they had lost three times at Wembley, including two Football League Cup Finals. Their 1969 defeat to Third Division Swindon Town had been particularly embarrassing. In the semi-finals, they had come back from being two goals down at half-time. The previous year, they had won the European Fairs Cup. Liverpool had won the F.A. Cup for the first time in 1965. Just five days earlier, Arsenal had clinched the League Championship, after coming from behind to pip Leeds United by a point. They were now on the verge of the 'double'. In their defence of the European Fairs Cup, they had reached the quarter-finals again, but had gone out on away goals to Cologne. Liverpool finished 5th in the First Division, for the second year in succession. They had reached the European Fairs Cup semi-finals for the first time, before losing by the only goal, on aggregate, to the eventual winners, Leeds United.

Semi–Finals, Saturday 27th March 1971

Arsenal	2:2	**Stoke City**	(Hillsborough, Sheffield)	
Storey 2 (1 penalty)		Smith, Ritchie		
Everton	1:2	**Liverpool**	(Old Trafford, Manchester)	
Ball		Evans, Hall		
Arsenal	2:0	**Stoke City**	(Villa Park, Birmingham)	Replay (Wednesday 31st March 1971)
Graham, Kennedy				

The Match

Neither side could find a breakthrough in the first 90 minutes, on a hot day. But in only the second minute of extra time, substitute Thompson sent Steve Heighway away on the left, and as Wilson prepared for a cross, the winger beat him at the near post to put Liverpool ahead. Arsenal, whose teamwork and resilience were their great strengths, were now faced with their sternest test of character. Incredibly, they responded. Nine minutes later, Radford's overhead kick produced a goalmouth scramble. Substitute Eddie Kelly got a touch, which went through Smith's legs, and rolled towards Clemence. Graham ran in, swung at the ball and missed, but wrong-footed Clemence, and the ball continued on its path, under his body and gently into the net. Arsenal's determination then had its reward, with nine minutes left. Radford played a one-two with Charlie George, and then cut inside to return it to the weary striker, whose shot took a slight deflection off Lloyd, to elude Clemence's reach. George lay down in exhaustion after securing the elusive 'double' for a team which refused to accept defeat throughout a remarkable season.

Arsenal	**2:1**	**Liverpool**
Kelly, George	**(AET)**	Heighway

Arsenal:
R. Wilson, Rice, McNab, Storey, McLintock (Captain), Simpson, Armstrong, Graham, Radford, R. Kennedy, George, Kelly (Sub), Bertie Mee (Manager)

Liverpool:
Clemence, Lawler, Lindsay, Smith (Captain), Lloyd, E. Hughes, Callaghan, Evans, Heighway, Toshack, Hall, P. Thompson (Sub), Bill Shankly (Manager)

Referee: N. Burtenshaw (Great Yarmouth)
Attendance: 100,000

Arsenal reached the final again a year later. As League Champions, they entered the European Cup, leaving Liverpool to take their place in the European Cup Winners Cup, where they were beaten in the last 16 by Bayern Munich. Liverpool won both the League Championship and the U.E.F.A. Cup in 1973, and then returned in 1974 to win the F.A. Cup.

CHALLENGE CUP COMPETIT

CENTENARY YEAR

1872

FINAL

SATURDAY 6th MAY 1972 ...... KICK-OFF 3 p.m.

1972

WANDERERS

BOLTON WANDERERS

NEWCASTLE UNITED

OLD ETONIANS

BRADFORD

CHARLTON ATHLETIC

CHELSEA

SHEFFIELD UNITED

B

SUNDERLAND

PORTSMOUT

ASTON VILLA

ARSENAL

EVERTO

TOTTENHAM HOTSPUR

NOTTS COUNTY

WEST HAM UNITED

BLACKBURN ROVERS

WOLVERHAMPTON WANDERERS

MANCHESTER CITY

OXFORD UNIVERSITY

BARNSLEY

PRESTON NORTH END

OLD CARTHUSIANS

WEST BROMWICH ALBION

SHEFFIELD WEDNESDAY

BLACKBURN OLYMPIC

ROYAL ENGINEERS

BURNLEY

NOTTINGHAM FOREST

CARDIFF CITY

BLACKPOOL

CLAPHAM ROVERS

DERBY COUNTY

MANCHESTER UNITED

HUDDERSFIELD TOWN

LIVERPOOL

ARSENAL v LEEDS UNITED

EMPIRE **WEMBLEY** STADIUM

Official

Arsenal v Leeds United

F.A. Cup Final, Saturday 6th May 1972

Holders Denied

Preview

Arsenal were the holders clinching the 'double' in the previous year's final. In the last 16, they had beaten Derby County, who were to succeed them as League Champions, and they had beaten the Football League Cup winners in the semi-finals, after losing their goalkeeper with an injury for the last 15 minutes of the first game. They had beaten the same opponents the previous year, also after a replay. Leeds were appearing in their second final in three years, having drawn at Wembley in 1970. They had still to win the F.A. Cup. In an earlier round, they had knocked out the previous year's finalists, Liverpool. Leeds had beaten Arsenal at Wembley, in the 1968 Football League Cup Final.

Arsenal finished 5th, in their defence of the League Championship, and reached the European Cup quarter-finals before losing both legs to the holders, and eventual winners, Ajax Amsterdam. Leeds, having won the European Fairs Cup the previous year, went out in the first round of the renamed U.E.F.A. Cup. They rested the first team for the second leg, at home, and lost 4-0 to Lierse, after winning 2-0 in Belgium. After finishing League runners-up for two successive years, Leeds had been demolishing their opponents in the league, and surely had the greatest team in their history. They were one point away from the League Championship.

Semi–Finals, Saturday 15th April 1972

Arsenal Armstrong	1:1	**Stoke City** Simpson o.g.	*(Villa Park, Birmingham)*
Birmingham City	0:3	**Leeds United** Jones 2, Lorimer	*(Hillsborough, Sheffield)*
Arsenal George (penalty) Radford	2:1	**Stoke City** Greenhoff (penalty)	*(Goodison Park, Liverpool)* Replay *(Wednesday 19th April 1972)*

The Match

The two sides were fierce rivals and the tackles came flying in, with neither team wanting to give an inch. Four players were booked, but it was not a dirty game and there were also a few near misses. The opening goal, in the 54th minute, proved enough to win the F.A. Cup in its centenary year. A cross from Jones (who dislocated his shoulder in the last attack of the match) was met by a diving header from Allan Clarke and the ball flew past Barnett, into the net. Leeds had won the trophy for the first time, repeating their League Cup win of 1968, by the same score.

Arsenal	0:1	**Leeds United** Clarke

Arsenal:
Barnett, Rice, McNab, Storey, McLintock (Captain), Simpson, Armstrong, Ball, George, Radford, Graham, R. Kennedy (Sub),
Bertie Mee (Manager)

Leeds United:
Harvey, Reaney, Madeley, Bremner (Captain), Charlton, Hunter, Lorimer, Clarke, Jones, Giles, E. Gray, Bates (Sub),
Don Revie (Manager)

Referee: D. Smith (Gloucester)
Attendance: 100,000

Arsenal reached the semi-finals for the third consecutive year in 1973, but they did not reach the final again until 1978. Leeds failed to emulate Arsenal's 'double' of the previous year. Just two days after Wembley, needing only a point to win the League Championship on goal average, they were surprisingly beaten by Wolverhampton Wanderers, and Derby County lifted the title. Leeds were runners-up for the third year in succession. They reached the F.A. Cup Final again the following year, and also reached the European Cup Winners Cup Final, losing to Milan in Salonika. Their victory at Wembley was, sadly, overshadowed by their numerous near misses.

SUNDERLAND

WEMBLEY '73

the official brochure of SUNDERLAND F.C. player

Leeds United v Sunderland

F.A. Cup Final, Saturday 5th May 1973

Shock Of The Century

Preview

Leeds, the holders for the first time, were appearing in their third final in four years. Sunderland's only previous Wembley visit was in winning the F.A. Cup for the first time, in 1937. It had been 42 years since a Second Division club had won the trophy (West Bromwich Albion), but Sunderland had beaten the previous year's finalists, in the semi-finals.

Leeds finished 3rd in the First Division. Incredibly, it was their lowest position in five years. They had also reached the final of the European Cup Winners Cup. Sunderland finished 6th in the Second Division, in their third season since relegation. They had begun badly, but new manager Bob Stokoe had revitalised the team.

Semi–Finals, Saturday 7th April 1973

Arsenal George	1:2	**Sunderland** Halom, Hughes	**(Hillsborough, Sheffield)**
Leeds United Bremner	1:0	**Wolverhampton W.**	**(Maine Road, Manchester)**

The Match

Leeds were overwhelming favourites, and very few, outside Sunderland, dared to predict an upset. In the 32nd minute, Sunderland went ahead. Hughes' corner fell to Halom, who knocked it forward. Ian Porterfield controlled it with his knee, and had time to turn and blast it over Harvey's head into the roof of the net. Leeds fought back, but were up against a Sunderland team prepared to die for the cause. The most memorable moment came 20 minutes from the end, when Jim Montgomery saved from Cherry, and left Lorimer with an open goal. With an amazing display of agility, Montgomery managed to throw himself, from his prone position, to deflect Lorimer's shot onto the underside of the bar, and out again. Leeds' players stared in disbelief, and this save, more than the goal, convinced them that it was not going to be their day. Sunderland had pulled off possibly the biggest shock in the history of the F.A. Cup.

Leeds United	0:1	**Sunderland** Porterfield

Leeds United:
Harvey, Reaney, Cherry, Bremner (Captain), Madeley, Hunter, Lorimer, Clarke, Jones, Giles, E. Gray, Yorath (Sub),
Don Revie (Manager)

Sunderland:
Montgomery, Malone, Guthrie, Horswill, Watson, Pitt, Kerr (Captain), Hughes, Halom, Porterfield, Tueart, Young (Sub),
Bob Stokoe (Manager)

Referee:	K. Burns (Stourbridge)
Attendance:	100,000

Eleven days later, Leeds lost the European Cup Winners Cup Final, in suspicious circumstances, to Milan in Salonika. There were allegations that the Greek referee had been bribed. It was the ninth time, in nine years, that Leeds had finished runners-up in a major competition. One of their great traits, however, was their powers of recovery, and the following season they set a new league record of 29 games unbeaten from the start of the season. This time they went on to win the League Championship for the second time. They returned for Wembley's first F.A. Charity Shield. Sunderland went out in the last 16 of the following season's European Cup Winners Cup, to Sporting Lisbon, and it was not until 1976 that they won the Second Division Championship to return to the top flight. They were back at Wembley, for the Milk Cup Final, in 1985 and were back in the Second Division when they next reached the F.A. Cup Final, in 1992.

Liverpool v Newcastle United
F.A. Cup Final, Saturday 4th May 1974

Reds Supreme

Preview

Liverpool's only F.A. Cup win had been in 1965, but they had lost the 1971 Final in extra time and had gone on to win a League Championship and U.E.F.A. Cup 'double' the previous year. Newcastle had not appeared at Wembley since their three F.A. Cup wins in five years in the 1950s, but they were unbeaten at the stadium, and were aiming to equal Aston Villa's record seven F.A. Cup wins.

In their defence of the League Championship, Liverpool finished runners-up to Leeds United, their ninth successive season in the top five. They were disappointing in the European Cup, however, losing both legs to Red Star Belgrade in the last 16. They also reached the quarter-finals of the Football League Cup, before losing to the eventual winners, Wolverhampton Wanderers. Newcastle finished 15th in the First Division, their lowest position for seven years, and only escaped relegation by two points.

Semi–Finals, Saturday 30th March 1974

Burnley	*0:2*	*Newcastle United* *Macdonald 2*	*(Hillsborough, Sheffield)*	
Leicester City	*0:0*	*Liverpool*	*(Old Trafford, Manchester)*	
Leicester City *Glover*	*1:3*	*Liverpool* *Hall, Keegan* *Toshack*	*(Villa Park, Birmingham)*	*Replay (Wednesday 3rd April 1974)*

The Match

After 58 minutes, Liverpool took the lead. Hall ducked underneath Smith's cross and the ball fell for Kevin Keegan, to tee it up before firing past McFaul. Liverpool clinched victory 17 minutes later. From Clemence's kick, Toshack's back-header was picked up by Steve Heighway, who ran on to notch the second with an expert finish. With two minutes left, the demoralised Newcastle United side were ripped apart for the final time, as Liverpool put on an exhibition display of 11 consecutive passes around the pitch, culminating in Smith's low cross, which eluded McFaul, and left Keegan to tap in his second goal of the game.

Liverpool *Keegan 2* *Heighway*	*3:0*	*Newcastle United*

Liverpool:
Clemence, Smith, Lindsay, P.B. Thompson, Cormack, E. Hughes (Captain), Keegan, Hall, Heighway, Toshack, Callaghan, Lawler (Sub),
Bill Shankly (Manager)

Newcastle United:
McFaul, Clark, Kennedy, McDermott, Howard, Moncur (Captain), Smith, Cassidy, Macdonald, Tudor, Hibbitt, Gibb (Sub),
Joe Harvey (Manager)

Referee:	*G. Kew (Amersham)*
Attendance:	*100,000*

Liverpool's great manager, Bill Shankly, retired after leading them out for the F.A. Charity Shield at Wembley, three months later. Incredibly, his successor, Bob Paisley, was to surpass his achievements. In the following season's European Cup Winners Cup, however, they went out in the last 16, to the Hungarians of Ferencvaros, on away goals. They were back in the F.A. Cup Final in 1977. Newcastle were back at Wembley two years later, for their first Football League Cup Final, but didn't appear in another F.A. Cup Final until 1998.

Kevin Keegan was a lively hard-working striker, whose infectious enthusiasm for the game made him the most famous British player of his generation. He started out at Scunthorpe United and was soon spotted by the big clubs, Bill Shankly signing him for Liverpool in 1971. Combining well with John Toshack, Keegan's career flourished at Anfield, and he won his first England cap in his second season with them. Liverpool were League Champions in 1973, and Keegan scored twice as they added the UEFA Cup to the title.

The following year, he again netted twice, as Liverpool destroyed Newcastle in the F.A. Cup Final. His passionate temperament also came to the fore, however, in three well-publicised moments during the next 12 months. Firstly, he was beaten up by Yugoslavian security officers after fooling around in Belgrade airport whilst on tour with England. Then he became the first English player to be sent off at Wembley, after clashing with Leeds' Billy Bremner in the F.A. Charity Shield. Bremner was also dismissed and because they both threw off their shirts in disgust, the F.A. came down hard on them, banning them for five weeks. At the end of that season, Keegan walked out on England after Don Revie had dropped him for a British Championship match against Wales, before being persuaded to return.

Meanwhile Liverpool were being moulded by Bob Paisley into a side feared throughout Europe and 1975-76 was the beginning of a 15-year period of domination. Keegan and Toshack's striking partnership took them to the League Championship, with Keegan scoring a vital equaliser in the last game at Wolves, as they clinched the title. He had already been voted Footballer of the Year and captained England. Liverpool also won the UEFA Cup again and Keegan scored twice in the final, as he had done in 1973. His second proved to be the winner.

The following season, Liverpool retained the title and almost won the 'treble', losing the F.A. Cup Final to Manchester United before memorably winning the European Cup in Rome, four days later, with Keegan's run leading to the penalty which gave them their third goal. Having won everything with Liverpool, he needed a new challenge and signed for Hamburg, in the West German Bundesliga, for a record £500,000. After a slow start, his football took on a new dimension. Playing in midfield, he was everywhere, controlling games and the Germans loved him, making him their Footballer of the Year in his first season.

His reputation grew even more and he was European Footballer of the Year at the end of 1978. England benefited greatly from his play and began to almost depend on him, amidst fears that they were becoming a one-man team. Hamburg won the Championship in 1979, and Keegan was European Footballer of the Year again. They reached the European Cup Final, the following year, only to lose to Nottingham Forest, but Keegan now wanted to return home. After a disappointing European Championship for England, he joined Southampton, a surprise choice, when he could have signed for several much bigger clubs. Typically, he was an inspiration.

In 1982, he was the First Division's top scorer and the Professional Footballers Association named him their Player of the Year. Now aged 31, a decade at the top had had its cost and Keegan's legs and knees had been involved in more than their fair share of crunching tackles, but it was his back which was to deny him the chance to shine on the biggest stage of all. By the time he was fit enough to play, England were facing an exit from the 1982 World Cup, needing to beat the hosts, Spain, by two clear goals to reach the semi-finals. Keegan came on as substitute for the last 27 minutes, and apart from a header, which went wide, couldn't inspire the side to make the vital breakthrough.

His international career was over and he dropped into the Second Division, with Newcastle United, but he still had the Midas touch. The Geordies, starved of success for so long, took him to their hearts, and they were promoted in his second season. With the future much brighter for Newcastle, Keegan decided to retire and emigrated to Spain, for a well-earned rest with his family. After eight years, he was tempted back to Newcastle, who were next to the bottom of the Second Division. Keegan came in as manager, they escaped relegation and he had embarked on a new career, which was to prove as equally dramatic as his playing days had.

The club was transformed almost overnight by Keegan's arrival and they began the next season by winning their first 11 league games, winning the title in style. This particular brand of attacking football then took the Premier League by storm. In January 1996, Newcastle held a 12-point lead at the top and seemed set to win their first Championship since 1927. Man United gradually broke it down though and Keegan's all-out attacking approach cost them several vital points in the run-in. The strain showed towards the end as Keegan allowed himself to be psyched out by his rival at Old Trafford, Alex Ferguson. Newcastle finished as runners-up. He then dropped a huge bombshell by resigning in January 1997, re-emerging the following season as Second Division Fulham's Chief Operating Officer.

At the end of the season, he had obviously caught the bug again, and took over as manager. Yet again, he had an immediate effect. Fulham won the Second Division Championship with 101 points, although Keegan had been enticed away to his dream role, in charge of England, and had to quit the Cottagers at the end of the season. England were in a state of disarray after Glenn Hoddle's tenure and in danger of failing to qualify for the European Championship.

Keegan steadied the ship, took them to a successful play-off victory against Scotland and led them on to Belgium and Holland. His lack of international managerial experience proved his downfall, however, and England lost vital leads against Portugal and Romania, although they did at least beat Germany in a major tournament for once. Keegan resigned after England then lost to Germany in Wembley's final match, a World Cup qualifier.

He returned to the more familiar surroundings of club management, at Manchester City in 2001. After the previous season's relegation, a typical Keegan rollercoaster ride ended in another title, as City went straight back to the Premier League, having scored 108 league goals. His main criticism as a manager has been that he neglects his defence, preferring to concentrate on scoring more goals than the opposition, but City are establishing themselves again in the top flight and there are sure to be more twists and turns in the never boring Kevin Keegan story.

FINAL

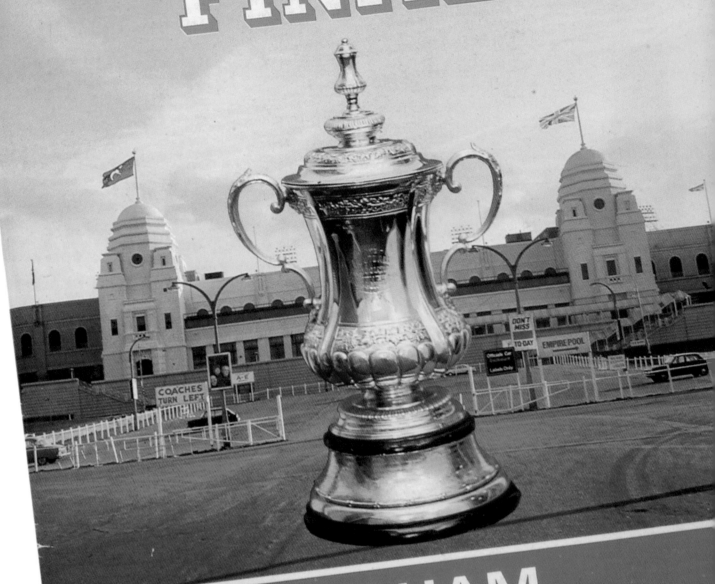

FULHAM
VERSUS
WEST HAM UNITED

SATURDAY, 3rd MAY, 1975   Kick-off 3

Official Souvenir Programme . . . 20p

WEMBLEY STAD

Fulham v West Ham United
F.A. Cup Final, Saturday 3rd May 1975

Hammers Taylor-Made

Preview

Fulham were appearing in their first final, were at Wembley for the first time and had never won a major trophy. They had knocked West Ham out of the Football League Cup earlier in the season though. West Ham had won the F.A. Cup once before, in 1964, and had returned the following year to win the European Cup Winners Cup.

Fulham finished 9th in the Second Division, the best they had managed since promotion from the Third Division in 1971. They were the third club from the Second Division to reach a Wembley Final that season, and they were hoping to match Sunderland's feat of two years earlier. West Ham finished 13th in the First Division, a considerable improvement on the previous year, when they had escaped relegation only by a point.

Semi–Finals, Saturday 5th April 1975

Birmingham City Gallagher	*1:1*	**Fulham** Mitchell	*(Hillsborough, Sheffield)*	
Ipswich	*0:0*	**West Ham United**	*(Villa Park, Birmingham)*	
Birmingham City	*0:1* *(AET)*	**Fulham** Mitchell	*(Maine Road, Manchester)*	*Replay (Wednesday 9th April 1975)*
Ipswich Jennings o.g.	*1:2* *(AET)*	**West Ham United** A. Taylor	*(Stamford Bridge, London)*	*Replay (Wednesday 9th April 1975)*

The Match

Fulham had played well in the first half, but fell behind on the hour. Cutbush lost the ball to Holland, who sent Jennings away to shoot. Mellor palmed it out, but Alan Taylor sent the rebound through his legs and into the net. Four minutes later, Mellor failed to hold Paddon's shot, and Taylor was there again, to smash the ball into the net. The Cup was won by a man who had scored twice in the quarter-finals, the semi-finals, and now the final, after starting the season with Fourth Division Rochdale.

Fulham	*0:2*	**West Ham United** A. Taylor 2

Fulham:
Mellor, Cutbush, Lacy, Mullery (Captain), Fraser, Moore, Conway, Slough, Mitchell, Busby, Barrett, Lloyd (Sub),
Alec Stock (Manager)

West Ham United:
Day, McDowell, Lampard, Bonds (Captain), T. Taylor, Lock, Jennings, Paddon, A. Taylor, Brooking, Holland, Gould (Sub),
John Lyall (Manager)

Referee:	*P. Partridge (Bishop Auckland)*
Attendance:	*100,000*

Five years later, Fulham dropped back into the Third Division, and never appeared at Wembley again. West Ham reached the following year's European Cup Winners Cup Final, before losing 4-2 to Anderlecht in an exciting game in Brussels. They were relegated in 1978, but won the F.A. Cup, as a Second Division side, two years later.

FOOTBALL ASSOCIATION CHALLENGE CUP COMPETITION

FINAL

MANCHESTER UNITED

SOUTHAMPTON

WEMBLEY STADIUM

Saturday 1st May 1976. Kick off 3pm.

Official Souvenir Programme 20p

Manchester United v Southampton

F.A. Cup Final, Saturday 1st May 1976

Saints Cast Out Red Devils

Preview

United had reached the semi-finals four times since winning the F.A. Cup in 1963, although they had won the European Cup, at Wembley, in 1968. Southampton were the second successive Second Division club to reach the final, and the third in four years. They had never won the Cup, but had reached two finals in three years as a Southern League club, at the turn of the century. In the second of these, in 1902, they took Sheffield United to a replay, before losing 2-1 at Crystal Palace, London.

United had won the Second Division Championship the previous year, and in their first season back in the top flight finished 3rd, their highest position since 1968. Southampton finished 6th in the Second Division, after relegation two years earlier, with United. Southampton had not beaten United, though, since 1970. Both teams had finished in the same league positions, as Leeds United and Sunderland, in the famous giantkilling final of 1973.

Semi–Finals, Saturday 3rd April 1976

Crystal Palace	**0:2**	**Southampton**	**(Stamford Bridge, London)**
		Gilchrist	
		Peach (penalty)	
Derby County	**0:2**	**Manchester United**	**(Hillsborough, Sheffield)**
		Hill 2	

The Match

Although they were in the Second Division, Southampton had more players with big match experience. They did their homework, and nullified United's young strikeforce. Then, with seven minutes left, McCalliog sent Bobby Stokes away, to outpace United's defenders and shoot past Stepney into the corner. Another sensational victory for the underdogs had given Southampton their first major trophy.

Manchester United	**0:1**	**Southampton**
		Stokes

Manchester United:
Stepney, Forsyth, Houston, Daly, B. Greenhoff, Buchan (Captain), Coppell, McIlroy, J.S. Pearson, Macari, Hill, McCreery (Sub),
Tommy Docherty (Manager)

Southampton:
Turner, Rodrigues, Peach, Holmes, Blyth, Steele, Gilchrist, Channon, Osgood, McCalliog, Stokes, Fisher (Sub),
Lawrie McMenemy (Manager)

Referee: C. Thomas (Treorchy)
Attendance: 100,000

Manchester United knocked Southampton out of the following year's F.A. Cup, and went on to win the trophy, as underdogs themselves. Southampton reached the European Cup Winners Cup quarter-finals, before losing to the holders and eventual finalists, Anderlecht.

Manchester United fans at Wembley

Liverpool v Manchester United

F.A. Cup Final, Saturday 21st May 1977

United Halt Liverpool Charge

Preview

Liverpool had won the F.A. Cup for the second time in 1974, and had won the F.A. Charity Shield, at Wembley, twice since then. United were appearing in their second successive Final, and had knocked out the holders, Southampton, in the last 16 to avenge their shock defeat the previous year. In the quarter-finals, they had beaten Aston Villa, who were to win the Football League Cup. Their third and last F.A. Cup win had been in 1963.

Liverpool retained the League Championship, were now on the verge of the elusive 'double' and, as they had also reached the European Cup Final, the amazing 'treble' was still a possibility. United finished 6th, in their second season back in the First Division. They had not beaten Liverpool since 1972. In the U.E.F.A. Cup, they had lost to Juventus, the eventual winners.

Semi–Finals, Saturday 23rd April 1977

Everton	2:2	Liverpool	(Maine Road, Manchester)	
McKenzie		McDermott		
Rioch		Case		
Leeds United	1:2	Manchester United	(Hillsborough, Sheffield)	
Clarke (penalty)		J. Greenhoff		
		Coppell		
Everton	0:3	Liverpool	(Maine Road, Manchester)	Replay (Wednesday 27th April 1977)
		Neal (penalty)		
		Case, Kennedy		

The Match

After a goalless first half, United struck the first blow in the 51st minute. Jimmy Greenhoff's header sent Stuart Pearson through, to beat Clemence at the near post with a low drive. Two minutes later, Liverpool, typically, were level. Jones crossed and Jimmy Case collected it on his thigh, before turning sharply to blast an unstoppable shot past Stepney. After a further two minutes, United restored their lead with a fortunate deflection. As Jimmy Greenhoff and Smith battled for possession in the penalty area, the ball fell for Macari whose shot would have gone wide, had it not hit Greenhoff's chest and looped over Clemence into the net. Liverpool fought back strongly, but the 'double', and consequently the 'treble', slipped away.

Liverpool	1:2	Manchester United
Case		Pearson,
		J. Greenhoff

Liverpool:
Clemence, Neal, J. Jones, Smith, R. Kennedy, E. Hughes (Captain), Keegan, Case, Heighway, Johnson, McDermott, Callaghan (Sub), Bob Paisley (Manager)

Manchester United:
Stepney, Nicholl, Albiston, McIlroy, B. Greenhoff, Buchan (Captain), Coppell, J. Greenhoff, J.S. Pearson, Macari, Hill, McCreery (Sub), Tommy Docherty (Manager)

Referee: R. Matthewson (Bolton)
Attendance: 100,000

Liverpool responded like the Champions they were, by beating Borussia Munchengladbach 3-1 in Rome to win the European Cup just four days later. The only other English club to win the trophy had been United, nine years earlier. Despite all their success, Liverpool would have to wait a further nine years before they reached another F.A. Cup Final. United were beaten in the last 16 of the European Cup Winners Cup the following season, despite scoring five at home against Porto. They would be back to contest their third F.A. Cup Final in four years, in 1979.

Paisley

Bob Paisley was the introverted reluctant manager, who conquered Europe with Liverpool's greatest ever side. He started out as an amateur wing half just before the war and was in the Bishop Auckland side which won the F.A. Amateur Cup, in 1939 at Sunderland. Liverpool signed him up, but he was 27 before he could make his league debut, because of the hostilities. It was a long drawn-out season with ice and snow causing hundreds of postponements, but it was an exciting one for Liverpool, with the Reds eventually clinching the first post-war League Championship in June 1947. They had also reached the F.A. Cup semi-finals, before losing to Second Division Burnley, Paisley's first disappointment in the only competition to consistently elude him, both as player and manager.

Liverpool had another good Cup run in 1950, and Paisley's lob set them on their way to a 2-0 victory over Everton in the semi-final, at Maine Road. At last, he had a chance for F.A. Cup glory. Alas, he injured his knee a week later and missed Liverpool's defeat by Arsenal at Wembley. He retired in 1954, but stayed at the club, and trained as a physiotherapist. Five years later, he became Liverpool's trainer and when Bill Shankly arrived as manager, Paisley became more of a psychological tactician, part of the legendary 'boot room', who got together daily to plan their strategies. Shankly became a hero on Merseyside, bringing three League Championships and two F.A. Cups to Anfield, plus their first European trophy, the UEFA Cup.

In 1970, Paisley became assistant manager and when Shankly suddenly announced his retirement, after their second F.A. Cup win, Paisley was offered the job. At 55, this quiet man suddenly found himself thrust into the limelight as manager of one of the top sides in the country. His experience was more valuable than he probably thought.

He maintained the 'boot room' and set about strengthening the side in the Liverpool tradition, with lower league players being blooded in the reserves and crucially, converting Ray Kennedy from a striker to a midfielder. They failed to win anything in his first season and his doubters were quick to suggest that it was impossible to follow the great Bill Shankly.

Twelve months later, they were silenced as Paisley's Liverpool took the League Championship and the UEFA Cup, his players responding magnificently to clinch the title at Wolves, after being a goal down and recovering from a two goal deficit in the UEFA Cup Final against Bruges. Shankly had been highly critical of the need for a defensive approach to European games and much preferred a more attacking style, but Paisley embraced it and re-modelled the Reds on a strong defence, with the ability to frustrate and slow things down, especially in hostile foreign surroundings.

In 1976-77, they came agonising close to winning the 'treble'. The Championship was retained fairly comfortably, and Paisley's side fought off the challenge of Everton to reach his only F.A. Cup Final as a manager. Fearful of avoiding a replay, which would have had to take place in late June, he changed his selection plans for the final against Manchester United and rested 35-year-old Ian Callaghan, because the European Cup Final was only four days after Wembley. Paisley had hoped Callaghan could control the midfield against United. Liverpool were narrowly beaten 2-1, and Paisley had to lift them for the biggest game of their careers.

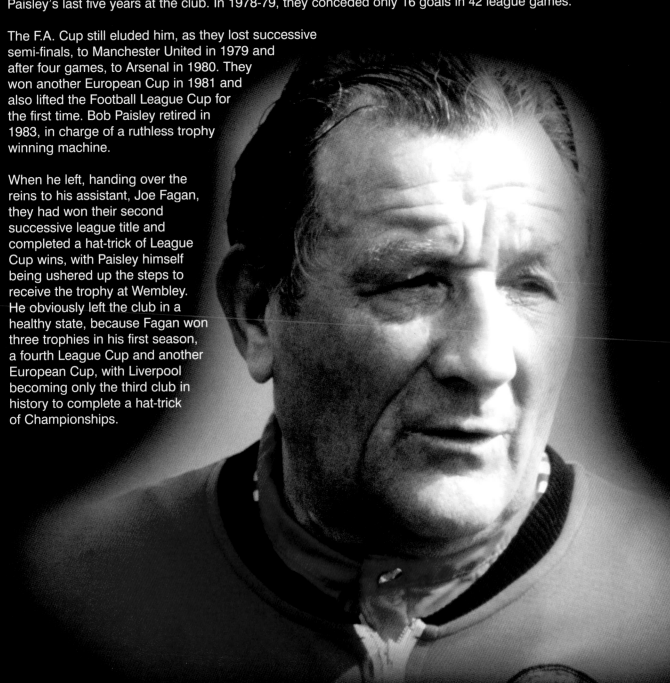

On the night, they were magnificent, beating Borussia Munchengladbach 3-1 in Rome. Paisley then had to replace Kevin Keegan, who left for Hamburg. Kenny Dalglish proved more than capable as his replacement. In 1978, they retained the European Cup, the first British side to win it twice, and it was Dalglish who scored the only goal, in the Wembley final, Paisley's first triumph under the twin towers. They lost the title to Nottingham Forest that year, but Liverpool were to win four more Championships in Paisley's last five years at the club. In 1978-79, they conceded only 16 goals in 42 league games.

The F.A. Cup still eluded him, as they lost successive semi-finals, to Manchester United in 1979 and after four games, to Arsenal in 1980. They won another European Cup in 1981 and also lifted the Football League Cup for the first time. Bob Paisley retired in 1983, in charge of a ruthless trophy winning machine.

When he left, handing over the reins to his assistant, Joe Fagan, they had won their second successive league title and completed a hat-trick of League Cup wins, with Paisley himself being ushered up the steps to receive the trophy at Wembley. He obviously left the club in a healthy state, because Fagan won three trophies in his first season, a fourth League Cup and another European Cup, with Liverpool becoming only the third club in history to complete a hat-trick of Championships.

...L ASSOCIATION CHALLENGE CUP COMPE...

CUP FINA...

50th WEMBLEY FA CUP FINAL

ARSENAL v IPSWICH TOWN

Saturday 6th May 1978 Kick off 3pm

Wembley Stadium

Official Souvenir Programme 50p

Arsenal v Ipswich Town

F.A. Cup Final, Saturday 6th May 1978

Roger And Out

Preview

Arsenal were appearing in their third final of the decade, having won the 'double' in 1971 and then losing the following year. Ipswich had reached their first final, but had previously appeared at Wembley, 50 years earlier, in the Southern Amateur League, beating Ealing Association 4-0.

Arsenal finished 5th in the First Division, their highest position since finishing runners-up in 1973. They also reached the Football League Cup semi-finals. Ipswich had been only a point away from the League Championship the previous year, but finished 18th, their lowest position since 1971 and just three points clear of relegation. In the UEFA Cup, they reached the last 16, before losing on penalties, in Barcelona after winning the first leg 3-0.

Semi–Finals, Saturday 8th April 1978

Arsenal *Macdonald 2, Rix*	*3:0*	**Leyton Orient**	**(Stamford Bridge, London)**
Ipswich *Talbot, Mills* *Wark*	*3:1*	**West Bromwich Albion** *T. Brown (penalty)*	**(Highbury, London)**

The Match

Ipswich surprisingly dominated the match, hitting the woodwork three times, before finally breaking through after 77 minutes. A low cross from Geddis went behind the Arsenal defence and Young could only turn it into the path of Roger Osborne, who drove it past Jennings. The emotion of the occasion was too much for Osborne. He went off immediately, exhausted, to be substituted, but his one moment of glory had given Ipswich a very popular and deserved victory.

Arsenal	*0:1*	**Ipswich Town** *Osborne*

Arsenal:
Jennings, Rice (Captain), Nelson, Price, O'Leary, Young, Brady, Hudson, Macdonald, Stapleton, Sunderland, Rix (Sub),
Terry Neill (Manager)

Ipswich:
Cooper, Burley, Mills (Captain), Talbot, Hunter, Beattie, Osborne, Wark, Mariner, Geddis, Woods, Lambert (Sub),
Bobby Robson (Manager)

Referee: *D. Nippard (Christchurch)*
Attendance: *100,000*

Arsenal returned to win the F.A. Cup the following year, in one of the most dramatic finals in the history of the competition.
Ipswich reached the quarter-finals of the European Cup Winners Cup, before again losing a first leg lead,
to Barcelona. This time, they went out on away goals, and Barcelona went on to win the trophy.

Bobby Robson, son of a Durham miner, joined Fulham in 1950, only to suffer relegation to the Second Division two years later. Although the club never really challenged for promotion, the young striker's formative years were spent in an environment where expression was encouraged. Fulham were always entertaining and a number of their players were keen to discuss tactics. Robson took an F.A. coaching course, wanting to learn, particularly in view of England's recent humiliation at the feet of the Hungarians. In 1955, he made his Wembley bow, scoring for a London select side, in the European Fairs Cup against Frankfurt.

Fulham sold him to West Bromwich Albion later that season and he was converted to an attacking midfielder. West Brom almost made it to Wembley in 1957, leading twice in the semi-final against Aston Villa, before losing narrowly in the replay. This was the closest Robson got to playing in an F.A. Cup Final. He ended the year as an international, however, scoring twice at Wembley for England against France, alongside three Manchester United players (Byrne, Edwards and Taylor), who were making their last appearances before the tragedy of the Munich air disaster took their lives.

Robson played in the following year's World Cup in Sweden and won 20 caps in all, scoring four goals, including the first in the 9-3 thrashing of Scotland in 1961. Things turned sour at West Brom and Robson was sold back to Fulham, who were now in the First Division. Realising that coaching was his best option once his playing days were over, the Fulham captain looked for other opportunities. He coached Oxford University for a while and left Fulham in 1967 to manage a Canadian team, Vancouver Royals. This was a short-lived experience, as he was quickly ousted in favour of the great Ferenc Puskas, but in January 1968, he found himself as manager of a struggling Fulham side. They were relegated at the end of the season and Robson was sacked after a poor start to the next. He felt aggrieved that he hadn't been given a fair crack of the whip, but he applied for the manager's job at Ipswich Town and began 1969 with a further opportunity to learn his trade in the First Division.

At first, there were problems with player unrest, but this time Robson was given the time to sort things out and by the mid-1970s they had a side, which was consistently qualifying for Europe. In 1978, they finally hit the jackpot and Robson led them to their first F.A. Cup win. The UEFA Cup followed in 1981, when Ipswich should also have won the Championship in a season where they were challenging on three fronts up until April. After another season where they finished runners-up to Liverpool, Robson was chosen to succeed Ron Greenwood as England Manager. Again, he had to learn the ropes. He began with the difficult decision of ending Kevin Keegan's international career and when England failed to qualify for the 1984 European Championship, there were calls for Keegan's return. Robson rode the criticism and took England to Mexico for the World Cup. A poor start was rescued by Gary Lineker's hat-trick against Poland.

England went on to reach the quarter-finals before Diego Maradona's trickery ended their hopes. A disappointing European Championship followed, before Robson decided to bow out at the 1990 World Cup, in Italy. The media had criticised him heavily over the years, but he managed to go out on a high, taking England to the semi-finals, for the first time in a World Cup played abroad. They had ridden their luck at times, but there were also outstanding performances and they were genuinely unlucky not to beat the West Germans, before eventually going out on penalties.

He spent the next nine years abroad, thus avoiding the pressures of the English media, but gaining a reputation as one of the top coaches in the world. Robson spent two Championship-winning years, at PSV Eindhoven in Holland, where he had the Brazilian ace, Romario, scoring for him.

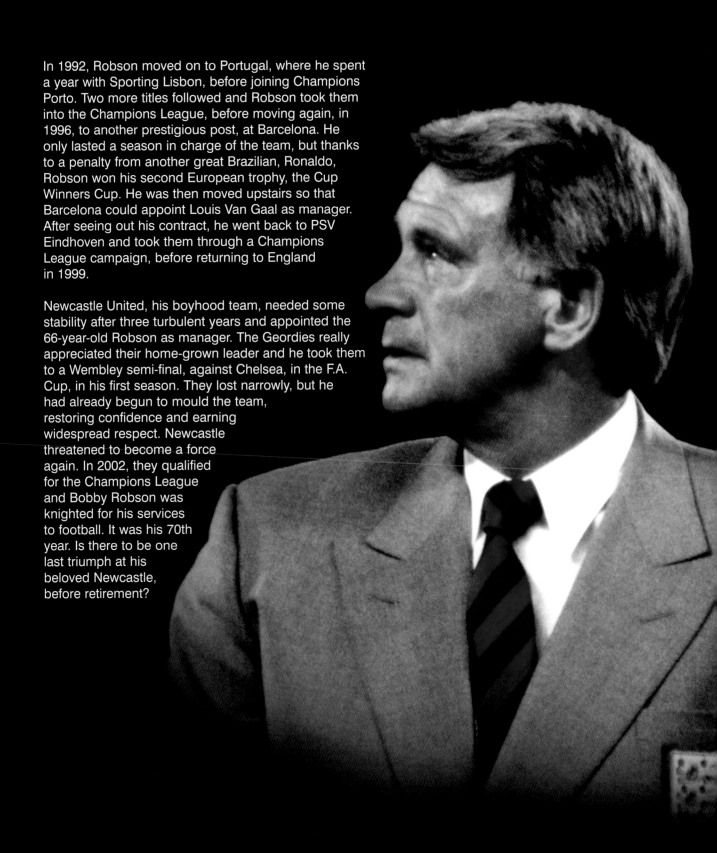

In 1992, Robson moved on to Portugal, where he spent a year with Sporting Lisbon, before joining Champions Porto. Two more titles followed and Robson took them into the Champions League, before moving again, in 1996, to another prestigious post, at Barcelona. He only lasted a season in charge of the team, but thanks to a penalty from another great Brazilian, Ronaldo, Robson won his second European trophy, the Cup Winners Cup. He was then moved upstairs so that Barcelona could appoint Louis Van Gaal as manager. After seeing out his contract, he went back to PSV Eindhoven and took them through a Champions League campaign, before returning to England in 1999.

Newcastle United, his boyhood team, needed some stability after three turbulent years and appointed the 66-year-old Robson as manager. The Geordies really appreciated their home-grown leader and he took them to a Wembley semi-final, against Chelsea, in the F.A. Cup, in his first season. They lost narrowly, but he had already begun to mould the team, restoring confidence and earning widespread respect. Newcastle threatened to become a force again. In 2002, they qualified for the Champions League and Bobby Robson was knighted for his services to football. It was his 70th year. Is there to be one last triumph at his beloved Newcastle, before retirement?

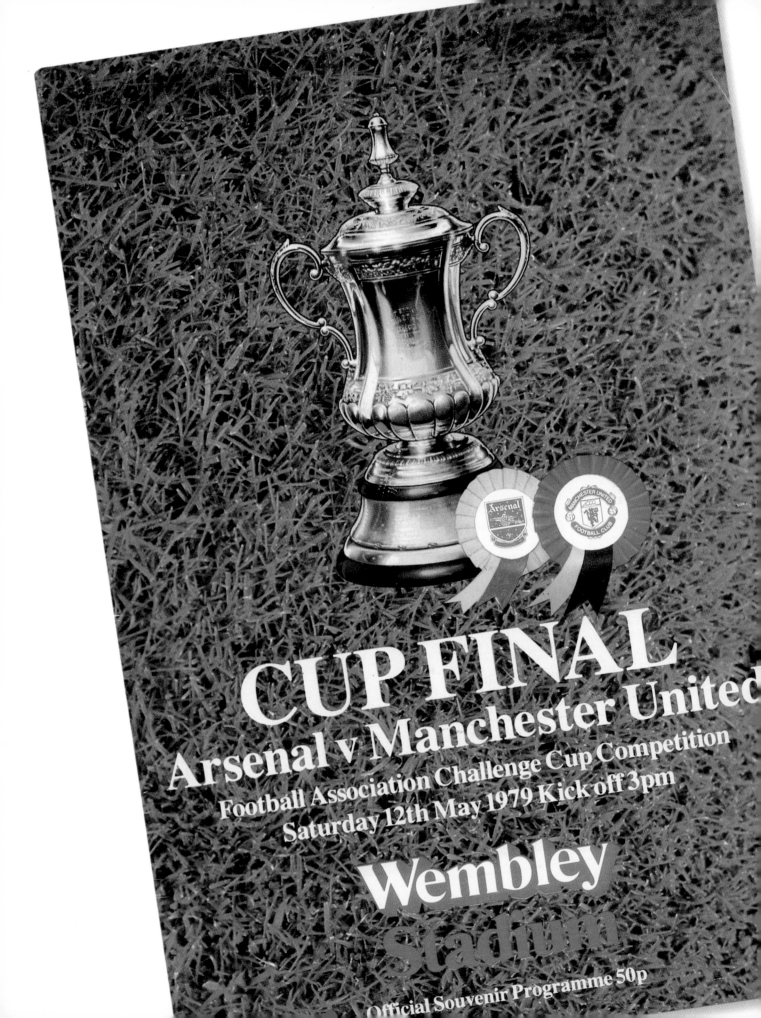

CUP FINAL
Arsenal v Manchester United

Football Association Challenge Cup Competition
Saturday 12th May 1979 Kick off 3pm

Wembley
Stadium

Official Souvenir Programme 50p

Arsenal v Manchester United

F.A. Cup Final, Saturday 12th May 1979

Four Minutes Without Warning

Preview

These two sides were evenly matched, with a wealth of experience between them. Arsenal had been well beaten in the previous year's final and were hell bent on winning the Cup for the first time since the 'double' triumph of 1971. In the last 16, they had won away, at Nottingham Forest, who went on to win both the Football League Cup and the European Cup. United were appearing in their third final in four years. After ending Liverpool's 'treble' dreams in 1977, they had beaten them again, in the semi-finals, leaving their opponents to concentrate on their third League Championship in four years. Arsenal finished 7th in the First Division, and reached the last 16 of the UEFA Cup, where they lost to the eventual finalists, Red Star Belgrade. United finished two places below them.

Semi–Finals, Saturday 31st March 1979

Arsenal *Stapleton, Sunderland*	*2:0*	*Wolverhampton W.*	*(Villa Park, Birmingham)*	
Liverpool *Dalglish* *Hansen*	*2:2*	*Manchester United* *Jordan* *B. Greenhoff*	*(Maine Road, Manchester)*	
Liverpool	*0:1*	*Manchester United* *J. Greenhoff*	*(Goodison Park, Liverpool)*	*Replay (Wednesday 4th April 1979)*

The Match

After 12 minutes, Liam Brady worked an opening and passed to Stapleton on the wing. Stapleton's through ball enabled Price to draw Bailey out of his goal and lay the ball back for two attackers and two defenders to fight for. Brian Talbot, who had helped Ipswich beat Arsenal in the previous year's final, just beat Buchan and Coppell, and his own team-mate, Sunderland, to force the ball past Nicholl on the line, to give Arsenal the lead. Two minutes before half-time, Arsenal appeared to clinch it, when Brady's supremely accurate cross was headed in by an unmarked Frank Stapleton (who was to score for United, in the 1983 final). Arsenal were thus coasting to victory, with four minutes left, when the whole stadium was thrown into turmoil, as United finally broke through. Coppell's free kick was knocked back into the goalmouth by Jordan and Gordon McQueen fired past Jennings, despite being surrounded by five Arsenal defenders, lazily waiting for the final whistle. United threw everything into attack, Arsenal panicked and United equalised, less than two minutes later. Coppell sent Sammy McIlroy away down the right. The Irishman cut inside, beating off desperate lunges from O'Leary and Walford, who had only come on as substitute a minute before United's first goal, and slipped the ball under the advancing Jennings. Pandemonium ensued. Arsenal were stunned, United euphoric. Yet there was to be a final twist. Brady galvanised Arsenal back into action, passing to Rix, out on the left. Rix's cross tempted Bailey out, but he could not reach it, and Alan Sunderland slid in, just ahead of Albiston, to restore Arsenal's lead. For United, it was a desperately cruel result. The last four incredible minutes were in complete contrast to the rather drab match which had been played out up until then. Comparisons were drawn to the 1953 final, but never had such emotions of triumph and despair been packed into such a short space of time, and still been completely exhaustive.

Arsenal *Talbot, Stapleton* *Sunderland*	*3:2*	*Manchester United* *McQueen* *McIlroy*	

Arsenal:
Jennings, Rice, Nelson, Talbot, O'Leary, Young, Brady, Sunderland, Stapleton, Price, Rix, Walford (Sub),
Terry Neill (Manager)

Manchester United:
Bailey, Nicholl, Albiston, McIlroy, McQueen, Buchan, Coppell, J. Greenhoff, Jordan, Macari, Thomas, B. Greenhoff (Sub),
Dave Sexton (Manager)

Referee:	*R. Challis (Tonbridge)*
Attendance:	*100,000*

Arsenal became the first club to reach three successive F.A. Cup Finals, at Wembley, the following year. They also reached the European Cup Winners Cup Final, but lost 5-4 on penalties, following a goalless draw after extra time, with Valencia in Brussels. This time, their luck deserted them at the crucial moment. United were League runners-up to Liverpool the following year and came back to Wembley in 1983, for both domestic Cup Finals.

Goalscorer Trevor Brooking celebrates the final whistle

Arsenal v West Ham United

F.A. Cup Final, Saturday 10th May 1980

A Step Too Far For The Gunners

Preview

Arsenal, the holders, had become the first club since Blackburn Rovers, in 1886, to reach three successive F.A. Cup Finals. In the longest semi-final of all time, they had eventually beaten the League Champions, to avenge their defeat in the F.A. Charity Shield the previous year. Their fifth F.A. Cup win had seen one of the most dramatic climaxes in the history of the competition. West Ham had won the Cup for the second time in 1975, but had lost at Wembley in the F.A. Charity Shield three months later.

In an exhausting season, Arsenal had also reached the European Cup Winners Cup Final for the first time and finished 4th in the First Division, their highest position since finishing runners-up in 1973. Both teams reached the quarter-finals of the Football League Cup, West Ham losing to the holders, and eventual finalists, Nottingham Forest, in extra time in the replay. Forest went on to retain the European Cup. Having been relegated two years earlier, and finishing only 7th in the Second Division, West Ham were aiming to become the lowest placed club to win the F.A. Cup, since Wolverhampton Wanderers in 1908.

Semi–Finals, Saturday 12th April 1980

Arsenal	*0:0*	**Liverpool**	*(Hillsborough, Sheffield)*	
Everton Kidd (penalty)	*1:1*	**West Ham United** Pearson	*(Villa Park, Birmingham)*	
Arsenal Sunderland	*1:1* *(AET)*	**Liverpool** Fairclough	*(Villa Park, Birmingham)*	*Replay (Thursday 16th April 1980)*
Everton Latchford	*1:2* *(AET)*	**West Ham United** Devonshire, Lampard	*(Elland Road, Leeds)*	*Replay (Wednesday 16th April 1980)*
Arsenal Sunderland	*1:1* *(AET)*	**Liverpool** Dalglish	*(Villa Park, Birmingham)*	*2nd Replay (Monday 28th April 1980)*
Arsenal Talbot	*1:0*	**Liverpool**	*(Highfield Road, Coventry)*	*3rd Replay (Thursday 1st May 1980)*

The Match

West Ham began well, on an extremely hot day. In the 13th minute, Devonshire's cross was pushed over to the far post by Jennings. Cross shot, but it was blocked by Young. The rebound fell to Pearson, whose shot flew across goal, where Trevor Brooking stooped to divert the ball past Jennings with his head. Arsenal looked jaded, and West Ham held on for a surprise   F.A. Cup win.

Arsenal	*0:1*	**West Ham United** Brooking

Arsenal:
Jennings, Rice (Captain), Devine, Talbot, O'Leary, Young, Brady, Sunderland, Stapleton, Price, Rix, Nelson (Sub), Terry Neill (Manager)

West Ham United:
Parkes, Stewart, Lampard, Bonds (Captain), Martin, Devonshire, Allen, Pearson, Cross, Brooking, Pike, Brush (Sub), John Lyall (Manager)

Referee: *G. Courtney (Spennymoor)*
Attendance: *100,000*

Four days later Arsenal lost on penalties to Valencia, following a goalless draw after extra time in the European Cup Winners Cup Final in Brussels. For all their efforts, they ended up with nothing. Arsenal finished 3rd the following year, but did not win honours again until 1987, when they captured the Littlewoods Cup for the first time. It was 1991, before they reached Wembley again, in the F.A. Cup. West Ham reached the European Cup Winners Cup quarter-finals the following year, where they lost to the eventual winners, Dynamo Tbilisi, despite winning the second leg in the U.S.S.R.

*The Wimbledon team celebrate their fantastic victory
over heavy favourites Liverpool in the 1988 F.A. Cup Final*

Chapter Seven
1981 - 90

Britain went to war with Argentina in 1982 over the Falkland Islands. The country rejoiced when Prince Charles married Diana Spencer, but the decade was blighted by a succession of disasters. A ferry capsized, a jumbo jet blew up in mid-air and crashed onto a housing estate and another crashed into a motorway embankment.

Football too, suffered three major disasters. A fire in an old wooden stand at Bradford killed 56 and a wall collapsed in Brussels before the European Cup Final, killing 39. Finally, an overcrowded terrace at Hillsborough, Sheffield before the F.A. Cup semi-final, led to 97 people losing their lives. Ground improvements suddenly became high priority. England graced the World Cup again, almost reaching the final in 1990. Liverpool continued to rule at home, but English clubs were banned from European competitions for five years.

Wembley saw a growing number of football matches and concerts over the decade. In 1990, the stadium became all-seated. Speedway was finally brought to a close, but American football became an annual event. In 1985, the Live Aid concert raised over £70 million for the starving in Africa.

Giantkillers and Bridesmaids

Telford United, regular visitors to Wembley in the F.A. Trophy Final have never beaten a top-flight club in the F.A. Cup, but in 1985, they became only the fourth non-league team to reach the last 16, since 1920. In the fifth round, they came up against the holders, Everton, at Goodison Park. Telford held them for 68 minutes, before the Merseysiders broke through to score three goals. Everton went on to reach the final and won both the League Championship and the European Cup Winners Cup.

Altrincham were one of the most consistent non-league clubs in the late 1970's and early 80's, but never made it into the Football League. They won the F.A. Trophy twice, at Wembley, and the Alliance Premier League (later known as the Conference) in each of its first two seasons. Altrincham were also a fine Cup side, beating nine league clubs in seven seasons, culminating in a 2-1 win at First Division Birmingham City, in 1986. This was only the second occasion since 1920, that a top-flight club had been beaten, at home, by a non-league side. Birmingham were relegated that season and suffered further humiliation when Robert Hopkins slid the ball past his own keeper, a young David Seaman, to put Altrincham into the fourth round.

When Sutton United, from the Conference, were drawn at home to First Division, Coventry City in the 1989 third round, they were not expected to stop a side, which had won the Cup less than two years earlier. Yet the Sky Blues fell to a couple of cleverly rehearsed set-piece moves from corner kicks. Captain, Tony Rains got the first, just before half-time. David Phillips fired Coventry level, only for Matthew Hanlan to volley Sutton in front again, six minutes later. Coventry bombarded the Sutton goal, but the Surrey part-timers held out to secure their place in the record books. Lower division clubs also made their mark in the decade. Plymouth Argyle, from the depths of the Third Division, reached the semi-finals in 1984, but pride of place has to go to Bournemouth, who beat the holders, Manchester United in the 1984 third round. This was the only defeat suffered by United in the Cup, between January 1982 and March 1986. They were Wembley winners in both 1983 and 1985, but were well beaten, 2-0, at Dean Court.

Southampton just managed to fall short of major honours, despite a star-studded line-up of Kevin Keegan, Alan Ball and Mike Channon. Peter Shilton arrived in 1982, and two years later, the Saints were riding high when they faced Everton in the F.A. Cup semi-final, where Adrian Heath's goal, three minutes from the end of extra time, knocked them out. In 1986, it was Liverpool who stood in their way, when Southampton reached the semi-finals again. After 37 minutes, England international defender, Mark Wright suffered a broken leg, in a collision with Shilton, but the Saints took the Reds to extra time, where two Ian Rush goals finally got the better of them. Liverpool went on to win the 'double'.

When Trevor Francis scored all four goals in a 4-0 win for Birmingham City against Bolton Wanderers, the only 16-year-old ever to score four in a league match, it was clear that he had a bright future. In his second season, the Blues were promoted to the First Division and reached the F.A. Cup semi-finals, where they lost, 3-0, to Leeds United. They lost another semi-final, to Second Division, Fulham, after a replay, in 1975 and the lightning pace of Francis would never again be as close to gracing the final. In 1979, he became the first million-pound player in Britain, when he signed for Nottingham Forest. Francis repaid a large chunk when he headed the only goal on his European debut, in the European Cup Final itself, in Munich.

Trevor Francis

He moved on to Manchester City, but was then lured to Sampdoria, where he won an Italian Cup winner's medal. He picked up a Scottish League Cup winner's medal for Rangers and was briefly player-manager of Queens Park Rangers. He was sacked at the end of 1989, but Ron Atkinson signed Francis as a player, for Sheffield Wednesday, only for the club to suffer relegation. They were promoted straight back to the First Division and when Atkinson left, Francis took his second job as player-manager. In 1993, now orchestrating from the bench, he masterminded a glorious run to both domestic Cup finals including a historic Sheffield derby victory in the F.A. Cup semi-final, at Wembley. Unfortunately, Wednesday lost both finals, to Arsenal. In the F.A. Cup, it was a heartbreaking last minute winner in extra time in the replay, which left his team without any reward from a marathon season. He was sacked in 1995, but Birmingham City lured him back into management, the following year, in an effort to win promotion to the Premier League. They were to suffer an agonising series of near misses, in three successive Play-Off semi-finals, twice losing on penalties and also losing the 2001 Worthington Cup Final, to Liverpool in a shootout. Francis was sacked in 2002, moving on to Crystal Palace. Birmingham meanwhile, won promotion after a penalty shootout, the final irony for Francis, who continues to search for long-overdue success as a manager.

In Celebration of The One-Hundredth
Football Association Challenge Cup Competitio[n]

FINAL TIE

Manchester
City
v
Tottenham
Hotspur

1981

THE FOOTBALL ASSOCIATION CHALLENGE CUP

100

ONE HUNDREDTH FOOTBALL ASSOCIATION
CHALLENGE CUP COMPETITION ©

Saturday
9th May 1981
Kick-off 3.00p.m.

Wembley
Stadium

Official Souvenir Programme
80p

Manchester City v Tottenham Hotspur

F.A. Cup Final, Saturday 9th May 1981

Ricky's Replay Revival

Preview

Both clubs had last won the F.A. Cup in the 1960s, City in 1969 and Tottenham in 1967. Both clubs had won the League Cup twice, in the 1970s. City had beaten the eventual UEFA Cup winners in the Semi-Finals. In the First Division, City finished 12th, while Tottenham finished two places above them, in their highest position since promotion in 1978.

Semi–Finals, Saturday 11th April 1981

Ipswich Town	*0:1*	**Manchester City**	*(Villa Park, Birmingham)*
	(AET)	Power	
Tottenham Hotspur	*2:2*	**Wolverhampton W.**	*(Hillsborough, Sheffield)*
Archibald, Hoddle	*(AET)*	Hibbitt, Carr (penalty)	
Tottenham Hotspur	*3:0*	**Wolverhampton W.**	*(Highbury, London)*	*Replay (Wednesday 15th April 1981)*
Crooks 2, Villa			

The Match

City denied Tottenham the space their creative midfield skills needed, and drew first blood, after half an hour of the 100th F.A. Cup Final. From Ranson's cross, Aleksic could not prevent Tommy Hutchison's diving header finding the corner of the net. Tottenham came back into it in the second half, but their equalising goal, ten minutes from the end, was terribly bad luck for the man whose goal separated the sides, up until then. A free kick, on the edge of the area was taken by Ardiles. The Argentinian tapped it to Perryman. The captain steadied it, and Hoddle chipped it over the defensive wall. Hutchison, anticipating where the ball was going to go, left the wall, but the ball struck his shoulder, and gave Corrigan no chance. Neither side could find a winner, as several players collapsed with cramp in extra time.

Manchester City	*1:1*	**Tottenham Hotspur**
Hutchison	*(AET)*	Hutchison o.g.

Manchester City:
Corrigan, Ranson, McDonald, Reid, Power (Captain), Caton, Bennett, Gow, Mackenzie, Hutchison, Reeves, Henry (Sub)
John Bond (Manager)

Tottenham Hotspur:
Aleksic, Hughton, Miller, Roberts, Perryman (Captain), Villa, Ardiles, Archibald, Galvin, Hoddle, Crooks, Brooke (Sub)
Keith Burkinshaw (Manager)

Referee: K. Hackett (Sheffield)
Attendance: 100,000

The Match

Wembley's first ever F.A. Cup Final replay sprung to life with two goals in the first ten minutes. After seven minutes Ricardo Villa fired Tottenham in front. City hit back within three minutes. Steve Mackenzie spectacularly volleyed a headed pass from Hutchison into the corner of the net. It was so quick and powerful that Aleksic never saw it. Five minutes after the interval, City took the lead. Bennett and Miller tussled for possession, and Bennett went down as Hughton also challenged. A penalty was given and Kevin Reeves found the corner of the net. Once again, Tottenham had to fight back. After 70 minutes, Archibald controlled a superb Hoddle lob and Garth Crooks stabbed it past Corrigan for the equaliser. With 13 minutes left, Galvin ran down the wing before passing to Villa. Five City defenders surrounded the Argentinian, but he beat both Caton and Ranson, and then cut in between them. As Caton then lunged, he stabbed it through Corrigan's legs for a brilliant individual goal. It was a fitting end to a highly entertaining game.

Manchester City	*2:3*	**Tottenham Hotspur**	*Replay (Thursday 14th May 1981)*
Mackenzie, Reeves (penalty)		Villa 2, Crooks	

The teams were the same as before with the exception of Tueart coming on as a substitute for Manchester City during the match.

Referee: K. Hackett (Sheffield)
Attendance: 92,000

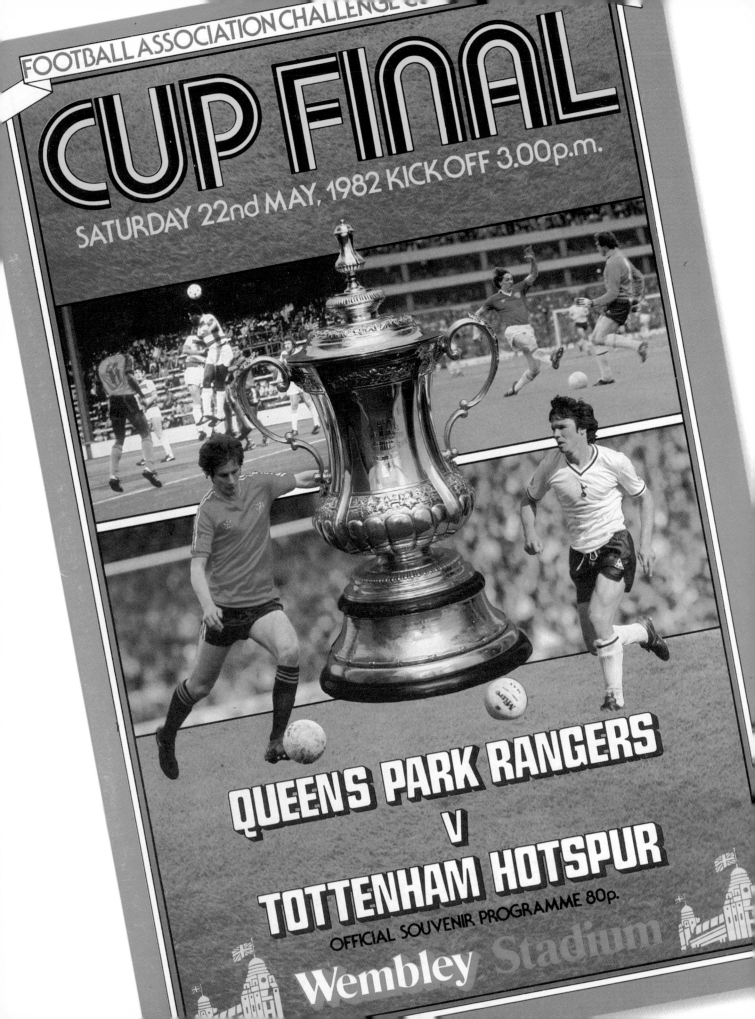

Queens Park Rangers v Tottenham Hotspur

F.A. Cup Final, Saturday 22nd May 1982

Anything But A Doddle For Hoddle

Preview

Rangers had never progressed beyond the quarter-finals of the competition before, but they had won the League Cup at Wembley as a Third Division club back in 1967. Tottenham, the holders, were aiming to equal Aston Villa's record of seven F.A. Cup wins. It was 20 years since any club had retained the F.A. Cup, but Tottenham were the last club to do it. Rangers finished 5th in their third season in the Second Division after relegation. They missed out on promotion by just two points, but were hoping to become the fourth Second Division club in the past decade to win the F.A. Cup. Tottenham had had an exhausting season. They finished 4th in the First Division, their highest position since 1971. They reached the European Cup Winners Cup semi-finals before losing to the eventual winners, Barcelona, and they almost won the Football League Milk Cup, losing in extra time to the holders, Liverpool. They had become the first club to reach both the League Cup and F.A. Cup Finals in the same season. The last thing they wanted was to face an F.A. Cup Final replay, as in the previous year.

Semi–Finals, Saturday 3rd April 1982

Leicester City	0:2	**Tottenham Hotspur**	(Villa Park, Birmingham)
		Crooks, Wilson o.g.	
Queen's Park Rangers	1:0	**West Bromwich Albion**	(Highbury, London)
Allen			

The Match

Tottenham were the stronger side, but could not find a way past Peter Hucker, Rangers' keeper and Wembley seemed set for its first goalless F.A. Cup Final. After 109 minutes, Glenn Hoddle played a one-two with Roberts and his shot deflected off Currie to beat Hucker. Rangers forced a replay with just five minutes remaining. From Stainrod's throw, Hazell back-headed it into the middle for Terry Fenwick to head over Clemence from inside the six-yard box. Five years later, he was to join Tottenham.

Queen's Park Rangers	1:1	**Tottenham Hotspur**
Fenwick	**(AET)**	Hoddle

Queen's Park Rangers:
Hucker, Fenwick, Gillard, Waddock, R. Hazell, Roeder (Captain), Currie, Flanagan, C. Allen, Stainrod, Gregory, Micklewhite (Sub)
Terry Venables (Manager)

Tottenham Hotspur:
Clemence, Hughton, Miller, Price, Hazard, Perryman (Captain), Roberts, Archibald, Galvin, Hoddle, Crooks, Brooke (Sub)
Keith Burkinshaw (Manager)

Referee:	C. White (Harrow)
Attendance:	100,000

The Match

After six minutes, Currie brought down Roberts and Glenn Hoddle sent Hucker the wrong way from the penalty spot to give Tottenham the best possible start. Unlike the first game, it was Rangers who impressed the most as they fought gallantly for the equaliser. This time it was not to be, despite creating several chances and Tottenham held out for a fortunate victory. Their endeavours over the season, however, perhaps warranted their good fortune at the end.

Queen's Park Rangers	0:1	**Tottenham Hotspur**	Replay (Thursday 27th May 1982)
		Hoddle (penalty)	

The teams were the same as before with the exception of Neill and Micklewhite replacing Roeder and Clive Allen in the Queen's Park Rangers starting line-up. Burke was the substitute.

Referee:	C. White (Harrow)
Attendance:	90,000

Rangers won the Second Division Championship the following year by a comfortable ten points, and were promoted back to the First Division. In 1986, they were back at Wembley, for the Milk Cup Final. Tottenham were well beaten in the last 16 of the following season's European Cup Winners Cup, by Bayern Munich. After seven Wembley appearances in 15 months, they would have to wait a further five years for their next visit, in the F.A. Cup Final.

Glenn Hoddle was one of the most skilful players of his generation. His superb long-range passing ability and shooting power made him much admired. At Tottenham Hotspur, he was a legendary figure. Yet he never really established himself in the England side, his main criticism being that he was a luxury player, with little inclination for the less creative tasks required from the team, such as tracking back.

Although Spurs were relegated in 1978, when Hoddle was only 18, his skills were already appreciated and he helped them win promotion the following year. In 1979, he made a dramatic first appearance on the international stage, by scoring from 20 yards with a stunning sidefooted strike, against Bulgaria at Wembley. It certainly helped his fellow professionals make him their Young Player of the Year. Hoddle even showed some goalkeeping prowess as he, incredibly, maintained a clean sheet, after taking over in goal against Manchester United at Old Trafford in an F.A. Cup replay, which Tottenham won 1-0 after extra time. Spurs were becoming a major force and after two successive quarter-final defeats, they won the F.A. Cup in 1981, in a thrilling replay. The following year, they retained it, with Hoddle scoring in both final games. His penalty in the replay was the only goal. UEFA Cup success followed, in 1984, but Hoddle's limited international appearances led to him wanting to move abroad.

The 1986 World Cup had given him an opportunity to shine on the big stage and he helped England reach the quarter-finals, but after losing in the following year's F.A. Cup Final with Spurs, he was signed by Arsene Wenger for Monaco. In his first season, they were French League Champions and Hoddle learned a lot about coaching and tactics from Wenger. Although his international career drew to a close, he was enjoying critical acclaim in France.

At the age of 33, he returned to England and joined Second Division Swindon Town as player-manager. It took him just two years to take them into the Premier League, after an exciting 4-3 Play-Off victory against Leicester City at Wembley, in which Hoddle scored the first goal, a typical sidefooted pass into the net. He didn't play for them in the Premier League, perhaps realising that they couldn't escape relegation. By the beginning of the following season, he had become Chelsea's player-manager and further enhanced his managerial reputation by leading his team to home-and-away victories over Manchester United, the team of the season. Chelsea beat Luton in a Wembley semi-final to book their place in the F.A. Cup Final, where they were to meet Manchester United. They held their illustrious opponents for an hour, before United ran out rather fortunate 4-0 winners. Hoddle's appearance as substitute failed to inspire them.

He retired from playing in 1995, and the following year the Football Association made the bold step of appointing 38-year-old Glenn Hoddle as England's youngest ever manager. The national side's World Cup hopes suffered an early blow, when Italy defeated them at Wembley, but Hoddle proved his worth as a coach and motivator, when his team resisted all Italian advances in the return in Rome and a goalless draw secured World Cup qualification. Unfortunately, Hoddle then showed his inexperience in the role with his handling of certain players.

In the finals, England were eliminated on penalties by Argentina, following a classic encounter in which England were reduced to ten men, after the dismissal of David Beckham just after half-time. Hoddle began to lose the respect of some of his players after publicly criticising them and was sensationally sacked in 1999, when he made some ill-judged comments about the disabled to the press. He took a year's break from the game before taking the manager's job at Southampton, where he reaffirmed his coaching credentials. In 2001, Tottenham Hotspur dismissed George Graham and Hoddle couldn't resist returning to the club where he knew he would be treated like the prodigal son. Time will tell if he can bring the glory days back to White Hart Lane.

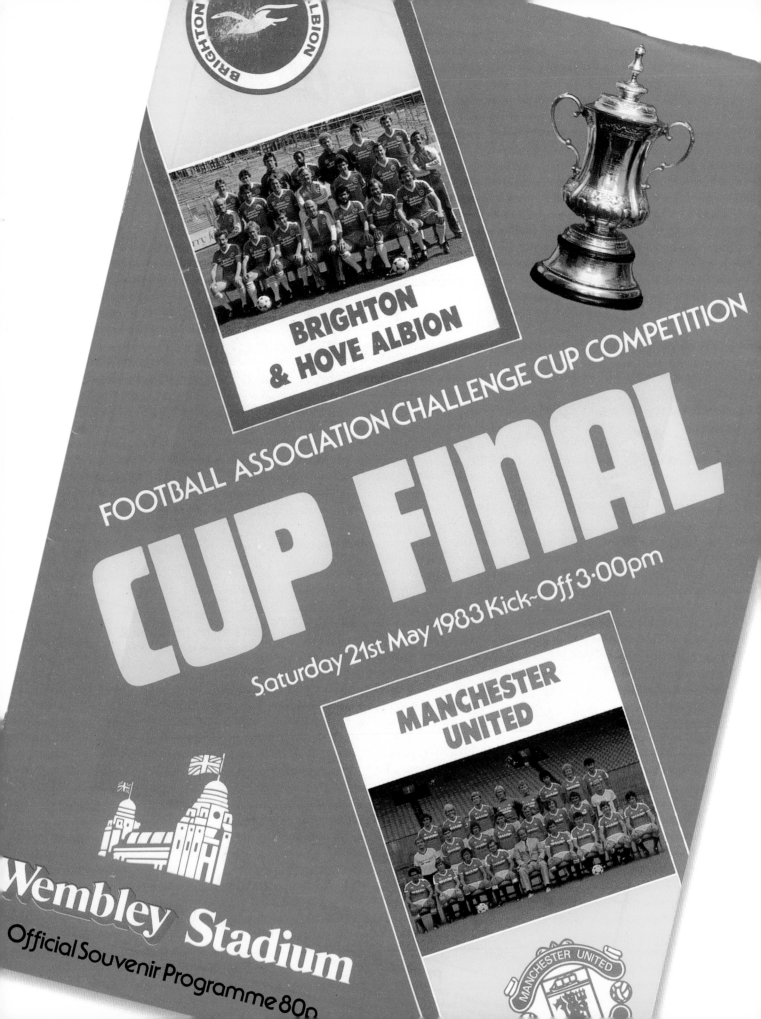

Brighton & Hove Albion v Man Utd

F.A. Cup Final, Saturday 21st May 1983

And Smith Must Score

Preview

Brighton had pulled off a sensational away win against the League Champions and Milk Cup holders, Liverpool, to reach the quarter-finals of the F.A. Cup for the first time. They were now appearing at Wembley for the first time and had never won a major trophy. United, by contrast, had won the F.A. Cup four times.

Brighton finished bottom of the First Division and were relegated after four seasons in the top flight. No club had ever won the F.A. Cup in a relegation season. United finished 3rd, for the second year in succession. In the UEFA Cup, they had gone out in the first round to Valencia of Spain.

Semi–Finals, Saturday 16th April 1983

Arsenal	1:2	*Manchester United*	*(Villa Park, Birmingham)*
Woodcock		Robson, Whiteside	
Brighton & Hove Albion	2:1	*Sheffield Wednesday*	*(Highbury, London)*
Case, Robinson		Mirocevic	

The Match

Brighton had nothing to lose and took a shock lead after 14 minutes. Howlett's cross went beyond Moran and Gordon Smith headed it beyond Bailey's reach. United equalised, ten minutes into the second half. Duxbury crossed and Whiteside dived to head the ball past Moseley and across the goalmouth, where Frank Stapleton beat Stevens to fire the ball into the roof of the net. He had scored against United, in the 1979 Final, for Arsenal. Nineteen minutes later, Muhren found Ray Wilkins in the clear with a long ball and the influential midfielder cut inside, as Pearce came to challenge, and curled a superb shot, which gave Moseley no chance and United the lead. The underdogs seemed beaten, but three minutes from the end, Case's corner found Grealish, outside the area. Gary Stevens ran on to his short pass, steadied himself and fired a dramatic equaliser to force extra time. In the last minute of the extra half-hour, Robinson found an unmarked Smith, with only Bailey to beat and a golden opportunity to give Brighton their first major trophy. A poor shot was safely gathered by the keeper, and United heaved a massive sigh of relief.

Brighton & Hove Albion	2:2	*Manchester United*	
Smith, Stevens	*(AET)*	Stapleton, Wilkins	

Brighton & Hove Albion:
Moseley, Ramsey, Pearce, Grealish (Captain), Stevens, Gatting, Case, Howlett, Robinson, Smith, Smillie, Ryan (Sub)
Jimmy Melia (Manager)

Manchester United:
Bailey, Duxbury, Albiston, Wilkins, McQueen, Moran, Robson (Captain), Muhren, Stapleton, Whiteside, Davies, Grimes (Sub)
Ron Atkinson (Manager)

Referee: A. Grey (Great Yarmouth)
Attendance: 100,000

The Match

After 24 minutes, Bryan Robson fired United ahead from a Davies pass. It was Davies who crossed for the second goal, five minutes later. Norman Whiteside rose to head powerfully past Moseley and Grealish, on the line. Brighton tried to respond but found themselves three goals down at the interval. Stapleton's header across goal just eluded McQueen and Foster, but Robson ran in unchallenged at the back post to destroy Brighton, with his second. After 62 minutes, Robson was held back by Stevens and Dutchman Arnold Muhren beat Moseley from the penalty spot to complete an emphatic victory for United.

Brighton & Hove Albion	0:4	*Manchester United*	**Replay (Thursday 26th May 1983)**
		Robson 2, Whiteside	
		Muhren (penalty)	

The teams were the same as before with the exception of Foster replacing Ramsey in the Brighton & Hove Albion starting line-up and taking over the captaincy, Gatting switched from centre back to right back

Referee: A. Grey (Great Yarmouth)
Attendance: 92,000

Bryan Robson was an aggressive dynamic midfielder, who scored many vital goals for club and country throughout his career. However, his willingness to be involved in everything led to numerous injuries, but he had great leadership qualities and captained both Manchester United and England. His first club was West Bromwich Albion, with whom he helped to win promotion to the First Division in 1976. Two broken legs were an ominous sign of things to come and set his progress back a little. This didn't stop him building a reputation in Ron Atkinson's successful side of the late 1970s though, and Robson played for England Under-21's as an over-age player at 22. A year later, he won the first of 90 England caps, against Ireland at Wembley, and when Ron Atkinson moved to Manchester United, in 1981, he spent £1.5 million to give Robson the opportunity to win major honours. His value soon multiplied.

In the 1982 World Cup, Robson scored twice in England's 3-1 win over France, his first coming after 27 seconds. He captained England for the first time later in the year. Domestic honours followed and 1983 was a magical year for United's new captain. They won the F.A. Cup, with Robson scoring twice in the replay. Six days later, he netted for England against Scotland at Wembley and then ended the summer by scoring both goals in United's Charity Shield victory against Liverpool, also at Wembley. They won the F.A. Cup again in 1985 and Robson led England to Mexico for the World Cup, the following year, only to damage an already weakened shoulder in the second game, which put him out of the rest of the tournament.

Back at Wembley, he scored twice in the Football League Centenary match and was one of the few players to come out of the 1988 European Championship, in Germany, with any credit. The injuries were taking their toll but Robson was still an inspirational figure. He showed that he was still quick off the mark in scoring England's fastest ever goal at Wembley, after 38 seconds of the stadium's last match of the 1980s, against Yugoslavia. Robson ended the season by becoming the first man to captain three winning F.A. Cup sides at Wembley and scored a goal as well. One last World Cup beckoned, but once again he limped out of the action in the second game and left for an operation on his Achilles.

With Alex Ferguson building a team which was to dominate for the next decade, the ageing injury-prone Robson was beginning to find his opportunities limited. He was still around to lead them to the European Cup Winners Cup, in 1991, but when United ended a 26-year wait for the title by winning the first Premier League Championship, in 1993, he was mainly being used as a substitute. The following year, when United won the 'double', Robson made his last appearance at Wembley, as a substitute in the F.A. Cup semi-final against Oldham, before ending his 13 years with the club to become Middlesbrough's player-manager.

His managerial talents came immediately to the fore and the club were promoted in his first season, as Football League Champions. Robson found that his reputation enabled him to attract world class stars to the north-east and the Juventus striker, Fabrizio Ravanelli, fresh from winning the European Cup, signed up alongside three Brazilians. The 1996-97 season was one that Boro's fans will never forget, but ultimately it backfired on Robson. Having never reached a major final before, Middlesbrough appeared in both domestic finals. Ravanelli gave them an extra-time lead in the Coca-Cola Cup Final, only for Leicester City to beat them after a replay. Despite a gallant fight, Boro were relegated before they met Chelsea in the F.A. Cup Final, where injuries and loss of form contributed to a poor performance on the day.

Robson, who had only made sporadic appearances in the first team as a substitute, finally retired from playing aged 40, and vowed to get them back to the Premier League. Twelve months later, he did just that, having signed Paul Gascoigne for the cause. They even reached another Coca-Cola Cup Final, although they again lost to Chelsea, after extra time. Boro found it a struggle to survive in the top flight on their return and in 2001, he finally relinquished the reins at the Riverside. Surely he will be back in football when the right opportunity comes along.

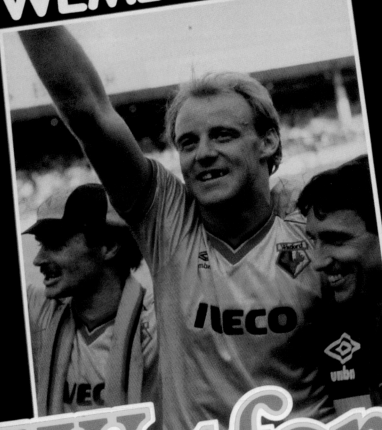

F.A. CUP FINAL
OFFICIAL SOUVENIR BROCHURE

WEMBLEY '84

Watford

Produced in conjunction with BENSKINS
Price: £1.50

EVERTON F.C
OFFICIAL HANDBOOK

FOOTBALL ASSOCIATION CHALLE

CUP
FINAL

SATURDAY 19 MAY
1984
KICK-OFF 3.00 p.m.

E·V·E·R·T·O·N
W·A·T·F·O·R·D

OFFICIAL SOUVENIR
PROGRAMME 80p

Everton v Watford

F.A. Cup Final, Saturday 19th May 1984

A Gray Day For The Hornets

Preview

Like Tottenham Hotspur and Manchester United in the two preceding years, the Milk Cup runners-up had returned to contest the F.A. Cup Final. Everton had held their mighty neighbours Liverpool to a goalless draw after extra time, two months earlier, before losing the replay. This was their first F.A. Cup Final since 1968, when they lost in extra time. Their last victory had been two years earlier, in 1966, when they came back from two goals down. Everton's last major trophy had been the League Championship in 1970. Watford were appearing in their first final and were at Wembley for the first time. In the last 16, they had beaten the previous year's finalists, Brighton and Hove Albion. Six years earlier, Watford had been Fourth Division Champions, beginning a meteoric rise up the Football League, which saw them finish runners-up in the top two divisions, in successive years.

Everton finished 7th in the First Division for the second year running, Watford finished 11th, having been League runners-up to Liverpool the previous year, in their first ever season in the First Division. Their first venture into European competition had seen them reach the last 16 of the U.E.F.A. Cup.

Semi–Finals, Saturday 14th April 1984

Everton	**1:0**	**Southampton**	**(Highbury, London)**
Heath	(AET)		
Plymouth Argyle	**0:1**	**Watford**	**(Villa Park, Birmingham)**
		Reilly	

The Match

Everton took the lead in the 38th minute. A cross from Richardson, who was transferred to Watford two years later, was headed out by Sinnott, but Steven knocked it back in to a now unmarked Graeme Sharp, who fired in off the post. After 52 minutes, the contest was effectively over, in very controversial circumstances. Sherwood leapt backwards to collect Steven's high cross, but Andy Gray headed it into the net before he could gather it. It could be argued that Gray had headed it out of Sherwood's hands, but the goal stood and Watford were beaten.

Everton	**2:0**	**Watford**
Sharp,		
Gray		

Everton:
Southall, Stevens, Bailey, Ratcliffe (Captain), Mountfield, Reid, Steven, Heath, Sharp, Gray, Richardson, Harper (Sub)
Howard Kendall (Manager)

Watford:
Sherwood, Bardsley, Price, Taylor (Captain), Terry, Sinnott, Callaghan, Johnston, Reilly, Jackett, Barnes, Atkinson (Sub)
Graham Taylor (Manager)

Referee: *J. Hunting (Leicester)*
Attendance: *100,000*

Everton won the European Cup Winners Cup the following year, with a 3-1 win against Rapid Vienna in Rotterdam and reached the F.A. Cup Final again. While Everton were to enjoy major successes in the next few years, Watford had reached their peak and were relegated back to the Second Division four years later. They were not to return to top-flight football until 1999, when they won the Play-Offs at Wembley.

Andy Gray played for four different teams in his five Wembley appearances and his goalscoring led to him winning a number of honours in a well-travelled career. This brave and fiery striker began with Dundee United and played in the club's first Scottish Cup Final in his first season. They were well beaten by Celtic, but Gray's goals earned him a move to Aston Villa in 1975 and he won his first Scotland cap at the end of the year.

The following season he was a revelation, although his international career stuttered to a halt when he was sent off in a World Cup qualifying match in Prague. Meanwhile, Villa were heading for the League Cup Final and Gray was voted the Player of the Year by his fellow professionals. He also picked up the Young Player of the Year award and finished the season as the First Division's leading scorer. Gray missed Villa's ultimate victory in the League Cup Final's second replay because of injury, an occupational hazard for a striker not afraid to put his head or his feet in, if there was a sniff of a chance.

He missed out on Scotland's disastrous World Cup in 1978, but won his place back and went on to win 20 caps. Villa would be European Champions by 1982, but they sold Gray to Wolverhampton Wanderers in 1979, for a British record fee of just under £1.5 million. Wolves won the League Cup at Wembley in his first season with them, and Gray scored the only goal in the final, a simple tap-in after a Nottingham Forest defensive mix-up. Gray proved just too expensive for them, however. They were relegated in 1982 and hit dire financial straits. Wolves were promoted straight back to the First Division, but were about to plunge headlong through the Football League, right down to the Fourth Division.

Gray was sold to Everton and, for once, he arrived at exactly the right time, just as Howard Kendall's side were about to become the dominant force in England. Cup-tied for the Milk Cup and denied an opportunity to play in a third League Cup Final, Gray grabbed another Wembley winner, against Watford as Everton lifted the F.A. Cup, their first major trophy for 14 years. It was a controversial headed goal, but it was the springboard to a glorious period in Everton's history.

They won the following year's League Championship and Gray's goals helped them into their first European final, with Gray getting the first in a 3-1 win in the Cup Winners Cup Final against Rapid Vienna, in Rotterdam. Having won two trophies, Everton returned to Wembley three days later, hoping to complete a fantastic 'treble' in the F.A. Cup Final. Sadly, it was all too much and a ten-man Manchester United side beat them in extra time.

With Gary Lineker joining for the following season, Andy Gray was surplus to requirements and returned to Aston Villa, who were relegated in 1987. He was loaned out to Third Division Notts County and then joined West Bromwich Albion, back in the Second Division, before a final swansong at his home-town favourite club, Rangers, as they won the first, of what was to be nine successive Scottish League Championships. Gray retired and became a hugely successful television pundit with an infectious

(left to right) Manchester United's Paul McGrath heads clear from Everton's Andy Gray

Everton v Manchester United

F.A. Cup Final, Saturday 18th May 1985

Norman's Conquest

Preview

Everton were the F.A. Cup holders and were hoping for as comfortable a victory as in the previous year's final. Since then, they had also won the F.A. Charity Shield at Wembley. United were attempting to regain the F.A. Cup for the second time in three years, after a convincing replay victory in 1983. Like Everton a year later, they had followed it up by beating Liverpool in the F.A. Charity Shield at Wembley.

Everton had won the League Championship for the first time since 1970 and were aiming to become the first team to win the 'double' since Arsenal in 1971. Three days earlier, they had beaten Rapid Vienna in Rotterdam to win the European Cup Winners Cup, their first European trophy, and so hoped to repeat Liverpool's three trophy wins of the previous year. United finished 4th in the First Division for the second year in succession. They lost at home to Everton in the Milk Cup, but reached the U.E.F.A. Cup quarter-finals, before losing on penalties to eventual finalists Videoton of Hungary.

Semi–Finals, Saturday 13th April 1985

Everton	**2:1**	**Luton Town**	*(Villa Park, Birmingham)*	
Sheedy, Mountfield	**(AET)**	*Hill*		
Liverpool	**2:2**	**Manchester United**	*(Goodison Park, Liverpool)*	
Whelan, Walsh	**(AET)**	*Robson, Stapleton*		
Liverpool	**1:2**	**Manchester United**	*(Maine Road, Manchester)*	*Replay (Wednesday 17th April 1985)*
McGrath o.g.		*Robson, Hughes*		

The Match

The sides had cancelled each other out, when a 78th minute incident transformed the game. Kevin Moran became the first player to be sent off in an F.A. Cup Final after a cynical foul on Reid, as he was clean through on goal. United's players were incensed with the harshness of the decision and were galvanised into action. With ten minutes left in extra time, Hughes sent Norman Whiteside away, down the right wing. The young Irishman cut inside and, faced with Van den Hauwe, managed to curl the ball round him and beyond Southall's dive for a magnificent goal. Everton's memorable season had finally caught up with them and their numerical advantage could not match United's determination.

Everton	**0:1**	**Manchester United**
	(AET)	*Whiteside*

Everton:
Southall, Stevens, Van den Hauwe, Ratcliffe (Captain), Mountfield, Reid, Steven, Gray, Sharp, Bracewell, Sheedy, Harper (Sub)
Howard Kendall (Manager)

Manchester United:
Bailey, Gidman, Albiston, Whiteside, McGrath, Moran, Robson (Captain), Strachan, Hughes, Stapleton, Olsen, Duxbury (Sub)
Ron Atkinson (Manager)

Referee:	*P. Willis (Meadowfield)*
Attendance:	*100,000*

Everton reached their third successive final the following year. United were denied the opportunity of competing in the European Cup Winners Cup by the Heysel Stadium disaster in Brussels, 11 days later and in the competition set up to replace the fixture gaps, the Screen Sport Super Cup, United were beaten home and away by the eventual finalists, Everton. They began the season with a determined run and won their first ten league games, yet they still could not win the Championship, finishing 4th for the third year in succession. In 1988, they were back at Wembley for the Football League Centenary Tournament, in which they beat Everton and, in 1990, they reached the F.A. Cup Final again.

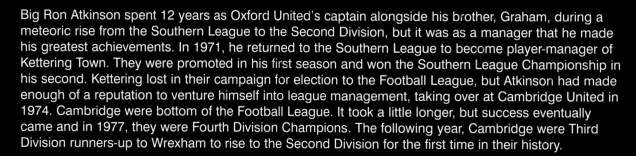

Big Ron Atkinson spent 12 years as Oxford United's captain alongside his brother, Graham, during a meteoric rise from the Southern League to the Second Division, but it was as a manager that he made his greatest achievements. In 1971, he returned to the Southern League to become player-manager of Kettering Town. They were promoted in his first season and won the Southern League Championship in his second. Kettering lost in their campaign for election to the Football League, but Atkinson had made enough of a reputation to venture himself into league management, taking over at Cambridge United in 1974. Cambridge were bottom of the Football League. It took a little longer, but success eventually came and in 1977, they were Fourth Division Champions. The following year, Cambridge were Third Division runners-up to Wrexham to rise to the Second Division for the first time in their history.

Atkinson had already left, before they clinched their second promotion, to take over at First Division West Bromwich Albion and he was celebrating himself. They qualified for the UEFA Cup for the first time, and also reached the F.A. Cup semi-finals by beating Nottingham Forest 2-0, one of only four games that the team of the season lost in all competitions. West Brom lost to Ipswich in the semi-final, but Atkinson was now a hot property. He had an exciting attacking team and allowed his players the freedom to express themselves on the field. The media loved him because he was always ready with a quick quip during interviews. All the qualities, in fact, that Manchester United traditionally looked for in a manager and when the relatively dour Dave Sexton was sacked by United in 1981, it was Atkinson who was approached to replace him. He was not out of his depth and their fans began to believe that this was the man who would bring the title back to Old Trafford.

In 1983, he took them to both major domestic finals, narrowly losing to Liverpool in extra time in the Milk Cup, before winning the F.A. Cup in a replay, after Brighton had almost pulled off a sensational victory in the first game. They won the Cup again in 1985 and after finishing a disappointing 4th in the First Division in successive years after promising more, this second Cup win raised hopes that they were now ready to maintain a sustained challenge. They began the following season like a train, winning their first ten league games and charging into a ten-point lead. Incredibly, they lost their way and finished 4th yet again. The disappointment was too much and Atkinson was dismissed the following season.

Alex Ferguson was to finally provide that much sought-after title, but it took him longer than Atkinson was given. This first dismissal was a blow to his pride, but he bounced back within a year, returning to West Bromwich Albion, now in the Second Division. His natural optimism was tested to the full as West Brom struggled, finishing only a point above the drop zone. Atkinson left after a year and moved to Spain to take over Atletico Madrid, where results were very favourable until he was inexplicably sacked, after just 96 days in charge, by their notorious president, Jesus Gil. Sheffield Wednesday provided Atkinson with some much needed stability in 1989 although his first full season ended disastrously, with relegation on goal difference after an unexpected end-of-season slump. This turned out to be a blessing in disguise, however. Atkinson set about putting things right and Wednesday won promotion straight back to the First Division, also remarkably winning the Rumbelows Cup at Wembley, beating, of all teams, Manchester United.

Aston Villa poached Atkinson before the start of the season, much to the disgust of the Hillsborough faithful, but for Atkinson, it was an opportunity too good to miss. He had begun his playing career at Villa, who had given him a free transfer in 1959 to Southern League Headington (later Oxford) United, after failing to break into the first team, thus ending his only chance of playing top-flight football.

Under Atkinson, Villa were challenging for the Premier League title within two years, but finally succumbed to Alex Ferguson's Manchester United, ending their 26-year quest for the title. Although the Championship was always a step too far for Atkinson, in 1994 he led Villa to the Coca-Cola Cup Final at Wembley, and once again, faced Manchester United, who were now the major force and chasing the domestic 'treble'. Atkinson got his tactics spot on, denying United the space their superior skills needed and Villa ran out surprise 3-1 winners.

It was his fourth Wembley triumph, with his third different club, and the two victories against the club which had sacked him eight years earlier must have given him immense satisfaction. It didn't last very long, however, and Atkinson was ousted from Villa Park after a poor start to the following season.

Now in his sixties, he had three more short-term managerial contracts before retiring to join the media as a football analyst and co-commentator.

Coventry City employed him after Villa, but after a dramatic escape from relegation, he became Director of Football whilst his assistant, Gordon Strachan, took over as manager. His old club Sheffield Wednesday took him on for seven months and he steered them clear of relegation. Nottingham Forest tried to do the same, the following year, but he had only three months and their plight was much worse than Wednesday's. They finished bottom, which was a sad end to Atkinson's managerial career, unless he can be tempted back by someone else.

Whiteside

Norman Whiteside was a record-breaking teenager, who achieved a lot in a career cut short by injury. This tall, aggressive and muscular striker was only 16 when he broke into Manchester United's first team and scored his first goal just eight days after his 17th birthday. He had a maturity far beyond his years and Billy Bingham was so impressed that he took the young starlet to the World Cup, where he won his first Northern Ireland cap, against Yugoslavia, becoming the youngest ever player in the tournament. Pele had previously held the record. Whiteside played in every match as the Irish beat the hosts, Spain, and came within one game of reaching the semi-finals.

With the encouragement of Ron Atkinson, he flourished in United's frontline, as they stormed through to two Cup Finals in 1983 and Whiteside set scoring records in both. He fired them into the lead against Liverpool, in the Milk Cup, becoming the youngest scorer in a Wembley final, before United lost in extra time.

Two months later, just after his 18th birthday, he became the youngest ever F.A. Cup Final scorer, when he headed United's second in a 4-0 replay victory against Brighton. It was clear he was a man for the big occasion. Later in the year, he scored the only goal as Northern Ireland pulled off a sensational victory against West Germany in Hamburg, in the European Championship, before losing out on goal difference to the Germans.

In 1985, having switched to midfield, he was back at Wembley to score the only goal in the F.A. Cup Final, against Everton, a superb curling effort in extra time, which enabled United to beat the odds after Moran was sent off. At the ripe old age of 21, Whiteside played in his second World Cup, and in 1987 he was on the mark at Wembley again, in the Football League Centenary match.

He seemed set for a long career. United sold him to Everton in 1989, but a knee injury forced him out of the game and he retired prematurely, aged 26, tragically young for such a great talent. Fortunately, because of his early development, he'd had time to win more trophies and medals than most players with longer careers had.

OFFICIAL SOUVENIR PROGRAMME £1·50

EVERTON∨LIVERPOOL

FOOTBALL ASSOCIATION CHALLENGE CUP COMPETITION

CUP FINAL

Everton v Liverpool
F.A. Cup Final, Saturday 10th May 1986

Rush's 'Double'

Preview

For the first time at Wembley, the F.A. Cup Final was contested between the top two teams in the league. Everton were appearing in their third successive final and hoping to regain the Cup for the second time in three years after comfortably beating Watford in 1984, but then failing to clinch the 'double' against ten men a year later. Liverpool had won the League Championship for the eighth time in 11 years, by two points from Everton, the previous year's League Champions. No player-manager had previously won a major honour, but Kenny Dalglish was now poised to lead his team to the first 'double', since Arsenal's in 1971. Remarkably, it was his first season in management, having taken over after the trauma of Brussels the previous year. The Merseyside rivals had met two years earlier, in the Milk Cup Final, with Liverpool winning the replay, but Everton had beaten them in the first of their two successive F.A. Charity Shield wins, five months later at Wembley. Liverpool had beaten the eventual Full Members Cup Winners, Chelsea, in the last 32 and were appearing in their first final since 1977, despite winning masses of other trophies since. Their last F.A. Cup win had been in 1974, Three days earlier, Liverpool had reached the Screen Sport Super Cup Final, where they would again meet Everton.

Semi–Finals, Saturday 5th April 1986

Everton *Harper, Sharp*	**2:1** **(AET)**	**Sheffield Wednesday** *Shutt*	*(Villa Park, Birmingham)*
Liverpool *Rush 2*	**2:0** **(AET)**	**Southampton**	*(White Hart Lane, London)*

The Match

Everton were determined to make up for losing the league title to Liverpool the previous week and took the lead in the 28th minute. A superb long ball from Reid found Gary Lineker, with only Grobbelaar to beat as Hansen gave chase. The keeper saved Lineker's first effort, but could not stop the rebound, despite a brave dive. Everton tried to finish Liverpool off by pushing for a second, but a Molby pass, in the 57th minute, transformed the game, as Ian Rush beat the offside trap, took the ball round Mimms and equalised against the run of play. Once Liverpool were back in the game, there was no stopping them. Six minutes later, Stevens' tackle on Molby, as he was about to centre, forced the ball behind Dalglish, but found Craig Johnston, who fired Liverpool into the lead. Everton pushed forward and Liverpool broke away to score a third, with six minutes left. Yet another important pass from the Dane Jan Molby sent Whelan away, down the left. He checked and lobbed the ball across to the unmarked Rush, who fired home his second. Perhaps Everton were a little unlucky, but Liverpool's past domination of English and European football deservedly warranted their inclusion in the list of 'double' winners.

Everton *Lineker*	**1:3**	**Liverpool** *Rush 2, Johnston*

Everton:
Mimms, Stevens, Van den Hauwe, Ratcliffe (Captain), Mountfield, Reid, Steven, Lineker, Sharp, Bracewell, Sheedy, Heath (Sub),
Howard Kendall (Manager)

Liverpool:
Grobbelaar, Lawrenson, Beglin, Nicol, Whelan, Hansen (Captain), Dalglish, Johnston, Rush, Molby, MacDonald, McMahon (Sub)
Kenny Dalglish (Player-Manager)

Referee: A. Robinson (Waterlooville)
Attendance: 98,000

The Screen Sport Super Cup Final was held over until the following season, but Liverpool once again came out on top, with a crushing 7-2 aggregate victory over Everton. With Liverpool also winning at Everton in the Littlewoods Cup quarter-finals the following year, they appeared to have the upper hand, but it was Everton who regained the League Championship, for the second time in three years, with Liverpool, inevitably, runners-up. In 1989, they met again in the F.A. Cup Final.

Kenny Dalglish, the most capped Scotsman of all time, with 102 caps, had a glittering career as a player and manager, winning a multitude of trophies and awards. He was revered by fans on both sides of the border, no mean achievement. Although he grew up a Rangers fan in Glasgow, it was European Champions Celtic who signed him in 1967. After impressing in the reserves, he became a first team regular in 1971. His first major cup final, in the Scottish League Cup, was a massive shock as Celtic were beaten 4-1 by Partick Thistle, although the young Dalglish scored their consolation goal. He did not have long to wait for a winner's medal. Celtic won the 'double' of Scottish League Championship and Scottish Cup and the youngster was also capped by Scotland for the first time. Dalglish was to win three more league titles with Celtic, scoring over 100 goals, and had four more cup wins. In 1977, he was captain when they won the 'double' again and he scored Scotland's Wembley winner against England, as he had done at Hampden Park the previous year. Having won all that he could in Scotland, he then took on an immense challenge by signing for Liverpool for a British record of £440,000.

The Reds had just won the European Cup and Dalglish was bought to replace Kevin Keegan. His debut was at Wembley in a goalless F.A. Charity Shield, but he wasted little time in proving his worth, banging in the goals and revealing his adeptness in controlling the ball in tight situations, before turning to curl the ball into the top corner, a Dalglish speciality. If there was to be only one direction Liverpool could go in after their successes of the previous year, it wasn't down. At the end of the season, they met Bruges at Wembley in their second European Cup Final and Dalglish scored the only goal of the game. It was a beauty. After running onto a through ball from Graeme Souness, Dalglish waited for the keeper to go down, before beating him with an exquisite lob.

The following season, Liverpool won the League Championship with a record 68 points and Dalglish was Footballer of the Year, scoring in an awesome Charity Shield performance at Wembley against Arsenal. He played in three World Cups, scoring in two of them, but never really shone at international level, despite equalling Denis Law's record of 30 goals. In 1981, he picked up another European Cup winner's medal. Dalglish went on to win four successive League Cups with Liverpool and six League Championships, forming a deadly partnership with Ian Rush.

In 1983, he was Footballer of the Year again and also picked up the P.F.A. Player of the Year award. He ended the year by scoring his 100th Football League goal and became only the second player to reach a century in both England and Scotland. Another European Cup was won that season, but in 1985, the Heysel Stadium disaster ended Liverpool's European adventures for six years and manager Joe Fagan retired.

The club surprisingly turned to the 34-year-old Dalglish in this traumatic period and he took over as player-manager. His first season was an undoubted success and did much to restore faith in the club. Dalglish not only became the first player-manager to win a major trophy, scoring the goal at Chelsea which clinched the title, but he capped it all by winning the F.A. Cup as well, a trophy which had eluded Liverpool since 1974. The 'double' at last and both achieved at the expense of Everton. It couldn't get any better for the fans on the Kop.

He won two more Championships with Liverpool and the F.A. Cup again, although their 1989 win was horrifically scarred by the Hillsborough disaster, a cruel blow coming just four years after Heysel. Dalglish played his last game in 1990 and then stunned the football world with a sudden resignation, the following year, citing the stress caused by trying to keep Liverpool at the top as the reason.

They have not won the Championship since. Dalglish reappeared later that year as manager of Second Division Blackburn Rovers and within two months had taken them to the top of the table. A late slump saw them drop into the Play-Off zone, but they recovered enough to win the Play-Off Final at Wembley against Leicester City. Thanks to the club's owner, Jack Walker, Dalglish had plenty of money to spend and Blackburn were able to challenge the big clubs in the Premier League, but it was their manager who bought wisely and shielded his players from the psychological media battles faced by the top clubs. In 1995, Blackburn won the Premier League Championship on a dramatic final day, their first title since 1914, with Dalglish becoming only the fourth manager to win the title with different clubs.

He then surprised everyone by handing over the manager's job to his assistant, Ray Harford, and became a remote Director of Football for the club. Harford was unable to maintain their success and was sacked after two years in charge. Dalglish moved on to Newcastle United in 1997, again stepping into Kevin Keegan's shoes. He took them into the Champions League and to the F.A. Cup Final, but his dour public manner won little favour with the Geordies and he was sacked after little more than 18 months in the job.

A brief spell in charge of Celtic followed in 2000, in which Dalglish took them to a Scottish League Cup win, but it was clear that his appetite for the job of manager was waning and he much preferred to avoid the pressure. He had, after all, won just about everything as a player and manager, with very little left to prove.

Wembley Greats
Gary Lineker
Everton, Tottenham Hotspur & England

Gary Lineker was one of the world's greatest predatory strikers, who worked hard to perfect his style. He rarely scored spectacular goals, but his speed of thought and immaculate timing brought him hundreds of goals in a 15-year career. Leicester City, his local club, signed Lineker straight from school. His first honour came in 1980, as Leicester won the Second Division Championship and the young Lineker got his first taste of the top flight, albeit brief, as they were relegated a year later. Nevertheless, Lineker worked on his game and when Leicester were promoted again, in 1983, he was the Second Division's top scorer.

International recognition followed and when Lineker topped the First Division scoring charts in 1985, Leicester could no longer hold on to their England striker. He was transferred to League Champions Everton, making his debut at Wembley in a Charity Shield victory against Manchester United. Within 12 months, he would be one of the most sought-after forwards in the world. Lineker had one of his best ever seasons. He was the Football League's top scorer with 30 goals, and won both the Footballer of the Year and the P.F.A. Player of the Year award. Unfortunately, it wasn't quite enough to win anything for Everton. Liverpool won the 'double' and Everton were double runners-up, despite Lineker putting them ahead in the F.A. Cup Final.

In the World Cup, Lineker rescued his country from an early exit by scoring a hat-trick against Poland and went on to grab the coveted Golden Boot as the tournament's top scorer. With sudden worldwide acclaim, Lineker was elevated to a new level and Terry Venables paid over £4.2 million to take him to Barcelona. He played well for the Catalan giants and earned much respect by scoring a hat-trick against Real Madrid. This was followed by an incredible performance in Madrid against Spain, for England, as Lineker scored all four goals in a 4-2 victory. He even appeared for the Rest of the World at Wembley, in the Football League Centenary match. In 1988, Barcelona won the Spanish Cup, but for the next season, new manager Johann Cruyff switched Lineker to the right wing and he was less effective. Although this unsettled him, he still helped the club to win the European Cup Winners Cup, before Terry Venables, now at Tottenham Hotspur, brought the ace striker back to England.

Lineker was still scoring regularly for his country and grabbed another four goals in the 1990 World Cup, where his big-match temperament was invaluable to Bobby Robson's side as they reached the semi-finals. It was Lineker who twice converted spot kicks in the quarter-final, one of which saved England from losing to Cameroon and the other proved to be the winner in extra time. He then popped up to equalise against West Germany in Turin, before England bowed out on penalties after a titanic struggle.

The following year, Lineker finally picked up a domestic honour in his home country as Spurs lifted the F.A. Cup, after two memorable Wembley encounters. He scored twice in the stadium's first semi-final, to guide his team-mates to a fantastic 3-1 victory against Arsenal, one of only three defeats suffered by the Gunners in all competitions. The final wasn't quite as memorable for Lineker, as his first half penalty was saved, but an exciting game went Spurs' way in extra time and the miss was forgotten. By now, he was closing in on Bobby Charlton's England goalscoring record of 49. A golden opportunity arose at Wembley, in May 1992, when England were awarded a penalty against Brazil. Lineker's casual chipped kick was saved and he remained on 48 goals, despite three subsequent appearances in the European Championship in Sweden.

He had already decided to retire from international football once the tournament ended. Lineker crowned his final season at Tottenham by winning the Footballer of the Year award for a second time and spent a further two years in Japan, before retiring to take up a broadcasting career with the B.B.C. With typical professionalism, he worked hard at his new career and was rewarded when he became the regular presenter of the Saturday night highlights show, 'Match of the Day'. Gary Lineker will undoubtedly, remain a household name for many years.

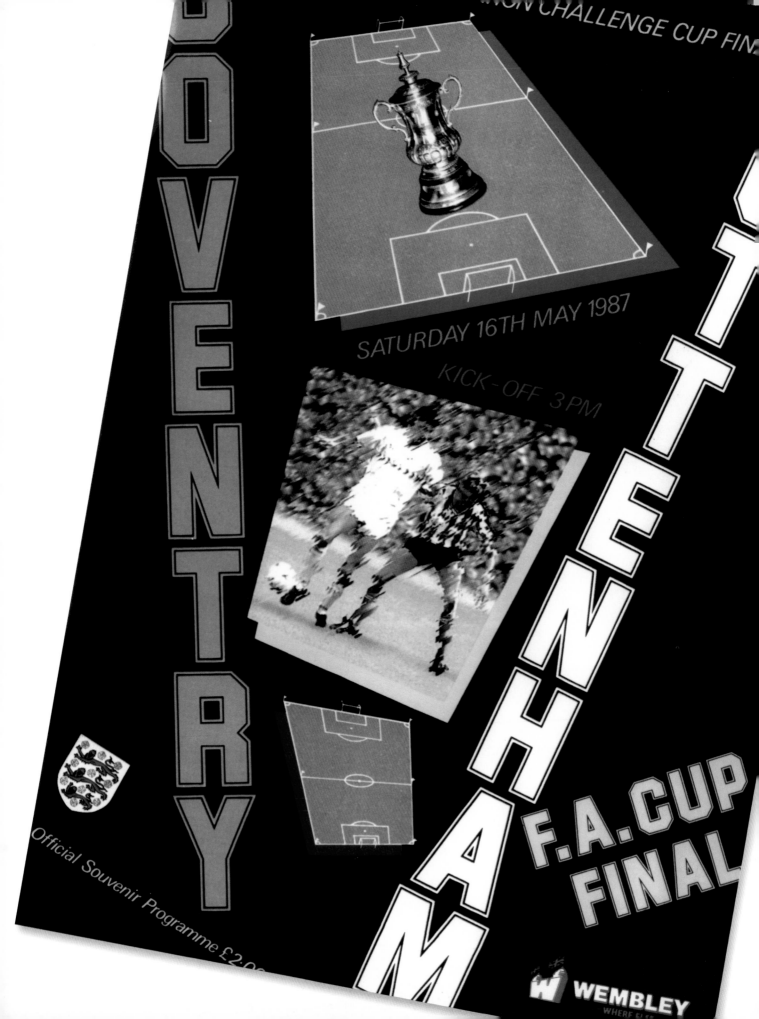

Coventry City v Tottenham Hotspur

F.A. Cup Final, Saturday 16th May 1987

Sky Blue Glory At Long Last

Preview

Coventry had never previously progressed beyond the Quarter-Finals, they had never appeared at Wembley before, and they had never won a major trophy. Tottenham, by contrast, were aiming to become the first club to win the F.A. Cup eight times. They had never lost a final and were chasing their third Cup win of the decade, after two replay wins, in 1981 and 1982. Victory would give them their fourth major triumph in seven years, following their 1984 UEFA Cup win, on penalties.

Coventry finished 10th in their 20th season in the First Division, their highest position since 1979. Tottenham finished 3rd, for the second time in three years, and reached the Littlewoods Cup semi-finals, where they won the away leg, went two up on aggregate in the home leg and led the replay, with eight minutes left. Incredibly they lost to eventual winners, Arsenal.

Semi–Final, Sunday 12th April 1987

Coventry City	**3:2**	**Leeds United**	(Hillsborough, Sheffield)
Gynn, Houchen	*(AET)*	Rennie	
Bennett		Edwards	

Semi–Final, Saturday 11th April 1987

Tottenham Hotspur	**4:1**	**Watford**	(Villa Park, Birmingham)
Hodge 2, C. Allen		Allen	
P. Allen			

The Match

Tottenham struck first, in the second minute. Waddle crossed and Clive Allen outjumped Peake to head the opener. Within seven minutes, Coventry had struck back. Downs' cross was flicked on by Houchen and seemed to be falling harmlessly for Clemence to collect. Dave Bennett nipped in to take the ball round him and fired past the covering Hodge. Five minutes before the interval, Tottenham, rather fortunately, regained the lead. Ogrizovic came for Hoddle's floated free kick, but checked and left himself in 'no man's land'. Mabbutt attempted to shoot, but connected instead with the back of Brian Kilcline's foot, which forced the ball in. Tottenham threatened to score again, but it was Coventry who replied again, after 63 minutes. An attack down the middle found Keith Houchen, who played the ball wide to Bennett. From the resulting cross, Houchen left his markers and dived to send a bullet header past Clemence. Coventry then secured a popular victory, six minutes into extra time. Gary Mabbutt did well to cut out McGrath's cross, but the ball flew up off his knee, and looped over Clemence for the winning goal.

Coventry City	**3:2**	**Tottenham Hotspur**
Bennett, Houchen	*(AET)*	C. Allen
Mabbutt o.g.		Kilcline o.g.

Coventry City:
Ogrizovic, Phillips, Downs, McGrath, Kilcline (Captain), Peake, Bennett, Gynn, Regis, Houchen, Pickering, Rodger (Sub), Sedgley (Sub)
John Sillett (Manager)

Tottenham Hotspur:
Clemence, Hughton, Thomas, Hodge, Gough (Captain), Mabbutt, C. Allen, P. Allen, Waddle, Hoddle, Ardiles, Claesen (Sub), Stevens (Sub)
David Pleat (Manager)

Referee:	*N. Midgley (Salford)*
Attendance:	*98,000*

After the Charity Shield, Coventry did not appear at Wembley again. Tottenham returned the following year, for the Wembley International Tournament, where they were beaten by great rivals Arsenal and in 1991, they faced the Gunners again, in Wembley's first F.A. Cup semi-final.

Wimbledon's Vinnie Jones shows his aggresive determination as he out battles Liverpool's John Barnes

Liverpool v Wimbledon

F.A. Cup Final, Saturday 14th May 1988

Dons' Delight

Preview

Liverpool had won the League Championship, for the seventh time in ten years, losing only two league games all season, and seemed set to win the 'double' for the second time in three years, having clinched it at Wembley in 1986. Since then, they had failed to win at Wembley, losing the previous year's Littlewoods Cup Final and making an early exit, on penalties, from the previous month's Football League Centenary Tournament, although they had beaten the winners of the tournament in the F.A. Cup semi-finals a week earlier. Wimbledon represented, surely, the most remarkable rags-to-riches story. Twenty-five years earlier, they had won the F.A. Amateur Cup at Wembley. They had only been in the Football League for 11 years and only five years earlier, they had been Fourth Division Champions. In their first ever F.A. Cup semi-final, they had beaten the eventual Littlewoods Cup winners. A week later, like Liverpool, they had made a first round exit, in the Football League Centenary Tournament, losing to Fourth Division Tranmere Rovers. Wimbledon finished 7th in only their second season in the First Division.

Semi–Finals, Saturday 9th April 1988

Liverpool	2:1	**Nottingham Forest**	(Hillsborough, Sheffield)
Aldridge 2 (1 Penalty)		Clough	
Luton Town	1:2	**Wimbledon**	(White Hart Lane, London)
Harford		Fashanu (penalty)	
		Wise	

The Match

While Wimbledon could not match Liverpool for skill, their team spirit was second to none and allied to clever tactics, they were more than a handful for anyone. Thus, they overcame a team that had been virtually unbeatable all season. After 37 minutes, Lawrie Sanchez rose above the Liverpool defence to head home Wise's free kick. In the 61st minute, Liverpool should have equalised. They were awarded a penalty, when Aldridge went down in the box, although Goodyear appeared to have taken the ball. Aldridge took the kick himself, but Dave Beasant pulled off a brilliant diving save, Wembley's first in an F.A. Cup Final. Liverpool really had no answer to Wimbledon's hurrying tactics and were well beaten in the end, but it was still the most unlikely result in an F.A. Cup Final since Sunderland's 1973 win.

Liverpool	0:1	**Wimbledon**
		Sanchez

Liverpool:
Grobbelaar, Gillespie, Ablett, Nicol, Spackman, Hansen (Captain), Beardsley, Aldridge, Houghton, Barnes, McMahon, Molby (Sub), Johnston (Sub)
Kenny Dalglish (Manager)

Ipswich:
Beasant (Captain), Goodyear, Phelan, Jones, Young, Thorn, Gibson, Cork, Fashanu, Sanchez, Wise, Scales (Sub), Cunningham (Sub)
Bobby Gould (Manager)

Referee: B. Hill (Kettering)
Attendance: 98,203

Liverpool won the F.A. Cup the following year, but had to endure the awful tragedy at Hillsborough, in the semi-final. Wimbledon's glory was brief and their return for the Charity Shield, was their last Wembley visit.

Liverpool fans at Wembley

Everton v Liverpool

F.A. Cup Final, Saturday 20th May 1989

Hillsborough Tribute

Preview

The F.A. Cup had been overshadowed by the tragedy at Liverpool's semi-final, at Hillsborough, Sheffield, when 96 people lost their lives on an overcrowded terrace. The match had been played three weeks later and Liverpool had beaten the Littlewoods and Simod Cup winners, for the second year in succession, to set up the second all-Merseyside F.A. Cup Final and their fifth Wembley meeting with Everton in five years. Everton had knocked out the holders, Wimbledon, in the quarter-finals and had reached their fourth final in six years, but had not won the Cup since 1984. They had beaten Liverpool in the F.A. Charity Shield three months later, but had surrendered their half-time lead to them in the 1986 Cup Final. Three months after that, in their last meeting at Wembley, it had finished all-square in another Charity Shield. Everton finished 8th in the First Division, their lowest position since 1982. They had been involved in the Simod Cup Final thriller, three weeks earlier, losing in extra time to Nottingham Forest at Wembley. Having failed to clinch the 'double' the previous year, Liverpool were making yet another attempt to win it for the second time. To retain the League Championship, they had to overcome Arsenal, whom they were to meet in their final match. Arsenal had beaten them in the Semi-Finals of the Football League Centenary Trophy, which they had gone on to win.

Semi–Final, Saturday 15th April 1989

Everton	**1:0**	**Norwich City**	**(Villa Park, Birmingham)**
Nevin			

Semi–Final, Sunday 7th May 1989

Liverpool	**3:1**	**Nottingham Forest**	**(Old Trafford, Manchester)**
Aldridge 2, Laws o.g.		Webb	

The Match

Liverpool took the lead in their first attack, after four minutes. McMahon ran on to Nicol's long ball and played it into the middle, where John Aldridge shot past Southall – a sweet moment, after the previous year's penalty miss. Liverpool could not add to their score and brought on Rush for Aldridge in the hope of producing a clincher. However, it was Everton's substitute who rescued them in the last minute. Grobbelaar could not hold Watson's shot and Stuart McCall just beat Nicol to stab the ball in. Just four minutes into extra time, Nicol crossed, Ian Rush controlled it on his chest, shielding it from Ratcliffe and then swivelled to hit the roof of the net and restore Liverpool's lead. Yet Everton still would not give up. Eight minutes later, Ratcliffe's free kick was headed out by Hansen. McCall took it on his chest and volleyed it over the defence and into the corner, to become the first substitute to score twice in an F.A. Cup Final. Liverpool's own scoring substitute was not to be denied. A minute before the extra-time break, Rush beat Southall again, with a glancing header from Barnes' cross and the man who had destroyed Everton with two goals in the 1986 final had repeated the dose.

Everton	**2:3**	**Liverpool**
McCall 2	**(AET)**	Aldridge, Rush 2

Everton:
Southall, McDonald, Van den Hauwe, Ratcliffe (Captain), Watson, Nevin, Steven, Bracewell, Sharp, Cottee, Sheedy, McCall (Sub), I. Wilson (Sub)
Colin Harvey (Manager)

Liverpool:
Grobbelaar, Nicol, Ablett, Staunton, Whelan (Captain), Hansen, Beardsley, Aldridge, Houghton, Barnes, McMahon, Venison (Sub), Rush (Sub)
Kenny Dalglish (Manager)

Referee: J. Worrall (Warrington)
Attendance: 82,800

Everton returned to Wembley two years later for the Zenith Cup Final, but were losers yet again. They would have to wait until 1995 to lift the F.A. Cup once more. It seemed a formality that Liverpool would win their second 'double', when they beat West Ham United, 5-1, three days later. This meant they had only to avoid a two-goal defeat at home to Arsenal, in their final match, three days after that, to retain the League Championship. When Arsenal scored first, Liverpool made the mistake of settling for a 1-0 defeat and the visitors grabbed a second, in injury time, to snatch the title from under their noses. Their goal differences were equal, but Arsenal had scored eight more goals. Arsenal beat them again, in the Makita Tournament Final at Wembley two months later but Liverpool recovered, as usual, and were League Champions again the following year.

Ian Rush was a phenomenal goalscoring legend in one of Europe's greatest club sides. The Welsh striker began his career with Chester City, from where the astute Bob Paisley signed him for Liverpool in 1980. As was Liverpool's style, Rush learned his trade in the reserve side, but was ready to be unleashed on the First Division by the following year, despite having already been capped by Wales. He soon won his first medal, in Liverpool's League Cup Final replay victory at Villa Park. As ever, Paisley had judged it just right and the 20-year-old's speed in the penalty area and lethal finishing made him the club's top scorer in his first full season, as Liverpool secured the League Championship.

Rush scored the goal that clinched their second successive League Cup, in extra time at Wembley. Liverpool were now far and away the strongest team in the land and Rush was being provided with hatfuls of chances in every game. They did not lose a match in which Rush scored, for seven years. In 1983, his fellow professionals voted him Young Player of the Year and he picked up a second Championship medal, as well as a Milk Cup winner's medal.

He even scored at Wembley for Wales, against England. The following season was even better. Rush was the First Division's top scorer as Liverpool, now under Joe Fagan, won their third successive title, plus the Milk Cup, before regaining the European Cup after a gruelling night in Rome. Their ace marksman scored one of the penalties as Liverpool overcame the hosts, Roma, in a shootout. For his part, Rush won both major individual awards. The P.F.A. elevated him to their Player of the Year, whilst the writers made him their Footballer of the Year.

1985 was a disappointment to all at the club, culminating in the Heysel Stadium disaster at the European Cup Final. Rush's striking partner Kenny Dalglish then became player-manager and guided the Reds back towards the title-winning path. A glorious week in May 1986 ended with Rush scoring twice at Wembley, to complete Liverpool's 'double' against the club he supported as a boy, Everton.

Twelve months later, he decided to test himself in the Italian League and signed with Juventus for £3.2 million. Rush found chances hard to come by. He was man-marked in every game and the club were still struggling to come to terms with Michel Platini's retirement, so there was no one to supply the telling passes that the Welshman would surely have thrived on. He returned to Liverpool after only a season in Italy. It wasn't quite the same back at Anfield, however. They had a new goalscorer in John Aldridge, who had topped the First Division scoring charts whilst he had been away. Rush would have to dislodge him if he was to reclaim his place, as Dalglish could not afford to offer him any sentiment.

His chances were limited in his first season back, not helped by a knee injury that required an operation. Rush watched from the substitute's bench as Aldridge gave Liverpool the lead in the F.A. Cup Final, against Everton. As Aldridge tired, Rush replaced him in the second half. Everton equalised in the last minute and suddenly he had a chance to take centre stage again.

Rush had always scored against their fellow Merseysiders, many of whom had played in the 1986 Final. To their horror, history was to repeat itself. Rush scored twice in extra time, proving that his old sharpness was back. Liverpool won 3-2, Aldridge was transferred four months later and Rush was back in pole position.

He won his fifth League Championship medal in 1990 and scored a record fifth F.A. Cup Final goal, as Liverpool won the Cup again in 1992. His goal in the Charity Shield that year was his 11th at Wembley, making him the highest scoring non-English player in the stadium's history. In 1995, Rush captained Liverpool to a Coca-Cola Cup win at Wembley, his last major honour, although he still went on to surpass Denis Law's post-war scoring record in the F.A. Cup, when he notched his 42nd goal.

He left Liverpool, aged 34, having scored 229 league goals from 449 games. He also finished as the all-time Welsh top scorer, with 28 goals. His last two seasons were spent at Leeds United and Newcastle United, where he managed one more F.A. Cup goal. To rub a final pinch of salt in the wound, it was the only goal of a third round tie, against Everton, at Goodison Park.

OFFICIAL MATCHDAY PROGRAMME £3.00

F.A. CUP FINAL

SATURDAY 12 MAY 1990

Crystal Palace
V
Manchester United

KICK OFF 3.00 p.m.

WEMBLEY
VENUE OF LEGENDS

Crystal Palace v Manchester United

F.A. Cup Final, Saturday 12th May 1990

Goals Galore

Preview

Palace had beaten the holders, and eventual League Champions to reach their first final, appearing at Wembley for the first time. United were aiming to equal the record of seven F.A. Cup wins set by Aston Villa and equalled by Spurs. Palace had won promotion the previous year by winning the Play-Offs. They finished 15th in their first season back in the First Division. United finished 13th, ahead of Palace only on goal difference.

Semi–Finals, Sunday 8th April 1990

Crystal Palace	**4:3**	**Liverpool**	*(Villa Park, Birmingham)*
Bright, O'Reilly	*(AET)*	*Rush, McMahon*	
Gray, Pardew		*Barnes (penalty)*	
Manchester United	**3:3**	**Oldham Athletic**	*(Maine Road, Manchester)*
Robson, Webb, Wallace	*(AET)*	*Barrett, Marshall, Palmer*	
Manchester United	**2:1**	**Oldham Athletic**	*(Maine Road, Manchester)* Replay (Wednesday 11th April 1990)
McClair, Robins	*(AET)*	*Ritchie*	

The Match

Palace were ahead after 19 minutes. Barber's free kick was headed in off Pallister's head by Gary O'Reilly. United equalised ten minutes before the break. McClair crossed and Bryan Robson's header was deflected past Martyn at the near post by Pemberton. United were fortunate again after 62 minutes, when they took the lead. Webb blocked Thorn's attempted clearance and it fell for Mark Hughes, who gave Martyn no chance with his shot. United appeared to have it won, but ten minutes later Palace struck back. From Bright's pass substitute Ian Wright raced away between Phelan and Pallister. Shrugging off Phelan's lunge he blasted the equaliser past Leighton. Extra time produced more thrills. After only two minutes, Salako's cross left Leighton in 'no man's land' and Wright charged in to volley Palace back in front. Now the pendulum swung Palace's way, but with only seven minutes remaining, Hughes ran on to Wallace's pass and tucked it into the corner past the advancing Martyn, as O'Reilly challenged.

Crystal Palace	**3:3**	**Manchester United**
O'Reilly, Wright 2	*(AET)*	*Robson, Hughes 2*

Crystal Palace:
Martyn, Pemberton, Shaw, Gray, O'Reilly, Thorn, Barber, Thomas (Captain), Bright, Salako, Pardew, Madden (Sub), Wright (Sub)
Steve Coppell (Manager)

Manchester United:
Leighton, Ince, Martin, Bruce, Phelan, Pallister, Robson (Captain), Webb, McClair, Hughes, Wallace, Blackmore (Sub), Robins (Sub)
Alex Ferguson (Manager)

Referee:	A. Gunn (South Chailey)
Attendance:	80,000

The Match

United goalkeeper Jim Leighton had been blamed for two of Palace's goals and was amazingly dropped for the replay. He never played for United again. His replacement was Les Sealey, on loan from Luton Town and making his debut in the biggest match of the season. Palace tried to unnerve Sealey in the opening exchanges with some unnecessarily physical challenges. Sealey shrugged them off and gave a faultless display. In the 59th minute, Lee Martin, who had been substituted in the first game, charged into the box with Gray in pursuit. He took Webb's pass on his chest and blasted the winner into the roof of the net.

Crystal Palace	**0:1**	**Manchester United**	Replay (Thursday 17th May 1990)
		Martin	

The teams were the same as before with the exception of Les Sealey replacing Jim Leighton in the Manchester United starting line-up.

Referee:	A. Gunn (South Chailey)
Attendance:	80,000

Chapter Eight

The break-up of the Berlin Wall in 1989 was the catalyst for a number of boundary changes in Eastern Europe, including the collapse of the Soviet Union. Britain and the United States joined forces to expel Iraq from Kuwait, but an accident in Paris in 1997 put the country in a severe state of shock. The death of the Princess of Wales brought an incredible outpouring of grief from far and wide.

After the gloom of football in the eighties, came the affluence of the nineties. Facilities had improved, attendances rose and the 1990 World Cup restored faith in the English game. The new Premier League enabled the elite to negotiate better television deals for themselves and the European Cup re-packaged itself as the Champions League to provide more financial security for the top clubs. Players became multi-millionaires. The 1990's signalled the end of Liverpool's domination and the rise of Manchester United to take their place.

Wembley's last decade saw the crowning of both Frank Bruno and the London Monarchs American football team as World Champions. In 1996, the European Championship was staged, evoking memories of thirty years earlier, but this time Germany took the honours and England lost in an unforgettable semi-final, after taking an early lead. League and Cup 'doubles' were clinched at the stadium on four occasions and Manchester United completed the second leg of a unique 'treble' in 1999. The following year, the stadium closed its doors for the last time, bringing to an end 77 years of magical memories.

Giantkillers and Bridesmaids

With the ever-widening gap between top and bottom, the elite few began to dominate the F.A. Cup, but there were still a few upsets on the rocky road to Wembley. In 1994, Kidderminster Harriers became the first non-league side to host a fifth round tie. They lost 1-0 at their Aggborough Stadium to West Ham United, yet when they won the Conference Championship at the end of that season, they were denied entry to the Football League because their ground was not up to standard and it was six years before they were finally admitted. Fourth Division, Cambridge United reached the Sixth Round, in 1990, before winning promotion in Wembley's first Play-Off final. The following year, they reached the sixth round again. Then, in 1992, came a result that reinforced the view that there was still life in the old tin pot.

Wrexham had finished bottom of the Football League in 1991, whilst Arsenal had won the League Championship, losing only one game. When they were drawn together, the following January, in the third round, they were a little closer, but still poles apart in terms of ability. The Gunners led at half-time through Alan Smith and were expected to take their place in the fourth round. Eight minutes remained when Wrexham were awarded a free kick, on the edge of the box. The much-travelled Mickey Thomas, once of Manchester United and Wales, stepped up and powered a shot, which flew past Seaman into the corner of the net. The 37-year-old's goal turned the game. With the Gunners still reeling, Steve Watkin nipped in to put Wrexham in front and the shock was complete.

In 1997, Chesterfield, of the Second Division, got closer to the F.A. Cup Final than any other lower division club had ever been. They had already won away at Bolton Wanderers, who went on to win the First Division Championship and defeated Premier League, Nottingham Forest, when they faced Middlesbrough in the semi-final at Old Trafford. Boro had Vladimir Kinder, their Slovakian defender, sent off in the first half and on the hour mark, Sean Dyche's penalty put Chesterfield into a sensational two-goal lead. Middlesbrough's experienced Italian, Fabrizio Ravanelli pulled one back, but the underdogs then had a clear goal disallowed when Jonathan Howard's shot crossed the line after hitting the bar, only to be ruled out. Boro stormed back and grabbed the lead in extra time, before Jamie Hewitt's last minute equaliser at least, brought the men from Derbyshire, the reward of a replay. Chesterfield were unable to repeat their heroics and lost, 3-0 at Hillsborough, nine days later.

Darren Anderton

Injuries and bad luck have blighted Darren Anderton's career, yet he keeps bouncing back and now, in his thirties, this talented and creative midfielder is at long last, experiencing an extended run in the Tottenham Hotspur side. He made his Wembley debut as a substitute for the England Under-19 side and a year later, he was playing for Portsmouth in the F.A. Cup semi-final against Liverpool. It was Anderton, who put the Second Division side ahead in extra time, only for Ronnie Whelan to rescue the Reds. Liverpool scraped through on penalties, after a goalless replay, in which Portsmouth hit the bar, with three minutes left. Tottenham Hotspur snapped up the impressive Anderton, who could play wide as well as central midfield, for £1.75 million and twelve months later, he was back at Wembley in another semi-final, as Spurs took on great rivals, Arsenal. Tony Adams' second-half winner denied him the opportunity of playing in the final, but he won his first England cap, in Terry Venables' first match in charge, in 1994. Tottenham Hotspur lost yet another semi-final, the following year, Everton beating them, 4-1. Anderton then missed most of the 1995-96 season with a groin injury but returned for the European Championship, helping England to the semi-finals, where yet again, he was to be disappointed. He almost became the hero, hitting the post in extra time, the rebound coming straight back into the German keeper's arms. Tottenham actually won a semi-final, in 1999, against Wimbledon and Anderton was in the side, which won the Worthington Cup, at Wembley, his first major honour. Three weeks later, they appeared in another F.A. Cup semi-final, only to lose in extra time, to Newcastle United. It was Anderton's fourth defeat at this stage and he seemed destined never to play in the showpiece event.

AL
HDAY
RAMME

1991 F. A. Cup Final

SATURDAY 18TH MAY
1991

WEMBLEY
VENUE OF LEGENDS

NOTTINGHAM FOREST
V
TOTTENHAM HOTSPUR
KICK-OFF 3.00pm

PRICE £4

Tottenham Hotspur
Football Club

F. A.
FI

Saturday, 1

NOTTINGHAM FOREST
V
TOTTENHAM HOTSPUR
WEMBLEY, MAY 18, 1991

Limited Edition £5.00

Nottingham Forest v Tottenham

F.A. Cup Final, Saturday 18th May 1991

When The Year Ends In One

Preview

Although this was Forest's first final since their second F.A. Cup win in 1959, they had become regular visitors to Wembley in recent years. Since 1988, they had won the Football League Centenary Tournament, the Simod Cup and two Littlewoods Cups. They had not lost at Wembley since the 1980 Football League Cup Final. Forest had begun the competition by defeating the previous year's finalists, Crystal Palace. Tottenham had beaten the eventual League Champions, in Wembley's first F.A. Cup semi-final to reach their first final since 1987. They were now hoping for a record eighth F.A. Cup win, their first since 1982.
Forest finished 8th, in the First Division, with Tottenham, two places below them.

Semi–Finals, Sunday 14th April 1991

Arsenal	1:3	**Tottenham Hotspur**	(Wembley Stadium, London)
Smith		Gascoigne, Lineker 2	
Nottingham Forest	4:0	**West Ham United**	(Villa Park, Birmingham))
Crosby, Keane			
Pearce, Charles			

The Match

After his stunning free kick goal in the semi-final, all eyes were on Paul Gascoigne, to see how he would handle his first final. The hyped-up character made the headlines for all the wrong reasons. The second of two horrific fouls on Forest players put him out of football for over a year with a serious knee injury. Worse still for Tottenham, was that Forest scored from the resultant free kick, after 15 minutes. Stuart Pearce curled it into the corner, although he was helped somewhat by Glover pushing Mabbutt off the end of the wall to leave a gap for Pearce's shot. After Gascoigne had been stretchered off, Tottenham set about getting back into the game. In the 32nd minute, Lineker ran on to Stewart's through ball and was brought down by Crossley, as he went round the keeper. Unfortunately for Lineker, Crossley brilliantly turned his spot kick over the bar. Tottenham deservedly levelled after nine minutes of the second half. Allen ran through the middle, drawing defenders towards him. He laid the ball off to his right, where Paul Stewart fired the equaliser past Crossley. Tottenham sensed victory, but Forest held out until extra time. Then, in the 94th minute, Spanish substitute, Nayim's corner was headed across to the far post by Stewart. Des Walker held off Mabbutt, but tragically for him, headed it into his own net. It was the winning goal and maintained Tottenham's curious record, of winning a major trophy in a year ending in the figure one. It was the fifth decade in succession that they had achieved this.

Nottingham Forest	1:2	**Tottenham Hotspur**
Pearce	*(AET)*	Stewart, Walker o.g.

Nottingham Forest:
Crossley, Charles, Pearce (Captain), Walker, Chettle, Keane, Crosby, Parker, Clough, Glover, Woan, Laws (Sub), Hodge (Sub)
Brian Clough (Manager)

Tottenham Hotspur:
Thorstvedt, Edinburgh, Van den Hauwe, Sedgley, Howells, Mabbutt (Captain), Stewart, Gascoigne, Samways, Lineker, P. Allen,
Nayim (Sub), Walsh (Sub)
Terry Venables (Manager)

Referee:	R. Milford (Bristol)
Attendance:	80,000

This defeat did not stop Forest from winning cup ties. They were back at Wembley twice more, the following year, winning the Zenith Cup, on their next visit and they beat Tottenham, to reach the Rumbelows Cup Final. Tottenham reached the quarter-finals of the European Cup Winners Cup, before losing to Feyenoord, of Holland, and in 1993, they were back at Wembley for another F.A. Cup semi-final against Arsenal.

Paul Gascoigne, or 'Gazza', as he is popularly known, was a crowd-pulling genius with an uncanny ability to self-destruct as well as to amaze with his outstanding skills. His first honour was the F.A. Youth Cup, with Newcastle United in 1985 and it was soon evident that this stocky midfielder was going to be one of the all-time greats. His ball control, passing and shooting were all first class, but his sharp footballing brain enabled him to produce the unexpected when his side most needed it. In 1988, he appeared at Wembley in the low-key Football League Centenary Tournament and was voted the P.F.A.'s Young Player of the Year.

When Terry Venables signed Gascoigne for Tottenham Hotspur, he became the first £2 million British player, a daunting label for a 21-year-old. He made his debut in the pre-season Wembley International Tournament as Tottenham lost 4-0 to Arsenal. The following month, he made his England debut as a Wembley substitute against Denmark, but took time to settle in London. He ended the season with a hyperactive display, again as substitute, as a stunning individual goal helped England to a World Cup qualifying victory against Albania, at Wembley.

His brilliance was now more evident and his inclusion in the 1990 World Cup squad was to change his life forever. As England made their way to the semi-finals, Gascoigne came of age as a world star, whilst also revealing his vulnerability to the watching millions. His tears as he picked up a yellow card, which would have ruled him out of the final had England qualified, were the abiding memory of the tournament and the nation took him to their heart.

Five months later, he was the BBC's Sports Personality of the Year, only the second footballer (after Bobby Moore) to win it. The confidence and youthful arrogance flowed as Tottenham reached the F.A. Cup semi-finals. Although he was still recovering from a stomach injury, a half-fit Gascoigne arrived at Wembley fired up. His superb goal from a free kick, after six minutes, knocked the stuffing out of Arsenal and they never recovered. Gascoigne came off after an hour. He tried to do the same in the final, but lost control and should have been dismissed before he tore his cruciate ligament in a second suicidal challenge. It was a year before he played again. With the media following him everywhere, Gascoigne moved to Italy, to play for Lazio for £3.5 million.

His off-field antics and pop star lifestyle did not suit Italian football, but his skills were admired. A broken leg in a training accident in 1994 signalled the beginning of the end of his Italian adventure. Rangers brought him back to Britain, the following year and Gascoigne settled quickly. He was Scottish Footballer of the Year, helping Rangers to win the 'double' of the Scottish League Championship and Scottish Cup. Rangers clinched the title with a Gascoigne hat-trick against Aberdeen.

The European Championship in England then gave him the chance to shine once more on the international stage. He had taken a lot of flak in the media for his occasional drinking excesses, but his goal, ironically against Scotland, at Wembley, silenced all the doubters. Flicking the ball over the head of Colin Hendry, before volleying past Andy Goram was a brilliant piece of skill at a crucial point in the match. Scotland had just missed a penalty and Gazza's goal was the final nail in the coffin. 11 days later, he was inches away from getting the final touch to an Alan Shearer cross, which would have put England into the final.

Only Gascoigne could have got away with returning to Scotland after his killer blow to their European Championship hopes, but his two goals helped Rangers to a Scottish League Cup victory and they went on to lift their ninth successive Championship, equalling Celtic's record. Gascoigne returned to his native north-east the following year, making his debut as a substitute for Middlesbrough in the Coca-Cola Cup Final. Boro lost, but went on to win promotion to the Premier League.

Gascoigne was dealt a huge blow to his pride when Glenn Hoddle axed him from his final World Cup squad at the end of the season. It would have been his last chance to play in a World Cup again and his fortunes took a turn for the worse. More injuries followed, including a broken arm sustained in a typically reckless challenge and his off-field activities seemed to interfere with his fitness.

In 2000, he joined Everton, before dropping back into the First Division for a brief spell with Burnley. Gascoigne was one of the game's true entertainers, never missing an opportunity to bring humour into his life. His moments of brilliance will live long in the memory, as will the question, "how much could he have achieved?"

Brian Clough was an extraordinarily prolific goalscorer, who went on to achieve astonishing success as a manager. As a player, with Middlesbrough, he was ruthless in his desire to score goals. In 1958-59, he was the Football League's top scorer, with 42 goals and won two England caps, no mean achievement for a Second Division player. He topped the divisional charts again, the following season, but Middlesbrough consistently failed to challenge for promotion and their arrogant and unpopular captain was eventually transferred to Sunderland where a serious knee injury cut short his career at the age of 25. Clough returned to play three First Division games, two years later, but he was a long way short of his previous standard and was eventually persuaded to take a job on the coaching staff.

In 1965, still only 29, he became the youngest manager in the league, when he took over at Fourth Division, Hartlepool United with his ex-team-mate, Peter Taylor as his assistant. Within two years, the young duo had taken one of the poorest clubs in the Football League up to the heady heights of 8th place. This was when Derby County offered them the opportunity to try out their new-found skills in the Second Division, where they had the luxury of money to spend on new players. Whilst their old club were building on the legacy of Clough and Taylor by winning promotion for the first time in their history, it was at Derby that Taylor's eye for a bargain and the pair's persuasive nature helped them to assemble a squad of players, which would win the Second Division Championship in 1969.

Clough proved that he was a master of motivation by taking the club onto new heights, whilst building up his own power within the club. In a remarkably close finish to the 1971-72 season, Derby came through to win the League Championship for the first time. They could even afford to go on holiday whilst Leeds and Liverpool were aiming to catch them in their final games. In 1973, Clough took Derby to the European Cup semi-finals, but his increasingly outspoken comments, which made great television, were also infuriating his chairman. Their relationship broke down and Clough resigned. The fans and players were outraged that their brilliant manager had been forced out.

After a six-month break, Clough and Taylor re-emerged at Third Division, Brighton and Hove Albion, an unusual choice of club, still recovering from the previous season's relegation. It soon became obvious that Clough regretted joining them. Leaving Taylor as manager, he succeeded Don Revie as the new Leeds United Manager, an even stranger appointment, after his previous public hatred of Revie's team. His new job began with Wembley's first Charity Shield, against Liverpool, but the players took an instant dislike to him and he was ousted after a mere 44 days. His next job was at Second Division, Nottingham Forest, where, realising that his managerial reputation was sliding, he turned to his old partner, Peter Taylor, who agreed to rejoin him.

It was to be the beginning of the most successful period in their careers. In their first season together, Forest were promoted. The duo immediately set about constructing a solid defence, signing England goalkeeper, Peter Shilton. Their taming of the rebellious Kenny Burns turned him into the find of the season. Forest won the Football League Cup, without the cup-tied Shilton, replacing him with 18-year-old Chris Woods, who remarkably kept out Liverpool in both the final (through extra time) and the replay, without a previous league appearance to his name. They remained unbeaten from November onwards and made Clough only the third manager to win the League Championship with different clubs. His achievement was unique in that neither of these east midlands sides had won the title before and he had taken them both out of the Second Division. Now he set about achieving what had been denied him at Derby.

Beating the holders, Liverpool in the first round, again without conceding a goal in both legs, Forest went on to win the European Cup at the first attempt, a phenomenal achievement. They were also only the second club to win the trophy unbeaten. Although they failed to retain the Championship, they did win the League Cup again and set a new Football League record of 42 consecutive games undefeated, the equivalent of a full season.

In 1980, they were European Champions again, after a brave 'backs to the wall' performance in the final against Kevin Keegan's Hamburg. Clough was often touted as a future England manager, but his abrasive style did not lend itself to the more diplomatic traditions of the Football Association and he was continually overlooked. Nor did it guarantee a long relationship with his partner, despite their success. Taylor retired in 1982, only to return as Derby County's new manager, the following season, dumping Forest out of the F.A. Cup third round in a shock win for the Second Division side. Clough struggled on alone throughout the 1980's.

Forest were always an entertaining side, but couldn't quite maintain a title challenge again. They reached two successive F.A. Cup semi-finals (the second was the Hillsborough disaster) but the Final always eluded him, until 1991. Clough had rediscovered some of the glory days and suddenly became a regular visitor to Wembley again. Forest won the Football League Centenary Tournament in 1988 and the following year, won the first of two successive Littlewoods Cups, which were to make him the first manager to win the League Cup, four times. His own son, Nigel, scored two of Forest's goals in a 3-1 win against Luton Town. They won a thrilling Simod Cup Final, three weeks later and became the first club to win two Wembley finals in the same season. Clough celebrated by climbing the steps to receive the trophy himself.

This fine run was ended by Spurs' recovery in the 1991 F.A. Cup Final, his last serious attempt at the 'big one'. Clough was criticised for remaining on the sidelines at the beginning of extra time, further indication that he was becoming more distant and leaving the motivation to his coaching staff. Nevertheless, they reached two more Wembley finals, the following year, winning the Zenith Cup and bringing his number of club trips to the stadium, to eight in five years. Clough was becoming ever more eccentric, his health was noticeably deteriorating and the club was probably relieved when he decided to retire in 1993. Forest were unfortunately, relegated in his last match, but he was held with such esteem and gratitude at the City Ground that it was all forgotten as he was given a rousing send-off.

THE F.A. CUP FINAL

LIVERPOOL
v
SUNDERLAND

SATURDAY 9th MAY 1992

KICK OFF 3.00 PM

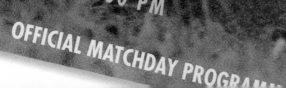

OFFICIAL MATCHDAY PROGRAMME

WEMBLEY
STADIUM

Liverpool v Sunderland

F.A. Cup Final, Saturday 9th May 1992

Reds' Brief Revival

Preview

The two teams were competing for a new trophy, after the old one, at 81 years old, was retired. Liverpool had reached their fourth final in seven years by winning the first semi-final to be decided on penalties. The last two of their four F.A. Cup wins, had both been against Everton. They had won their tenth League Championship in 15 years, in 1990, and shared the F.A. Charity Shield, on their last Wembley visit, but had won nothing since. Sunderland had twice won the F.A. Cup, with their 1973 triumph, as a Second Division club, providing great drama. They too, had last appeared at Wembley in 1990, when although they had lost the Second Division Promotion Play-Off Final to Swindon Town, they had been promoted due to financial irregularities at the Wiltshire club. Sunderland had been relegated straight back to the Second Division, however.

Liverpool finished 6th, in the First Division, their lowest position for an incredible 27 years. The season also marked their return to European competition for the first time since 1985. They reached the U.E.F.A. Cup quarter-finals before losing to Genoa of Italy. Sunderland had struggled in their first season back in the Second Division and finished 18th.

Semi–Finals, Sunday 5th April 1992

Liverpool	*1:1*	**Portsmouth**	**(Highbury, London)**
Whelan	*(AET)*	Anderton	
Norwich City	*0:1*	**Sunderland**	**(Hillsborough, Sheffield)**
		Byrne	
Liverpool	*0:0*	**Portsmouth**	**(Villa Park, Birmingham)** **Replay (Monday 13th April 1992)**
	(AET)		

Liverpool won 3:1 on penalties

The Match

Sunderland had looked dangerous in the first half, but it was Liverpool who scored after 47 minutes. Michael Thomas waited for McManaman's cross to bounce and then smacked a spectacular rising shot past Norman as he fell backwards. Liverpool fans must have instantly forgiven him for depriving them of the 'double' in 1989, with an injury-time goal for Arsenal at Liverpool. He had also played against Liverpool three times at Wembley for Arsenal. Sunderland could not respond and 21 minutes later, Thomas ran on to Saunders' through ball, took it round Ball and into the path of Ian Rush, who tucked it past Norman, into the corner. It was his fifth F.A. Cup Final goal, a new record.

Liverpool	*2:0*	**Sunderland**
Thomas		
Rush		

Liverpool:
Grobbelaar, R. Jones, Burrows, Nicol, Molby, Wright (Captain), Saunders, Houghton, Rush, McManaman, Thomas, Marsh (Sub), Walters (Sub)
Graeme Souness (Manager)

Sunderland:
Norman, Owers, Ball, Bennett, Rogan, Rush, Bracewell (Captain), Davenport, Armstrong, Byrne, Atkinson, Hardyman (Sub), Hawke (Sub)
Malcolm Crosby (Manager)

Referee:	P. Don (Hanworth Park)
Attendance:	79,544

The Match

This was to be the end of Liverpool's incredible 20-year run of success and they now embarked on a period of rebuilding. They were beaten in the last 16 of the following season's European Cup Winners Cup, losing home and away to Spartak Moscow and would not win another major honour until the 1995 Coca-Cola Cup, reaching the F.A. Cup Final, the following year. Sunderland struggled again and only escaped relegation by a point. In 1996, they won the Football League Championship, and were promoted to the F.A. Premier League, although they were relegated the following year.

Arsenal v Sheffield Wednesday

F.A. Cup Final, Saturday 15th May 1993

Dreary Marathon

Preview

This was Arsenal's first final since 1980. Arsenal were, by no means, strangers to Wembley though. Since 1980, they had made 13 appearances, which included two semi-finals against their North London rivals. Wednesday had beaten the previous year's finalists, Sunderland and had reached their first final since 1966, but it had been 58 years since they last won the F.A. Cup. Arsenal had beaten Wednesday in the previous month's Coca-Cola Cup Final, but had finished 10th, in the Premier League, their lowest position for 10 years. Wednesday finished 7th and were beaten in the last 32 of the UEFA Cup by Kaiserslautern.

Semi–Final, Sunday 4th April 1993

Arsenal	**1:0**	**Tottenham Hotspur**	**(Wembley Stadium, London)**
Adams			

Semi–Final, Saturday 3rd April 1993

Sheffield United	**1:2**	**Sheffield Wednesday**	**(Wembley Stadium, London)**
Cork	**(AET)**	Waddle, Bright	

The Match

Arsenal scored first, after 21 minutes. A Davis free kick into the box, was headed across goal by Linighan. It went beyond Warhurst to Ian Wright, who powered a header past Woods. Arsenal stayed in control until half-time. Wednesday came out more determined for the second half and were rewarded after 61 minutes. Sheridan's cross was flicked on by Bright, to Harkes. As Dixon came to challenge, Harkes unselfishly headed it across to David Hirst, who slid in the equaliser as Seaman advanced. Wednesday had chances to win it, but this disappointing final could produce no winning goal.

Arsenal	**1:1**	**Sheffield Wednesday**
Wright	**(AET)**	Hirst

Arsenal:
Seaman, Dixon, Winterburn, Davis, Linighan, Adams (Captain), Jensen, Wright, Campbell, Merson, Parlour, O'Leary (Sub), A. Smith (Sub)
George Graham (Manager)

Sheffield Wednesday:
Woods, Nilsson, Worthington, Palmer, Anderson (Captain), Warhurst, Harkes, Waddle, Hirst, Bright, Sheridan, Hyde (Sub), Bart-Williams (Sub)
Trevor Francis (Manager)

Referee:	K. Barratt (Coventry)
Attendance:	79,347

The Match

The replay followed a similar pattern to the first game. After 34 minutes, Smith sent Ian Wright away. Woods hesitated fatally and Wright tucked it past him. It was his fourth F.A. Cup Final goal in four appearances, in none of which he completed a full match. Once again, Wednesday came back in the second half. In the 69th minute, Bright and Linighan went up for a Harkes cross and the ball hit Linighan's shoulder. It bounced up off Dixon's knee to Chris Waddle, whose shot then deflected off Dixon's leg and beat Seaman for a bizarre equaliser. Again Wednesday had chances to win, but the final was heading for its first ever penalty shootout, when Arsenal won a corner in the last minute of extra time. Merson found the head of Andy Linighan, who powered a header, which Woods got his hands to, but could not keep out. Linighan had broken his nose and a finger, when colliding with Bright's elbow in the 18th minute, but he became the hero with the most dramatic of winners.

Arsenal	**2:1**	**Sheffield Wednesday**	**Replay (Thursday 20th May 1993)**
Wright, Linighan	**(AET)**	Waddle	

Team Changes:
For Arsenal; Alan Smith replaced Ray Parlour in the starting line-up and Selley was named as a substitute. For Sheffield Wednesday; Wilson replaced Anderson and Carlton Palmer took over the captaincy. The Referee remained the same and the 62,267 fans attended.

After becoming the first club to win both major domestic knockout trophies in the same season, Arsenal went on to win the European Cup Winners Cup the following year. In the final they defeated the holders Parma by a single goal in Copenhagen. They almost retained the Cup Winners Cup in 1995, but lost the final to Real Zaragoza in Paris, the winner coming from a speculative 50-yard lob in the last minute of extra time. Three years later, Arsenal returned to Wembley on the verge of a second 'double'. Wednesday's unsuccessful hunt for a trophy continued.

Wright

Ian Wright was a late developer, but from his late twenties onwards, he blossomed into a deadly striker, with a penchant for the big stage. He began in non-league football and was spotted by Crystal Palace, playing for Greenwich Boro of the Kent League, aged 21. In 1987-88, he scored 20 league goals and appeared at Wembley in the Football League Centenary Tournament. His partnership with Mark Bright went from strength to strength with both consistently hitting the target. Palace had been on the verge of promotion and in 1989, came from behind to win the Second Division Promotion Play-Offs, in a final against Blackburn Rovers which was settled in extra time.

His debut season in the top flight was hindered by a twice-broken shin bone and when Palace surprisingly defeated Liverpool in the F.A. Cup semi-finals, Wright had a desperate race to be fit for Wembley. After almost two months out, he did well to make the substitutes bench for the final. After 69 minutes, with Palace 2-1 down to Manchester United, he was sent on and scored a fantastic goal within three minutes. Determined to make the most of his limited opportunity, Wright was in electric form. Two minutes into extra time, he volleyed them in front, only for United to force a replay. Wright was still not match-fit however and he was again left on the bench for the replay. He came on, but was unable to reproduce his form of the first game and Palace went down to a single goal.

The following year, Wright again showed his big-match temperament, scoring twice as Palace won the Zenith Cup at Wembley and finished 3rd in the First Division, their highest ever placing. He also made his first England appearance, before Arsenal paid £2.5 million for him and it was at Highbury where he really made his mark.

In his first season with the Gunners, he was the Football League's top scorer with 29 goals and in 1993, he was back at Wembley as Arsenal won both the Coca-Cola Cup and the F.A. Cup. Wright scored in the F.A. Cup Final and the replay, bringing his goals tally in the final to four, even though he wasn't fully fit and was substituted in both games. He began the next season with a stunning goal against Manchester United in the Charity Shield, although he then missed a penalty, which would have given the Gunners, the silverware.

Wright missed the Cup Winners Cup Final in 1994, after a second yellow card of the competition in the semi-final, but played in the following year's final, which Arsenal lost. In his thirties, his volatile temperament often brought him into conflict with players and referees, but he left Highbury, a legend, in 1998, after his first-team chances became fewer in the side which won the 'double'.

After spells with West Ham United, Nottingham Forest and Celtic, he ended his career on a high by helping Burnley to win promotion from the Second Division. He retired to become a television presenter and chat show host where his lively personality could be more fully exploited.

OFFICIAL MATCHDAY PROGRAMME £5.00

THE 1994 F.A. CUP FINAL

WEMBLEY STADIUM LIMITED

CHELSEA
v
MANCHESTER UNITED
SATURDAY 14 MAY KICK-OFF

Chelsea v Manchester United

F.A. Cup Final, Saturday 14th May 1994

Eric Spot On For The 'Double'

Preview

Chelsea had won the Cup only once previously, in 1970, after drawing the final at Wembley, but they had won the Full Members Cup and the Zenith Cup at Wembley since. Earlier in the competition, they had knocked out the previous year's finalists, Sheffield Wednesday. United had beaten the same team in the semi-finals, as when they last won the Cup in 1990 and they had again needed a replay. They were now aiming to equal Tottenham Hotspur's record of eight F.A. Cup wins. Both sides had begun the season by winning silverware. Chelsea had won the Makita Tournament and United had won the F.A. Charity Shield on penalties, but while Chelsea finished 14th, in the F.A. Premier League, United retained the Premier League Championship, winning it by eight points from Blackburn Rovers. They were now favourites to clinch the first 'double' since Liverpool's 1986 success. They had also reached the Coca-Cola Cup Final but had lost to Aston Villa. Their big disappointment though, was in losing on away goals, to Galatasaray of Turkey in the last 16 of the European Cup.

Semi–Final, Saturday 9th April 1994

Chelsea	**2:0**	**Luton Town**	(Wembley Stadium, London)
Peacock 2			

Semi–Final, Sunday 10th April 1994

Manchester United	**1:1**	**Oldham Athletic**	(Wembley Stadium, London)
Hughes	**(AET)**	Pointon	

Manchester United	**4:1**	**Oldham Athletic**	(Maine Road, Manchester)	Replay (Wednesday 13th April 1994)
Irwin, Kanchelskis		Pointon		
Robson, Giggs				

The Match

Chelsea had completed a league 'double' over United without conceding a goal and again showed the qualities that had previously produced those two shock victories. Whereas Aston Villa, in the Coca-Cola Cup Final, had used similar tactics to stifle United and broke away to score, Chelsea failed to break through and one rush of blood, after an hour's play, was to prove their undoing. Newton upended Irwin, in the area and Eric Cantona sent the goalkeeper, Kharine the wrong way, from the penalty spot to give United the lead. Chelsea panicked and pushed players forward in an attempt to grab a quick reply. This proved fatal, as United now had the space previously denied them. Twice they broke and ripped Chelsea's defence wide open and after 65 minutes, Kanchelskis broke away and was knocked over by Sinclair's challenge. Although contact appeared to be outside the area, another penalty was given and Cantona again sent Kharine the other way. Three minutes later, Sinclair's misery was complete, as he slipped in the wet conditions, when attempting a clearance and accidentally put Mark Hughes through to fire into the corner. Hughes was to join Chelsea, the following year. In eight minutes, Chelsea had abandoned their previously successful game plan and paid the ultimate price. They bravely created more chances and were cruelly caught out again in injury time. This time it was Ince who broke away, rounded Kharine and left substitute, Brian McClair with an open goal. The scoreline was harsh on Chelsea, but United were always capable of over-running teams and the 'double' was just reward for a talented side.

Chelsea	**0:4**	**Manchester United**
		Cantona (2 penalties)
		Hughes, McClair

Chelsea:
Kharine, Clarke, Sinclair, Johnsen, Kjeldbjerg, Wise (Captain), Peacock, Burley, Newton, Spencer, Stein, Hoddle (Sub), Cascarino (Sub)
Glenn Hoddle (Player-Manager)

Manchester United:
Schmeichel, Parker, Irwin, Bruce (Captain), Pallister, Kanchelskis, Ince, Keane, Giggs, Hughes, Cantona, Sharpe (Sub), McClair (Sub)
Alex Ferguson (Manager)

Referee: D. Elleray (Harrow)
Attendance: 79,634

As United were again competing in the European Cup, Chelsea took their place in the European Cup Winners Cup and surprisingly reached the semi-finals, where they were beaten by the eventual winners, Real Zaragoza. United reached the F.A. Cup Final again the following year, while Chelsea won the Cup on their next visit, in 1997.

Mark Hughes made an incredible 16 appearances at Wembley for club sides, plus one for Wales Schoolboys. Hughes was an aggressive and determined striker, who played in the Manchester United youth team, alongside Norman Whiteside. His first team debut came in 1983, at the age of 19 and he quickly established himself in United's front line. At the end of his first season, he won the first of 72 caps for Wales and scored the only goal of the game, against England, at Wrexham, the town where he was born.

The following season brought him his first major honour, as he scored United's winning goal against Liverpool in the semi-final replay, before helping them beat Everton to win the F.A. Cup at Wembley. He also impressed with a stunning acrobatic volley for Wales against Spain in a World Cup qualifying match. Hughes' contribution during the season was honoured by his fellow professionals and he picked up the Young Player of the Year award.

Terry Venables paid £2.5 million for him in 1986 to take him to Barcelona, but even though he was partnered by Gary Lineker, Hughes' style was deemed too aggressive for the Spanish league and he couldn't settle. Bayern Munich took him on loan the following year, before Alex Ferguson brought him back to Old Trafford in 1988.

He was now a more mature all-round team player, expertly holding the ball and shielding it from defenders before laying it off to a team-mate. The P.F.A. voted him their Player of the Year in his first season back in English football. His return was very timely as United, under Ferguson, were about to sweep all before them. In the 1990 F.A. Cup Final, Hughes scored twice, including a late equaliser against Crystal Palace, which allowed United to regroup and return to win the replay. United were one of the first English clubs allowed back into European competition the following season after the six-year ban imposed after the Heysel Stadium disaster and stormed through to win the Cup Winners Cup.

The final was a personal triumph for Hughes as he scored both goals in a 2-1 win against his old club, Barcelona in Rotterdam. He also picked up the Player of the Year award, becoming the first to win it twice. It was his second in three years and the third occasion that he had been honoured by the P.F.A. More trophies followed.

The Rumbelows Cup in 1992 and United's long-awaited Championship the following year, gave Hughes' medal collection a further boost and 1993-94 was to see United launch an assault on the 'treble'. It began with Hughes scoring another spectacular volley, at Wembley in the Charity Shield and it was under the twin towers that he became a regular scorer. United lost the Coca-Cola Cup Final, but it was Hughes who grabbed their consolation effort. When they were in danger of losing the F.A. Cup Semi-Final to Oldham, it was Hughes who unleashed yet another volley, in injury time, to put them back on track and it was Hughes who slotted home United's third in the F.A. Cup Final to wrap up the 'double'.

He left United in 1995, to join Chelsea. Two years later, he scored twice against Wimbledon to take his new club to the F.A. Cup Final where Hughes picked up a fourth winner's medal, a Wembley record. Yet still, he was not finished. Three months later, he put Chelsea ahead at Wembley, against Manchester United in the Charity Shield, only for United to win on penalties.

In 1998, he helped Chelsea win the Coca-Cola Cup and his goal took them into the Cup Winners Cup Final, although he missed out on that one. Nevertheless, after spells at Southampton and Everton, his unsatiable desire for honours was further fulfilled in 2002, when at the grand old age of 38, he was in the Blackburn Rovers side, which won the Worthington Cup, his third victory in the competition, all with different clubs. By then, this quietly spoken man, contrary to his demeanour on the pitch, had found an unexpected further string to his bow.

He took on the daunting task of becoming Wales Manager, at a time when their fortunes were at an all-time low. Hughes proceeded to pick them up, turning them first, into a team, which was difficult to beat, thereby building up confidence and then launched an assault on qualification for the 2004 European Championship. On the way, they broke the Welsh record with their ninth consecutive game undefeated and Mark Hughes was set for as glittering a career in management as he had on the field of play.

THE 1995 F.A. CUP FINAL

SPONSORED BY LITTLEWOODS POOLS

Everton v Manchester United

SATURDAY 20 MAY KICK-OFF 3.00PM

Everton v Manchester United

F.A. Cup Final, Saturday 20th May 1995

United's 'Double Double' Foiled

Preview

Everton had lost five consecutive Wembley finals since their last F.A. Cup win in 1984. The following year saw the beginning of their unfortunate run, when a single goal in extra time, was enough for United to wrest the F.A. Cup from Everton's grasp, despite United having Kevin Moran sent off. Everton gained their revenge, three months later, in the F.A. Charity Shield, but a single goal was again enough for United to beat them at Wembley, in the Football League Centenary Tournament in 1988. Everton had appeared in two other losing F.A. Cup Finals, both to Liverpool, in the late 1980's and had not won a major trophy since the 1987 League Championship. United had won the F.A. Cup twice, since beating Everton in 1985. 1994 had been their best ever domestic year as they won the 'double' of Premier League Championship and F.A. Cup.

Everton had ended the previous season by dramatically hanging on to their Premier League status, but they had improved to finish 15th, in the season just ended. United had begun the season by retaining the F.A. Charity Shield, but they had failed to progress beyond the last 16 of the European Cup for the second year in succession, suffering a 4-0 humiliation in Barcelona. Their pursuit of a hat-trick of Premier League titles, had ended the previous week, when they failed, by a point, to overhaul Blackburn Rovers. United's attempt to lift the F.A. Cup for a record ninth time, was their last chance to avoid their first barren season for six years.

Semi–Finals, Sunday 9th April 1995

Crystal Palace	**2:2**	**Manchester United**	*(Villa Park, Birmingham)*
Dowie, Armstrong	*(AET)*	*Irwin, Pallister*	
Everton	**4:1**	**Tottenham Hotspur**	*(Elland Road, Leeds)*
Jackson, Stuart		*Klinsmann (penalty)*	
Amokachi 2			
Crystal Palace	**0:2**	**Manchester United**	*(Villa Park, Birmingham)* Replay (Wednesday 12th April 1995)
		Bruce, Pallister	

The Match

Everton took the lead on the half-hour mark. Stuart hit the underside of the bar, when given a glorious opportunity to score from Jackson's pass. Fortunately for him, Paul Rideout rose to head the rebound past United's Danish keeper, Schmeichel and Bruce, who was struggling with a hernia problem and was substituted at half-time. Rideout's goal was his sixth at Wembley in four games, the other five being at schoolboy level. United came back in the second half, but Neville Southall was on top form in Everton's goal. The holders ran out of ideas and finished the match looking jaded. For Joe Royle, Everton's manager, it was sweet revenge. United had twice beaten his previous club, Oldham Athletic in semi-finals, with United snatching a last minute equaliser in their Wembley meeting the previous year.

Everton	**1:0**	**Manchester United**
Rideout		

Everton:
Southall, Jackson, Watson (Captain), Unsworth, Ablett, Limpar, Home, Parkinson, Hinchcliffe, Stuart, Rideout, Amokachi (Sub), Ferguson (Sub), Kearton (Sub)
Joe Royle (Manager)

Manchester United:
Schmeichel, G. Neville, Bruce (Captain), Pallister, Irwin, Butt, Keane, Ince, Sharpe, McClair, Hughes, Giggs (Sub), Scholes (Sub), Walsh (Sub)
Alex Ferguson (Manager)

Referee: G. Ashby (Worcester)
Attendance: 79,592

Everton went out in the last 16 of the following season's European Cup Winners Cup, losing to Feyenoord. United recovered in spectacular style and returned the following year, on the verge of an unprecedented second 'double' in three years.

F.A. CUP FINAL 1996

SPONSORED BY LITTLEWOODS

F.A. CUP
LITTLEWOODS

WEMBLEY
STADIUM LIMITED

LIVERPOOL
v
MANCHESTER
UNITED

SATURDAY 11 MAY 1996

Liverpool v Manchester United

F.A. Cup Final, Saturday 11th May 1996

Eric Le Hero

Preview

Liverpool had last won the F.A. Cup in 1992, but this final brought back memories of the 1977 final, the first Wembley meeting between these two teams, when United denied Liverpool the 'double'. This was to be their sixth clash at the stadium and Liverpool's only victory had been in the 1983 Milk Cup Final, with their last encounter being the second of two F.A. Charity Shield draws in 1990. After two barren seasons without a trophy, Liverpool had lifted the Coca-Cola Cup, the previous year and were now hoping to follow it, by notching their sixth F.A. Cup win, after beating the new Coca-Cola Cup winners in the semi-finals. United were appearing in their third successive final and once again, were attempting to win a record ninth F.A. Cup. Two years earlier, they had clinched the 'double' at Wembley, by despatching Chelsea and had beaten them again, to reach the final. The previous season had ended in extreme disappointment, as a low-key United lost the F.A. Cup Final, a week after failing to complete a hat-trick of Premier League titles.

Both sides had taken early exits in the UEFA Cup. Liverpool reached the last 32, before losing at home to Brondby, after drawing in Denmark. United went out on away goals, in the first round, to Rotor Volgograd, after drawing in Russia. Both teams recovered strongly. Liverpool finished 3rd, in the Premier League, their best position for five years. United meanwhile, astonished all their critics the previous week, by clinching their third Championship in four years. Victory at Wembley would give them a record second 'double' in three years.

Semi–Finals, Sunday 31st March 1996

Aston Villa	0:3	**Liverpool** Fowler 2, McAteer		*(Old Trafford, Manchester)*
Chelsea Gullit	1:2	**Manchester United** Cole, Beckham		*(Villa Park, Birmingham)*

The Match

A final, which promised so much, delivered so little. Neither team got into their stride and extra time loomed, when one historic moment settled the issue. With five minutes remaining, Beckham's corner was punched out by James, but hit substitute, Rush, on the shoulder. It fell to Eric Cantona and with most of the Liverpool team between him and the goal, he took a step backwards and fired it, with poise and precision, between Jones and Scales, into the net. It was the culmination of a remarkable transformation in Cantona's career. He had begun the season, by completing an eight-month ban for attacking a spectator at Crystal Palace, the previous season. He had ended it as a reformed character. Cantona had become the first French winner of the Footballer of the Year award and he had captained a remarkable team to an unprecedented second 'double' in three years.

Liverpool	0:1	**Manchester United** Cantona	

Liverpool:
James, McAteer, Scales, Wright, Babb, Jones, McManaman, Redknapp, Barnes (Captain), Collymore, Fowler, Thomas (Sub), Rush (Sub), Warner (Sub)
Roy Evans (Manager)

Manchester United
Schmeichel, Irwin, May, Pallister, P. Neville, Beckham, Butt, Keane, Giggs, Cantona (Captain), Cole, G. Neville (Sub), Scholes (Sub), Sharpe (Sub)
Alex Ferguson (Manager)

Referee:	*D. Gallagher (Banbury)*
Attendance:	*79,007*

United had secured the 'double' with six of the team that clinched the first 'double', two years earlier. As United were competing in the European Cup, Liverpool were entered into the European Cup Winners Cup and reached the semi-finals, before losing to the holders, Paris St. Germain. They would not win the F.A. Cup again at this stadium, but won Cardiff's first final, in 2001. In 1999, United were back at Wembley, poised to become the first club to win the 'treble'.

Wembley's Other Finals

When the Football Association won the bidding to stage the 1996 European Championship in England, thoughts inevitably turned back to the World Cup of 30 years earlier. Could history repeat itself? Sadly, it couldn't, but 'Euro 96' was still a fantastic festival and football came home to a warm welcome. England almost made it to the final, but it was left to Germany and surprise package, the Czech Republic to contest the prize. The Czechs took a surprise lead, but inevitably it was the Germans who responded to win the tournament with Oliver Bierhoff getting the first ever 'golden goal' in an international final. For Germany, it was setting the record straight after the 'injustice' of 1966.

Eric Cantona spent only five years in English football, but achieved so much, not least in notoriety, that when he retired, it was a massive shock. His ability to surprise, as well as entertain the masses made him one of the most talked-about players in history. He was 25 when he came to England, after an astonishing catalogue of temper tantrums, which had resulted in the fiery Frenchman quitting his native country. Cantona had already played for five different clubs and had won the French League Championship and French Cup with Olympique Marseille, his hometown club. He had won 20 French caps, so he obviously had the talent. It was his violent confrontations with players and authorities, which made him an outcast, especially his insulting behaviour at disciplinary commissions, which made matters worse.

England was to rescue his career. Leeds United took him on loan from Nimes and he gave them the extra spark they needed to hold off Manchester United's challenge to win the League Championship. The fans loved him and he openly declared his feelings for them in return. The next season began with Cantona scoring a hat-trick at Wembley in the Charity Shield, against Liverpool. His goals were often spectacular and unpredictable, but Leeds couldn't hold onto him.

Howard Wilkinson was not prepared to build the team around Cantona, so after only nine months at Elland Road, he sensationally sold him, for £1.2 million, to Manchester United, where Alex Ferguson was prepared to give the Frenchman a free role. It was surely a decision that Wilkinson will always regret. The Championship went to Old Trafford and Cantona picked up his second successive title, his third overall, all with different clubs. United won the 'double' in 1994, with Cantona's penalties proving crucial in the F.A. Cup Final. His fellow professionals voted him their Player of the Year and at 27, he at last, felt settled. Although he had been sent off on the odd occasion, he had not been involved in serious confrontations yet and was well supported by his manager.

In 1994-95, Cantona's temperament began to fail him and he allowed himself to be drawn into more and more clashes, resulting in red cards. One such incident, in January 1995 led to a bizarre confrontation between Cantona and a fan, in which the Frenchman launched himself, kung-fu style, over the barrier, at his aggressor and the whole footballing world was outraged.

For a time, he was in danger of being imprisoned for assault, but ended up with community service and a nine-month ban from professional football. He took his punishment with dignity and watched as United failed to pick up a trophy in his absence. On his return, it was as if he'd never been away. He was back to his inspirational best and was even made United's captain.

In 1996, they won the 'double' for the second time and Cantona was named Footballer of the Year by the writers, the first Frenchman to win the award. His goal in the Charity Shield was his eighth, on his eighth and last appearance at Wembley, for at the end of that season, after winning his sixth Championship, he stunned United, by announcing his retirement. He was 30 years old and wanted to become an actor. It was typical of the flamboyance of one of the game's greatest ever performers.

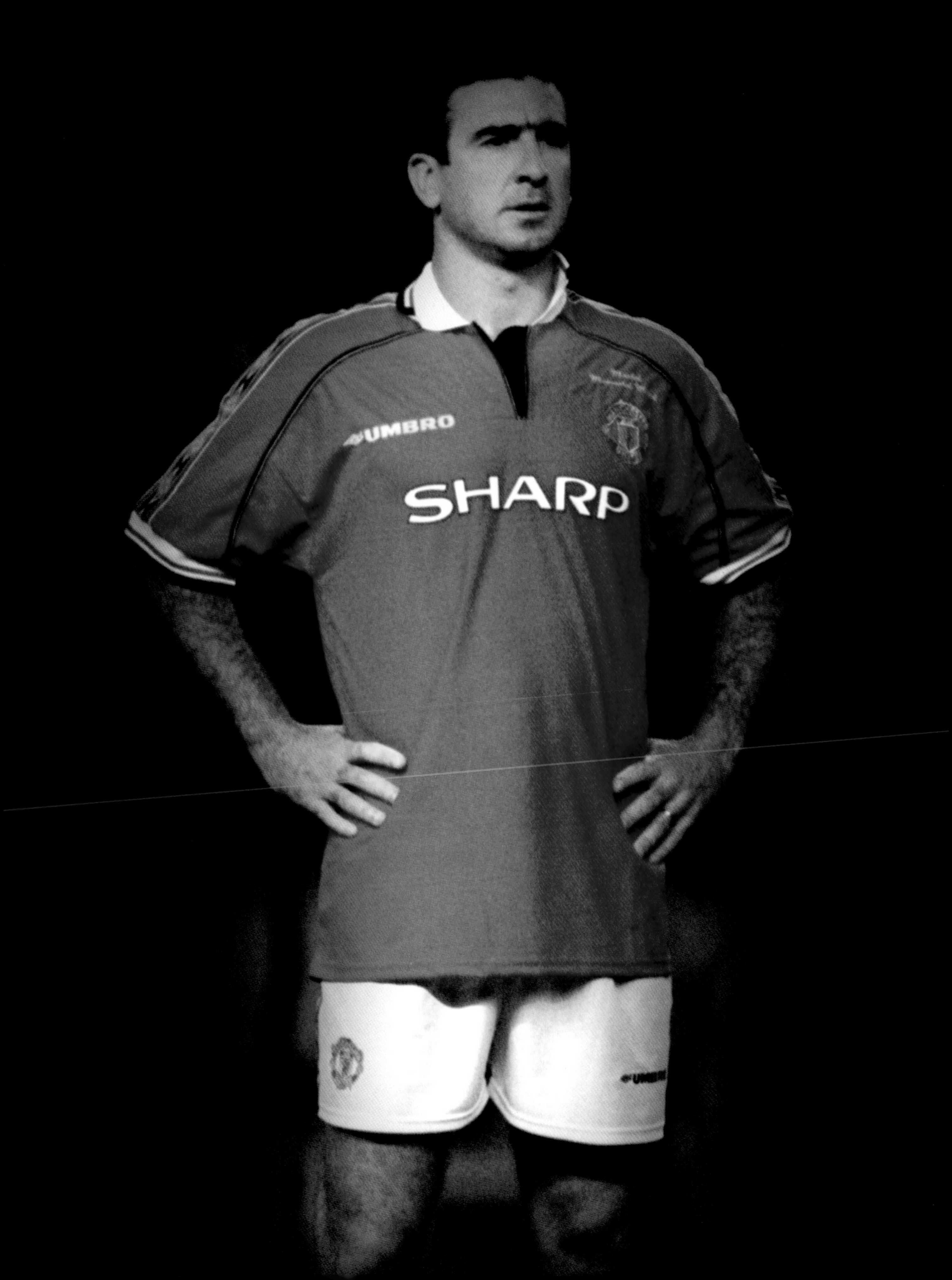
UMBRO
SHARP

THE F.A. CUP FINAL

SPONSORED BY
LITTLEWOODS

CHELSEA
v
MIDDLESBROUGH

F.A. CUP
LITTLEWOODS

SATURDAY 17TH MAY 1997
KICK-OFF 3.00PM
OFFICIAL MATCHDAY PROGRAMME £6.00

Wembley

Chelsea v Middlesbrough

F.A. Cup Final, Saturday 17th May 1997

Boro Feel The Blues

Preview

It had been 27 years since Chelsea's only F.A. Cup win and the drawn final had meant they had never lifted the trophy at Wembley. They had made five visits since then, winning two other competitions at the stadium. Chelsea had even won a semi-final at Wembley, but lifting the F.A. Cup there, had continued to elude them. Chelsea finished 6th, in the F.A. Premier League, their highest position for seven years. Middlesbrough were about to complete the most eventful season by far, in their history. What should have been a proud and joyous end to an unforgettable season, was now their only hope of consolation, amidst tears of heartbreak and frustration. The previous month, in their first ever Coca-Cola Cup Final, they had been three minutes away from the trophy, when victory was snatched from their grasp. They lost an exhausting replay, three days after the F.A. Cup semi-final and their two magnificent cup runs meant that league fixtures were piling up in their battle against relegation. Vital points were then lost as the strength sapped out of them. They were forced to play their last four matches in the space of nine days and despite remaining unbeaten in all of them, they finished 19th and were relegated back to the Football League after two years in the top flight. Their last match, just six days before the F.A. Cup Final, saw them finish two points adrift of safety, a fact even more heartbreaking, because of the fact that they had been deducted three points for postponing a fixture at Blackburn in December due to illness and injury.

Semi–Final, Sunday 13th April 1997

Chelsea Hughes 2, Zola	**3:0**	**Wimbledon**	(Highbury, London)
Chesterfield Morris, Dyche (penalty) Hewitt	**3:3** **(AET)**	**Middlesbrough** Ravanelli Hignett (penalty), Festa	(Old Trafford, Manchester)
Chesterfield	**0:3**	**Middlesbrough** Beck, Ravanelli, Emerson	(Hillsborough, Sheffield) Replay (Tuesday 22nd April 1997)

The Match

The quickest ever goal in a Wembley F.A. Cup Final got the match off to a sensational start. Chelsea's Roberto Di Matteo, one of five Italians to play in this final, received the ball in his own half from Wise and ran straight down the middle of the field. Hughes bundled the experienced Italian defender, Festa out of the way and from 30 yards out, Di Matteo unleashed a vicious dipping shot, which sailed over Roberts and in off the crossbar. It was timed at 42 seconds. Middlesbrough's recent bad luck continued to kick them in the teeth. Two players went off injured in the first half-hour, including their influential star Italian striker, Ravanelli and although the goal was all that divided the teams until eight minutes from the end, Middlesbrough never really threatened. Eddie Newton started the move, which sunk them for the last time and left their fans in tears. He passed to the Romanian, Petrescu, who crossed to the far post where it was met by the first Italian winner of the Footballer of the Year award, Zola. His exquisite back-flick with his heel, set Newton up to beat Roberts, via a deflection off Pearson's arm. It was a sweet moment for the scorer, who had conceded the crucial first penalty in the 1994 final.

Chelsea Di Matteo, Newton	**2:0**	**Middlesbrough**

Chelsea:
Grodas, Sinclair, Lebeouf, Clarke, Minto, Petrescu, Newton, Di Matteo, Wise (Captain), Zola, Hughes, Vialli (Sub), Myers (Sub), Hitchcock (Sub)
Ruud Gullit (Manager)

Middlesbrough:
Roberts, Blackmore, Pearson (Captain), Festa, Fleming, Stamp, Emerson, Mustoe, Hignett, Juninho, Ravanelli, Vickers (Sub), Kinder (Sub), Beck (sub)
Bryan Robson (Manager)

Referee: S. Lodge (Barnsley)
Attendance: 79,160

Chelsea went on to win the European Cup Winners Cup, the following year, in Stockholm, with a single goal victory in the final against Stuttgart. It was their first European trophy since winning the same competition in 1971. Chelsea were to win the F.A. Cup again in Wembley's last final in 2000. Middlesbrough bounced straight back to the Premier League the following year, by finishing as Football League runners-up and they also returned to Wembley, only to lose to Chelsea yet again, in their second successive Coca-Cola Cup Final.

Wembley Greats
Roberto Di Matteo
Chelsea & Italy

Di Matteo

Roberto Di Matteo seemed to be inspired by Wembley Stadium, because on three separate occasions, he cropped up to score the winning goal in a cup final. Although he was born in Switzerland and won the Swiss League Championship with Aarau, his parents were Italian and in 1993 he was transferred to the Italian club Lazio, where he played alongside Paul Gascoigne. This brought him to the attention of Arrigo Sacchi, who picked Di Matteo for the Italian national side.

He played in England in the 1996 European Championship, before Chelsea signed him for £4.9 million. In his first season, he was in the Italian team which beat England in a World Cup qualifying match at Wembley Stadium and went on to score the quickest ever Wembley Cup Final goal, as Chelsea lifted the F.A. Cup.

Despite missing a penalty in the Charity Shield shoot-out against Manchester United, he went on to collect more medals, scoring in extra time in the Coca-Cola Cup Final and helping Chelsea win the European Cup Winners Cup, before playing for Italy in the World Cup. An ankle injury kept him out of the side in 1999 and after returning to first-team action, he was soon sidelined again by a broken arm.

The popular midfielder fought his way back into the side as Chelsea converged on Wembley again   and when David James' clearance fell invitingly for Di Matteo, he didn't waste the opportunity to score one more Wembley winner. It was the last goal ever scored in the F.A. Cup at the stadium.

Four months later, Di Matteo's career was brought abruptly to an end, at the age of 30, when he sustained a badly broken leg in a UEFA Cup tie. Ironically, it was at St. Gallen in the country where his career began, Switzerland.

Newcastle United's Alan Shearer smashes a shot against David Seaman's post

Arsenal v Newcastle

F.A. Cup Final, Saturday 16th May 1998

Unstoppable Gunners

Preview

Arsenal had twice lost F.A. Cup Finals to Newcastle, either side of the war, but faced them on this occasion as overwhelming favourites. It had been five years since they had last won the Cup. In 1994 they had won the European Cup Winners Cup, but had suddenly struck a rich vein of form to wrest the Premier League Championship from Manchester United and now stood on the verge of emulating United's two 'double' triumphs. They had taken a tough route to Wembley, however. Twice, they had progressed on penalties, away from home and also won away against the previous year's finalists, Middlesbrough. Newcastle's last Cup win had been back in 1955 and their more recent Wembley visits had been woeful. They were humiliated in the 1974 final and suffered an even worse fate in the 1996 F.A. Charity Shield, losing 4-0 to Manchester United.

As Arsenal were sprinting towards their first title since 1991, Newcastle were finishing 13th, their lowest position since promotion in 1993. This was a big disappointment after two successive runners-up placings had raised hopes of long overdue silverware. In their first ever European Cup campaign, they had defeated the European Cup Winners Cup holders, Barcelona, but had failed to qualify for the quarter-finals. Arsenal, meanwhile, had taken a shock first round exit from the UEFA Cup at the hands of P.A.O.K. Salonika, but had reached the Coca-Cola Cup semi-finals for the second time in three years, before losing to the eventual winners, Chelsea.

Semi–Finals, Sunday 5th April 1998

Arsenal	1:0	Wolverhampton W.	(Villa Park, Birmingham)
Wreh			
Newcastle United	1:0	Sheffield United	(Old Trafford, Manchester)
Shearer			

The Match

Arsenal broke through after 23 minutes, when Petit, who was to clinch the World Cup for France, two months later, sent Marc Overmars through. The Dutchman held off the Italian, Pistone to slot the opener through Given's legs. With 21 minutes left, the historic 'double' was clinched when the young French striker, Nicolas Anelka ran on to Parlour's long ball and fired into the corner. Anelka went on to score three more Wembley goals in the nine months, including two that beat England.

Arsenal	2:0	**Newcastle United**
Overmars		
Anelka		

Arsenal:
Seaman, Dixon, Keown, Adams (Captain), Winterburn, Parlour, Vieira, Petit, Overmars, Wreh, Anelka, Platt (Sub), Bould (Sub), Grimandi (Sub), Wright (Sub), Manninger (Sub)
Arsene Wenger (Manager)

Newcastle United:
Given, Pistone, Dabizas, Howey, Pearce, Barton, Lee (Captain), Batty, Speed, Ketsbaia, Shearer, Andersson (Sub), Watson (Sub), Barnes (Sub), Albert (Sub), Hislop (Sub)
Kenny Dalglish (Manager)

Referee:	P. Durkin (Portland)
Attendance:	79,183

Arsenal's second 'double' was secured by an unexpected unstoppable run of form in the second half of the season. They had won both honours comfortably in the end, unlike their 1971 counterparts, who had had to battle and come from behind to triumph. With Arsenal qualifying for the European Cup and playing home games at Wembley, Newcastle took their place in the European Cup Winners Cup. However, their first appearance in the competition was a brief one, as Partizan Belgrade eliminated them in the first round, on away goals. There was almost a repeat of this final, the following year, when both sides reached the semi-finals again, but only Newcastle made it back to Wembley.

Adams

No player has appeared at Wembley Stadium, more times than Tony Adams. His 60th game was when captaining England against Germany at Wembley stadium's last fixture in 2000. Adams was a rock at the heart of the defence for both Arsenal and England, captaining both. He was a natural leader who graduated into a regular in the Arsenal first team when George Graham became manager at Highbury.

In 1987, he won his first England cap at the age of 20 and instantly impressed in a 4-2 win against Spain in Madrid. Two months later he was in the Arsenal side which beat Liverpool at Wembley to win the Littlewoods Cup and Adams was the players' choice as Young Player of the Year. He captained Arsenal in their defence of the Littlewoods Cup at the 1988 final, but Luton Town beat them 3-2 in a thriller.

Adams ended the season at the European Championships in Germany, where England flopped, although the young defender scored against the U.S.S.R. He lost his place in the England side in the following season as Bobby Robson preferred the centre-back pairing of Terry Butcher and Des Walker, but Adams still led Arsenal to a sensational League Championship victory, won at the death, with a 2-0 success against Liverpool, at Anfield. Missing out on a World Cup place, his off-field excesses began to spiral out of control and he was jailed at Christmas 1990 for a drink-driving offence. Adams was released two months later and able to captain Arsenal to their second title in three years.

He was also brought back into the England fold by Graham Taylor, despite calls for him to be banned. Adams kept his head down and concentrated on restoring his battered image. Arsenal won both domestic cup competitions in 1993, although Adams was mortified when he accidentally broke Coca-Cola Cup hero, Steve Morrow's arm during the immediate after-match celebrations. The following year, the Gunners lifted the Cup Winners Cup and Adams became the England captain for the first time, leading his country into their heroic European Championship campaign in 1996, which finally ended at the semi-final hurdle.

Two years later, Arsenal won the 'double' and Adams took the familiar path up the Wembley steps to receive the F.A. Cup, before heading off to France to play in his first and only World Cup. Thanks to Arsenal's participation in pre-season tournaments and the Champions League at Wembley, Adams passed Peter Shilton's record of 58 appearances in 2000, marking the occasion by scoring against the Ukraine.

As he reached his mid-thirties, his appearances in Arsenal's first team began to dwindle, due to more injuries and intense competition from a very high quality squad, built by Arsene Wenger. Adams retired in 2002, after Arsenal had won the 'double' for the third time.

Shearer

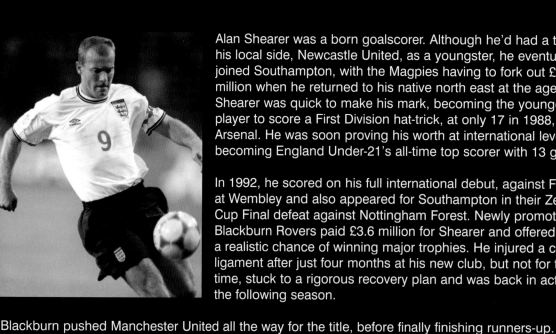

Alan Shearer was a born goalscorer. Although he'd had a trial for his local side, Newcastle United, as a youngster, he eventually joined Southampton, with the Magpies having to fork out £15 million when he returned to his native north east at the age of 25. Shearer was quick to make his mark, becoming the youngest player to score a First Division hat-trick, at only 17 in 1988, against Arsenal. He was soon proving his worth at international level, becoming England Under-21's all-time top scorer with 13 goals.

In 1992, he scored on his full international debut, against France at Wembley and also appeared for Southampton in their Zenith Cup Final defeat against Nottingham Forest. Newly promoted Blackburn Rovers paid £3.6 million for Shearer and offered him a realistic chance of winning major trophies. He injured a cruciate ligament after just four months at his new club, but not for the first time, stuck to a rigorous recovery plan and was back in action for the following season.

Blackburn pushed Manchester United all the way for the title, before finally finishing runners-up. Shearer was voted Footballer of the Year. Chris Sutton was signed in the summer of 1994 to partner him and the 'SAS', as they were known took Blackburn to the Premier League Championship, with Shearer scoring at Liverpool, on a dramatic final day as Manchester United failed to catch them. It was his 34th league goal of the season, the highest total in all four divisions and his fellow professionals made him their Player of the Year.

Blackburn failed to capitalise on this success but Shearer was, once again, the leading scorer in all four divisions with 31 goals, the next season. Strangely enough, he had failed to score a single goal for England for almost two years, when he joined the European Championship squad in 1996 and was under pressure for his place. Perhaps it was because England hadn't played a competitive game in that period, but he netted the opening goal of the tournament and went on to finish as top scorer with five goals. Shearer scored after two minutes of the semi-final against Germany, but England were defeated on penalties after a dramatic two hours.

After the tournament, he could not resist the call of Kevin Keegan, who took him back home to Newcastle for a world record transfer fee of £15 million. His debut was back at Wembley in the Charity Shield, but Newcastle were well beaten. Shearer ended his third successive season as the Premier League's top scorer, although Keegan had resigned and the Magpies then went through a transitional period. They still managed to reach two consecutive F.A. Cup Finals though, with Shearer getting the goals in both semi-finals and hitting the inside of the post in the 1998 final.

In 1999, he was captain. Newcastle were unlucky that they came up against 'double' and 'treble' winning sides on each occasion. Shearer has survived a number of bad leg injuries and in 2000, after getting his 30th England goal, as captain, at the European Championship, he decided to quit international football to concentrate the remainder of his career on guiding Newcastle back to the top. Under the astute managership of 70-year-old Sir Bobby Robson, Shearer holds the record for goals scored in the Premier League and continues to add to his total.

Wembley
NATIONAL STADIUM LTD

THE F.A. CUP SPONSORED BY AXA - FINAL TIE

MANCHESTER UNITED
v
NEWCASTLE UNITED

SATURDAY 22 MAY 1999
KICK OFF 3PM

Manchester United v Newcastle United

F.A. Cup Final, Saturday 22nd May 1999

Team Of The Century

Preview

United were chasing their fourth F.A. Cup win of the decade and a record tenth overall. Six days earlier, they had clinched their fifth Premier League Championship in seven years, by a point, from Arsenal, the previous year's 'double' winners. Now United had the opportunity to secure an unbelievable third 'double' and all within the 1990's. Their opponents, Newcastle were appearing in their second successive final and were again attempting to prevent the 'double' being achieved. In the previous year's final, they had been outplayed and were anxious to avoid another Wembley defeat. They had not won the Cup since 1955 and United had destroyed them in the 1996 F.A. Charity Shield at Wembley. In the semi-finals, Newcastle had beaten the Worthington Cup winners, while United had survived an injury-time penalty in the replay (which would have put them out) to beat the holders, before also pipping them to the Championship. There had been no indication that this would be such a record-breaking season for United, when they were comprehensively beaten in the F.A. Charity Shield by Arsenal, but they had also reached the European Cup Final for the first time since 1968. They had even reached the Worthington Cup quarter-finals, only losing to the eventual winners. Newcastle finished 13th, in the Premier League, for the second year in succession.

Semi–Finals, Sunday 11th April 1999

Arsenal	*0:0*	**Manchester United**	*(Villa Park, Birmingham)*	
	(AET)			
Newcastle United *Shearer 2 (1 penalty)*	*2:0* *(AET)*	**Tottenham Hotspur**	*(Old Trafford, Manchester)*	
Arsenal *Bergkamp*	*1:2* *(AET)*	**Manchester United** *Beckham, Giggs*	*(Villa Park, Birmingham)*	*Replay (Wednesday 14th April 1999)*

The Match

United lost their captain, Roy Keane, who went off injured after only nine minutes, but incredibly, it was his substitute, who put them ahead, less than two minutes later. Striker Teddy Sheringham played a one-two with Scholes, before firing through Harper's legs, as the French defender, Charvet made a desperate final lunge. After a brief Newcastle revival at the beginning of the second half, the same players combined to add United's second. With his back to goal, Sheringham laid it into the path of Paul Scholes, whose sweetly struck shot went through Charvet's legs before beating Harper. Manchester United then strolled to victory and their third 'double'.

Manchester United *Sheringham* *Scholes*	*2:0*	**Newcastle United**

Manchester United:
Schmeichel, G. Neville, May, Johnsen, P. Neville, Beckham, Keane (Captain), Scholes, Giggs, Solskjaer, Cole, Sheringham (Sub), Stam (Sub), Yorke (Sub), Blomqvist (Sub), Van der Gouw (Sub)
Alex Ferguson (Manager)

Newcastle United:
Harper, Griffin, Charvet, Dabizas, Domi, Lee, Hamann, Speed, Solano, Shearer (Captain), Ketsbaia, Ferguson (Sub), Maric (Sub), Glass (Sub), Barton (Sub), Given (Sub)
Ruud Gullit (Manager)

Referee:	*P. Jones (Loughborough)*
Attendance:	*79,101*

Alex Ferguson had built a team, which was now rewriting the record books. Three of them, Schmeichel, Keane and Giggs had played in all three Cup Finals, which clinched the 'doubles', whilst only the two Norwegians, Johnsen and Solskjaer, of the starting eleven, had not played in the 1996 Final. Ferguson's policy of resting key players at various points of the season was now reaping its rewards. United were unbeaten in all competitions during 1999 and had ended the season in unstoppable form. Four days later came their greatest triumph of all. In the European Cup Final in Barcelona, they were a goal down to Bayern Munich in injury time, when their two substitutes, Sheringham and Solskjaer both scored to snatch victory from the Germans. United had won the 'treble' and their manager was rewarded with a knighthood, the following month. Their European Cup success meant that they would not defend the F.A. Cup, competing instead in F.I.F.A.'s Club World Championship in Brazil. Newcastle were back at Wembley the following year, attempting to reach their third successive final. In the UEFA Cup, they reached the third round, before losing narrowly to Roma.

Alex Ferguson was a useful striker who topped the Scottish First Division scoring charts in 1966, with Dunfermline Athletic. He spent two years at Rangers, but was criticised after his performance in the 4-0 defeat by Celtic in the 1969 Scottish Cup Final and was soon on his way out of Ibrox. In 1975, his managerial career began at Second Division, East Stirling, when he was only 33, having retired because of injury. He quickly moved on to St. Mirren and won promotion to the Premier Division in his first season with them, as they won the First Division Championship.

The ambitious Ferguson saw limited opportunities at Love Street and moved on again, after two years, to the northern outpost of Aberdeen, where he saw the potential to challenge Celtic and Rangers.

His motivational skills coming to the fore, he took the Dons to two successive Scottish League Cup Finals, before sensationally taking the Scottish League Championship outside Glasgow for the first time in 15 years. It was Aberdeen's first title for 25 years. This was no 'flash in the pan'. They also won the Scottish Cup, three years in succession and in 1983, became the first Scottish club outside Glasgow to win a European trophy, after a sensational 2-1 victory in extra time against Real Madrid in the Cup Winners Cup Final.

Two more Championships followed and both domestic cup competitions were won in 1986, Ferguson's last season before he was tempted over the border. It was also the year that he took Scotland to the World Cup, after the untimely death of Jock Stein. The tournament was not a success for the Scots and he declined to take the job on in a permanent role. Instead, he joined Manchester United, a club that had consistently failed to deliver a league title to its increasingly impatient board.

Ferguson needed to take time to rebuild and he was given it. Removing the old guard, establishing a good youth policy and splashing out on some big signings, but by 1989, they were still falling short and Ferguson's job seemed under threat. A 5-1 defeat at Manchester City was almost the final straw. The F.A. Cup rescued him. After drawing the final at Wembley, he bravely dropped his experienced keeper, Jim Leighton, who never forgave him, and introduced Les Sealey, a seasoned campaigner himself, for a sensational debut. It paid off and so began more than a decade of endless success for United.

They won the European Cup Winners Cup in 1991, Ferguson's second and the Rumbelows Cup, the following year, before finally ending the 26-year wait with the first Premier League Championship, Ferguson's signing of Eric Cantona, from rivals Leeds United, proving to be the deal of the decade for him. Cantona was an inspiration to younger players, if a little too volatile at times and Ferguson was fiercely defensive of his side, building up an 'us and them' mentality in the dressing room. They won the 'double' in 1994 and again in 1996.

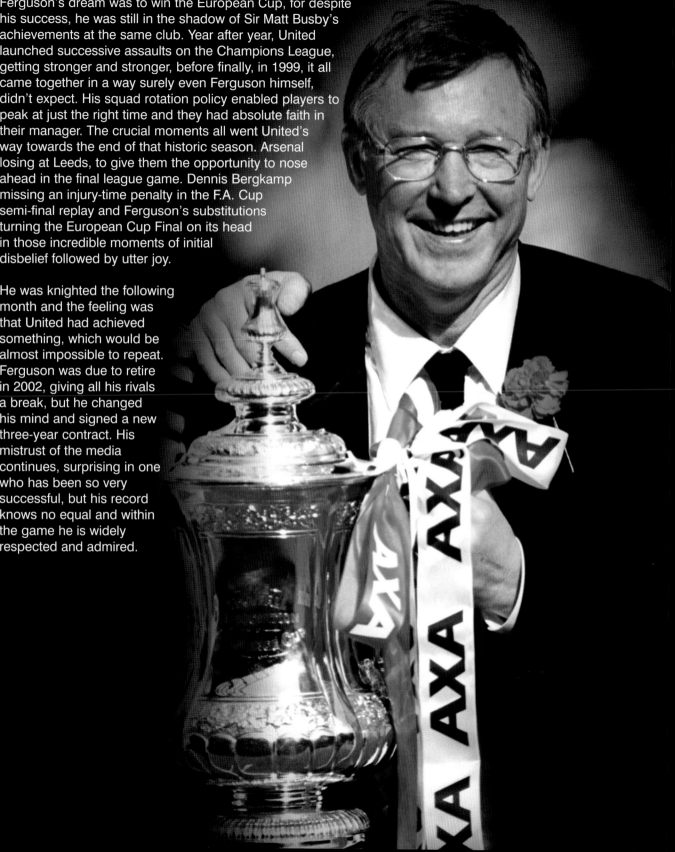

Ferguson's dream was to win the European Cup, for despite his success, he was still in the shadow of Sir Matt Busby's achievements at the same club. Year after year, United launched successive assaults on the Champions League, getting stronger and stronger, before finally, in 1999, it all came together in a way surely even Ferguson himself, didn't expect. His squad rotation policy enabled players to peak at just the right time and they had absolute faith in their manager. The crucial moments all went United's way towards the end of that historic season. Arsenal losing at Leeds, to give them the opportunity to nose ahead in the final league game. Dennis Bergkamp missing an injury-time penalty in the F.A. Cup semi-final replay and Ferguson's substitutions turning the European Cup Final on its head in those incredible moments of initial disbelief followed by utter joy.

He was knighted the following month and the feeling was that United had achieved something, which would be almost impossible to repeat. Ferguson was due to retire in 2002, giving all his rivals a break, but he changed his mind and signed a new three-year contract. His mistrust of the media continues, surprising in one who has been so very successful, but his record knows no equal and within the game he is widely respected and admired.

Aston Villa v Chelsea

F.A. Cup Final, Saturday 20th May 2000

The End Of An Era

Preview

After 77 years of magical memories, Wembley Stadium hosted its last F.A. Cup Final before being rebuilt. Villa had not won the trophy since 1957, their seventh victory. Chelsea had won it twice, most recently in 1997. Villa had needed penalties to defeat a First Division side in the semi-finals, whilst Chelsea were fortunate to prevent their opponents from reaching a third successive final. Chelsea had also knocked out the eventual Worthington Cup winners, Leicester City, in the last 16.

Both clubs had just missed out on European qualification from the F.A. Premier League. Villa finished 6th, for the second year in succession and Chelsea finished a place above them, having also reached the European Cup quarter-finals at the first attempt, where they took Barcelona to extra time before crashing out.

Semi–Final, Sunday 2nd April 2000

Aston Villa	**0:0**	**Bolton Wanderers**	**(Wembley Stadium, London)**
	(AET)		

Aston Villa won 4:1 on penalties

Semi–Final, Sunday 9th April 2000

Chelsea	**2:1**	**Newcastle United**	**(Wembley Stadium, London)**
Poyet 2		Lee	

The Match

Sadly, the old Wembley's last Cup Final was not very memorable. The first half was poor, but Chelsea began to pressurise Villa, after the interval and deservedly scored after 72 minutes. Zola sent a free kick into a crowded penalty area. James managed to reach it, but his punch out, rebounded off Southgate and Roberto Di Matteo crashed it into the roof of the net. Wembley was a happy place for the Italian. He had scored a sensational first minute goal in the 1997 Final and had netted in the following year's Coca-Cola Cup Final. Villa failed to reply, but at least Wembley could proudly claim that it never staged a goalless F.A. Cup final. The abiding memory of this game is of Chelsea's captain, Dennis Wise taking his son of four months with him to receive the Cup.

Aston Villa	**0:1**	**Chelsea**	
		Di Matteo	

Aston Villa:
James, Ehiogu, Southgate (Captain), Barry, Delaney, Boateng, Merson, Taylor, Wright, Dublin, Carbone, Stone (Sub), Hendrie (Sub), Joachim (Sub), Samuel (Sub), Enckelman (Sub)
John Gregory (Manager)

Chelsea:
De Goey, Melchiot, Desailly, Lebeouf, Babayaro, Poyet, Wise (Captain), Deschamps, Di Matteo, Zola, Weah, Morris (Sub), Flo (Sub), Terry (Sub), Harley (Sub), Cudicini (Sub)
Gianluca Vialli (Manager)

Referee:	*G. Poll (Tring)*
Attendance:	*78,217*

Didier Deschamps went on to captain World Champions, France to European Championship success in Rotterdam, two months later. Desailly also played in the final. Chelsea's recent good European form deserted them in the following season's UEFA Cup and they were surprisingly knocked out in the first round by St. Gallen of Switzerland.

The Records

The Teams

Most Wins
9 – Manchester United

Most Appearances
14 – Manchester United (plus two replays and a semi-final)

FA Cup Wins In Successive Years
Newcastle United – 1951, 52
Tottenham Hotspur – 1961, 62
Tottenham Hotspur – 1981, 82

Finalists In Three Successive Years
Arsenal – 1978-80
Everton – 1984-86
Manchester United – 1994-96
(Newcastle United appeared in two successive finals followed by a Wembley semi-final)

Same Opponents In Three Finals
Arsenal v. Newcastle United – 1932, 52, 98

Most Consecutive Wins
5 – Newcastle United (first five visits)
(Tottenham Hotspur won their first five finals at Wembley, but two of them needed replays)

Beaten Finalists In Successive Years
Manchester United – 1957, 58
Everton – 1985, 86
Newcastle United – 1998, 99

Most Consecutive Defeats
4 – Leicester City (have never won the Cup)
(Newcastle United lost three finals and a semi-final in successive visits)

League Championship & FA Cup 'Double' Winners
1961 – Tottenham Hotspur
1971 – Arsenal
1986 – Liverpool
1994 – Manchester United
1996 – Manchester United
1998 – Arsenal
1999 – Manchester United (also won European Cup – the 'treble')

FA Cup & Football League Cup Winners In The Same Year
1993 – Arsenal (beat Sheffield Wednesday in both finals)

FA Cup Winners & Football League Cup Finalists In The Same Year
1982 – Tottenham Hotspur
1983 – Manchester United
1984 – Everton
1994 – Manchester United

Beaten Finalists In FA Cup & Football League Cup In Same Year
1993 – Sheffield Wednesday
1997 – Middlesbrough

FA Cup Winners & Football League Runners-Up In Same Year
1948 – Manchester United
1954 – West Bromwich Albion
1960 – Wolverhampton Wanderers
1972 – Leeds United
1974 – Liverpool
1989 – Liverpool

Beaten Finalists & League Champions In Same Year
1957 – Manchester United
1977 – Liverpool (also European Cup finalists)
1985 – Everton (also won European Cup Winners Cup)
1988 – Liverpool

Runners-Up In League & FA Cup In Same Year
1928 – Huddersfield Town
1932 – Arsenal
1939 – Wolverhampton Wanderers
1962 – Burnley
1965 – Leeds United
1970 – Leeds United
1986 – Everton (Liverpool won both)
1995 – Manchester United

Finalists In Other Competitions In Same Year
1977 – Liverpool (European Cup Winners)
1980 – Arsenal (European Cup Winners Cup)
1985 – Everton (European Cup Winners Cup Winners)
1986 – Liverpool (Screen Sport Super Cup Winners)
1986 – Everton (Screen Sport Super Cup)
1989 – Everton (Simod Cup)
1999 – Manchester United (European Cup Winners)

Relegated Finalists
1926 – Manchester City
1969 – Leicester City
1983 – Brighton and Hove Albion
1997 – Middlesbrough

Second Division Winners (League Position In Brackets)
1931 – West Bromwich Albion (promoted as runners-up)
1973 – Sunderland (6th)
1976 – Southampton (6th)
1980 – West Ham United (7th)

Second Division Beaten Finalists (League Position In Brackets)
1923 – West Ham United (promoted as runners-up)
1936 – Sheffield United (3rd)
1947 – Burnley (promoted as runners-up)
1949 – Leicester City (19th)
1964 – Preston North End (3rd)
1975 – Fulham (9th)
1982 – Queen's Park Rangers (5th)
1992 – Sunderland (18th)

Arsenal
1927...0-1 Cardiff City
1930...2-0 Huddersfield Town
1932...1-2 Newcastle United
1936...1-0 Sheffield United
1950...2-0 Liverpool
1952...0-1 Newcastle United
1971...2-1 Liverpool (AET)
1972...0-1 Leeds United
1978...0-1 Ipswich Town
1979...3-2 Manchester United
1980...0-1 West Ham United
(lost 1991 Semi-Final 1-3 to Tottenham Hotspur at Wembley)
1993...1-1 Sheffield Wednesday (AET) Replay 2-1 (AET)
1998...2-0 Newcastle United

Aston Villa
1924...0-2 Newcastle United
1957...2-1 Manchester United
2000...0-1 Chelsea
(beat Bolton Wanderers 4-1 on penalties in Semi-Final at Wembley)

Birmingham City
1931...1-2 West Bromwich Albion
1956...1-3 Manchester City

Blackburn Rovers
1928...3-1 Huddersfield Town
1960...0-3 Wolverhampton Wanderers

Blackpool
1948...2-4 Manchester United
1951...0-2 Newcastle United
1953...4-3 Bolton Wanderers

Bolton Wanderers
1923...2-0 West Ham United
1926...1-0 Manchester City
1929...2-0 Portsmouth
1953...3-4 Blackpool
1958...2-0 Manchester United
(lost 2000 semi-final 1-4 on penalties at Wembley)

Brighton & Hove Albion
1983...2-2 Manchester United *(AET)*
Replay 0-4

Burnley
1947...0-1 Charlton Athletic *(AET)*
1962...1-3 Tottenham Hotspur

Cardiff City
1925...0-1 Sheffield United
1927...1-0 Arsenal

Charlton Athletic
1946...1-4 Derby County *((AET)*
1947...1-0 Burnley *(AET)*

Chelsea
1967...1-2 Tottenham Hotspur
1970...2-2 Leeds United *(AET)*
(won replay 2-1 A.E.T. at Old Trafford, Manchester)
1994...0-4 Manchester United
(beat Luton Town 2-0 in semi-final at Wembley)
1997...2-0 Middlesbrough
2000...1-0 Aston Villa
(beat Newcastle United 2-1 in semi-final at Wembley)

Coventry City
1987...3-2 Tottenham Hotspur *(AET)*

Crystal Palace
1990...3-3 Manchester United *(AET)* Replay 0-1

Derby County
1946...4-1 Charlton Athletic *(AET)*

Everton
1933...3-0 Manchester City
1966...3-2 Sheffield Wednesday
1968...0-1 West Bromwich Albion *(AET)*
1984...2-0 Watford
1985...0-1 Manchester United *(AET)*
1986...1-3 Liverpool
1989...2-3 Liverpool *(AET)*
1995...1-0 Manchester United

Fulham
1975...0-2 West Ham United

Huddersfield Town
1928...1-3 Blackburn Rovers
1930...0-2 Arsenal
1938...0-1 Preston North End *(AET)*

Ipswich Town
1978...1-0 Arsenal

Leeds United
1965...1-2 Liverpool *(AET)*
1970...2-2 Chelsea *(AET) (lost replay 1-2 AET at Old Trafford, Manchester)*
1972...1-0 Arsenal
1973...0-1 Sunderland

Leicester City
1949...1-3 Wolverhampton Wanderers
1961...0-2 Tottenham Hotspur
1963...1-3 Manchester United
1969...0-1 Manchester City

Liverpool
1950...0-2 Arsenal
1965...2-1 Leeds United *(AET)*
1971...1-2 Arsenal *(AET)*
1974...3-0 Newcastle United
1977...1-2 Manchester United
1986...3-1 Everton
1988...0-1 Wimbledon
1989...3-2 Everton *(AET)*
1992...2-0 Sunderland
1996...0-1 Manchester United

Luton Town
1959...1-2 Nottingham Forest *(lost 1994 semi-final 0-2 to Chelsea at Wembley)*

Manchester City
1926...0-1 Bolton Wanderers
1933...0-3 Everton
1934...2-1 Portsmouth
1955...1-3 Newcastle United
1956...3-1 Birmingham City
1969...1-0 Leicester City
1981...1-1 Tottenham Hotspur *(AET)*
Replay 2-3

Manchester United
1948...4-2 Blackpool
1957...1-2 Aston Villa
1958...0-2 Bolton Wanderers
1963...3-1 Leicester City
1976...0-1 Southampton
1977...2-1 Liverpool
1979...2-3 Arsenal
1983...2-2 Brighton and Hove Albion *(AET)*
Replay 4-0
1985...1-0 Everton *(AET)*
1990...3-3 Crystal Palace *(AET)*
Replay 1-0
1994...4-0 Chelsea
(drew 1-1 AET with Oldham Athletic in semi-final at Wembley)
1995...0-1 Everton
1996...1-0 Liverpool
1999...2-0 Newcastle United

Middlesbrough
1997...0-2 Chelsea

Newcastle United
1924...2-0 Aston Villa
1932...2-1 Arsenal
1951...2-0 Blackpool
1952...1-0 Arsenal
1955...3-1 Manchester City
1974...0-3 Liverpool
1998...0-2 Arsenal
1999...0-2 Manchester United
(lost 2000 semi-final 1-2 to Chelsea at Wembley)

Nottingham Forest
1959...2-1 Luton Town
1991...1-2 Tottenham Hotspur *(AET)*

Oldham Athletic
(drew 1994 semi-final 1-1 AET with Manchester United at Wembley)

Portsmouth
1929...0-2 Bolton Wanderers
1934...1-2 Manchester City
1939...4-1 Wolverhampton Wanderers

Preston North End
1937...1-3 Sunderland
1938...1-0 Huddersfield Town *(AET)*
1954...2-3 West Bromwich Albion
1964...2-3 West Ham United

Queen's Park Rangers
1982...1-1 Tottenham Hotspur *(AET)*
Replay 0-1

Sheffield United
1925...1-0 Cardiff City
1936...0-1 Arsenal
(lost 1993 semi-final 1-2 AET. to Sheffield Wednesday at Wembley)

Sheffield Wednesday
1935...4-2 West Bromwich Albion
1966...2-3 Everton
1993...1-1 Arsenal *(AET)*
Replay 1-2 *(AET)*
(beat Sheffield United 2-1 AET in semi-final at Wembley)

Southampton
1976...1-0 Manchester United

Sunderland
1937...3-1 Preston North End
1973...1-0 Leeds United
1992...0-2 Liverpool

Tottenham Hotspur
1961...2-0 Leicester City
1962...3-1 Burnley
1967...2-1 Chelsea
1981...1-1 Manchester City *(AET)*
Replay 3-2
1982...1-1 Queen's Park Rangers *(AET)*
Replay 1-0
1987...2-3 Coventry City *(AET)*
1991...2-1 Nottingham Forest *(AET)*
(beat Arsenal 3-1 in Semi-Final at Wembley)
(lost 1993 semi-final 0-1 to Arsenal at Wembley)

Watford
1984...0-2 Everton

West Bromwich Albion
1931...2-1 Birmingham City
1935...2-4 Sheffield Wednesday
1954...3-2 Preston North End
1968...1-0 Everton *(AET)*

West Ham United
1923...0-2 Bolton Wanderers
1964...3-2 Preston North End
1975...2-0 Fulham
1980...1-0 Arsenal

Wimbledon
1988...1-0 Liverpool

Wolverhampton Wanderers
1939...1-4 Portsmouth
1949...3-1 Leicester City
1960...3-0 Blackburn Rovers

The Players

Most Wins: 4 – Mark Hughes *(Manchester United 1985, 90, 94, Chelsea 97)*

Most Appearances (Including Replays) 6:
Ray Clemence *(Liverpool 1971, 74, 77, Tottenham Hotspur 1982 and replay, 87)*
Frank Stapleton *(Arsenal 1978, 79, 80, Manchester United 1983 and replay, 85)*
Glenn Hoddle *(Tottenham Hotspur 1981 and replay, 82 and replay, 87, Chelsea 1994)*
Mark Hughes *(Manchester United 1985, 90 and replay, 94, 95, Chelsea 1997)*
(Joe Hulme 1927, 30, 32, 36, 38, Johnny Giles 1963, 65, 70, 72, 73
and Pat Rice 1971, 72, 78, 79, 80 also played in five finals)

Most Final Goals: 5 – Ian Rush *(Liverpool 1986, 89, 92)*
(also all-time top scorer in F.A. Cup with 43 goals)

Only Hat-trick: Stan Mortensen *(Blackpool 1953)*

Most Defeats: 4 – Paul Bracewell *(Everton 1985, 86, 89, Sunderland 1992)*

Youngest Finalist: Paul Allen *(West Ham United 1980)*
17 years, 256 days

Youngest Captain: David Nish *(Leicester City 1969)*
21 years, 7 months

Youngest Goalkeeper: Peter Shilton *(Leicester City 1969)*
19 years, 7 months

Youngest Scorer: Norman Whiteside *(Manchester United 1983 replay)*
18 years, 19 days

Won Successive Finals With Different Clubs:
Brian Talbot *(Ipswich Town 1978, Arsenal 1979)*

Played In Finals For Three Different Clubs:
Ernie Taylor *(Newcastle United 1951, Blackpool 1953, Manchester United 1958)*
John Barnes *(Watford 1984, Liverpool 1988, 89, 96, Newcastle United 1998)*

Scored In More Than One Final:
David Jack *(Bolton Wanderers 1923, 26)*
Stan Mortensen *(Blackpool 1948, 53)*
Jackie Milburn *(Newcastle United 1951, 55)*
Nat Lofthouse *(Bolton Wanderers 1953, 58)*
Bobby Johnstone *(Manchester City 1955, 56)*
Bobby Smith *(Tottenham Hotspur 1961, 62)*
Steve Heighway *(Liverpool 1971, 74)*
Frank Stapleton *(Arsenal 1979, Manchester United 1983)*
Norman Whiteside *(Manchester United 1983, 85)*
Ian Rush *(Liverpool 1986, 89, 92)*
Ian Wright *(Crystal Palace 1990, Arsenal 1993)*
Mark Hughes *(Manchester United 1990, 94)*
Eric Cantona *(Manchester United 1994, 96)*
Roberto Di Matteo *(Chelsea 1997, 2000)*

Penalties Converted:
George Mutch *(Preston North End 1938)*
Eddie Shimwell *(Blackpool 1948)*
Ronnie Allen *(West Bromwich Albion 1954)*
Danny Blanchflower *(Tottenham Hotspur 1962)*
Kevin Reeves *(Manchester City 1981 replay)*
Glenn Hoddle *(Tottenham Hotspur 1982 replay)*
Arnold Muhren *(Manchester United 1983 replay)*
Eric Cantona *(Manchester United 1994)* - twice

Penalties Saved:
Dave Beasant
(Wimbledon from John Aldridge of Liverpool 1988)
Mark Crossley
(Nottingham Forest from Gary Lineker of Tottenham Hotspur 1991)

Own Goals:
Bert Turner
(for Derby County v. Charlton Athletic 1946)
Tommy Hutchison
(for Tottenham Hotspur v. Manchester City 1981)
Brian Kilcline
(for Tottenham Hotspur v. Coventry City 1987)
Gary Mabbutt
(for Coventry City v. Tottenham Hotspur 1987)
Des Walker
(for Tottenham Hotspur v. Nottingham Forest 1991)

Scored In Every Round
Ellis Rimmer *(Sheffield Wednesday 1935)*
Frank O'Donnell *(Preston North End 1937)*
Stan Mortensen *(Blackpool 1948)*
Jackie Milburn *(Newcastle United 1951)*
Nat Lofthouse *(Bolton Wanderers 1953)*
Charlie Wayman *(Preston North End 1954)*
Jeff Astle *(West Bromwich Albion 1968)*
Peter Osgood *(Chelsea 1970)* – scored in final replay and not at Wembley

Only Dismissal
Kevin Moran *(Manchester United 1985)*

First Substitution
Dennis Clarke for John Kaye *(West Bromwich Albion 1968)*

Scoring Substitutes
Eddie Kelly *(Arsenal 1971)*
Stuart McCall *(Everton 1989)* – first to score twice
Ian Rush *(Liverpool 1989)* – scored twice
Ian Wright *(Crystal Palace 1990)* – scored twice
Brian McClair *(Manchester United 1994)*
Teddy Sheringham *(Manchester United 1999)*

Your F.A. Cup
Glorious Giggs Takes Nationwide's F.A. Cup Accolade

Nationwide Building Society has asked the country's football fans: "What is the greatest F.A. Cup moment during the competition's 131-year history?".

Nearly 10,000 football fans responded to Nationwide - an Official Partner of the F.A. Cup - and the answer was clear.

Ryan Giggs' wonder goal against Arsenal in the semi-final replay at Villa Park in 1999 raced ahead of the other magic moments on the shortlist and has been crowned the F.A. Cup's Greatest Moment.

Peter Gandolfi, Nationwide's Head of Sports Marketing, said: "As an official partner of the F.A. Cup, Nationwide was delighted to host this fascinating debate. It is a survey which has stimulated many discussions around the country at matches, at home and in bars over the last month. We decided that we wanted to give every football fan in the country the opportunity to vote for their most treasured moment in the World's most famous domestic cup competition and Ryan's amazing goal is a worthy winner."

A Full list of the results of the survey is as follows:

19.4%	*Ryan Giggs' mazy run against Arsenal in the semi-final*	*Arsenal 1:2 Manchester United, 1999*
11.5%	*Ricky Villa's amazing run to make City blue*	*Manchester City 2:3 Tottenham Hotspur, 1981*
8.4%	*Alan Sunderland's winner to give the Gunners the Cup*	*Arsenal 3:2 Manchester United, 1979*
8.1%	*Michael Owen's last gasp goal to overcome the Gunners*	*Arsenal 1:2 Liverpool, 2001*
6.9%	*Paul Gascoigne's stunning free-kick to take Spurs to the final*	*Arsenal 1:3 Tottenham Hotspur, 1991*
5.8%	*Ronnie Radford's wonder strike in the mud at Edgar Street*	*Hereford United 2:1 Newcastle United, 1972*
5.6%	*Dave Beasant's penalty save to give the 'Crazy Gang' the Cup*	*Liverpool 0:1 Wimbledon, 1988*
5.1%	*Charlie George's winning goal to clinch the double*	*Arsenal 2:1 Liverpool, 1971*
4.2%	*Roberto Di Matteo's quickest ever Wembley Cup Final goal*	*Chelsea 2:0 Middlesbrough, 1997*
4.1%	*The Matthews' Final - Sir Stan finally gets his winners' medal*	*Blackpool 4:3 Bolton Wanderers, 1953*
3.7%	*The Crowd Scene and White Horse at Wembley's first final*	*Bolton Wanderers 2:0 West Ham United, 1923*
3.5%	*Jim Montgomery's miraculous save to win the Cup*	*Leeds United 0:1 Sunderland, 1973*
2.9%	*Keith Houchen's diving header to send the Sky Blues crazy*	*Coventry City 3:2 Tottenham Hotspur, 1987*
2.4%	*Alan Pardew's deciding goal in a classic semi-final*	*Crystal Palace 4:3 Liverpool, 1990*
2.2%	*Harry's Cherries knock out the holders*	*Bournemouth 2:0 Manchester United, 1984*
1.7%	*Nigel Jemson's double strike for Shrewsbury against Everton*	*Shrewsbury Town 2:1 Everton, 2003*
1.2%	*Norman Whiteside beating Southall from the edge of the box*	*Everton 0:1 Manchester United, 1985*
1.1%	*Epic final that finally swings towards the Toffees*	*Everton 3:2 Sheffield Wednesday, 1966*
1.0%	*Non-league Matthew Hanlon shocks the recent winners*	*Sutton United 2:1 Coventry City, 1989*
1.0%	*Mickey Thomas' free-kick gives the Robins a platform for glory*	*Wrexham 2:1 Arsenal, 1992*

Giggs

Despite not being a Manchester United or Arsenal fan, this game, and Giggs goal would still be my 'Magic Moment'. Seeing Giggs drift past defenders with ease in the 120th minute of an action packed game between two of the best teams in the country and produce an unsavable shot is what makes you love football so much. It was an image you want to see over and over again, and attempt to relive on the Sunday football pitches. Seeing defenders twisting one way and turning another and being unable to do nothing but be bamboozled by Giggs feet at work. It is what the F.A. Cup is all about, producing moments unlikely to be seen again. A game that was full of everything, great goals, penalty saves, sending offs and a goal which could be described as the greatest ever, capping it off. An exciting and captivating moment for all football fans to love whatever club you support.
Neil Miles, Hants

Sunderland

Undoubtedly one of the greatest F.A. Cup Finals ever, after clawing back to 2-2 Manchester United looked like they'd gained extra-time. But Liam Brady picked up the ball in his own half and ran through the middle chased by Lou Macari. He played the ball out to Graham Rix on the left, the clock was ticking down. Rix crossed, Gary Bailey was stood near post. The ball floated high over him and there was Alan Sunderland, curly perm bouncing, to make it 3-2 in the dying seconds. What a moment - if you're an Arsenal fan, which I'm not! Even as a Manchester United fan, it was still a breathtaking moment to win a Cup Final.

Darren Evans, Berkshire

Owen

Liverpool had equalised and there was not much time left. I remember Arsenal were given a free-kick past the half-way line which was not very promising for us. The ball was swung in, nothing came of it and the ball broke for Patrick Berger who took one look up and sent a perfect ball down the field to Michael Owen who then ran on to it, held off Lee Dixon while running towards the Arsenal goal. You could hear the excitment in the Liverpool crowd, then Michael shot the ball across the face of David Seaman, just escaping a sliding challenge from Tony Adams and nestled in the right hand corner of the goal. The Liverpool crowd went absolutely mad, it was the best feeling that I've ever had.
Mark Samuel, Hampshire

Nationwide

Gascoigne

As a Spurs fan there have been few players that have outshone Paul Gascoigne in his prime, and no sweeter moment than that great day at Wembley. With the nation watching, Paul Gascoigne struck one of the greatest free-kicks the two towers ever saw. From 30 yards the ball was driven through the Arsenal wall and straight into ther top corner of the net. Even a fully stretched David Seaman had no chance with this one.

Jordan Barker, Middlesex

Houchen

I was a seven year old boy, interested in football and Coventry, my local team, the final had whipped up a frenzy around the city and I had never experienced such an atmosphere. As a boy I couldn't quite understand it all, it was only another footy match, but then things changed. When Houchen scored his magnificent diving header it was the one moment in time that I actually fell in love with football and Coventry City. Most people just grew into the game but I have a defining, turning point in my life that sunk deep into a little boy's heart and remains there ever since. That image of the goal is clearer to me than all other childhood memories, I can still feel the sun and taste the cherryade that I was drinking at the time. For me, that moment will always be the F.A. Cup magic, I can't watch a game of football, even a friendly, without thinking about it. F.A. Cup magic dead? Not in my heart!
Matthew Clarke, Cardiff

Whiteside

Everton were the new Merseyside supremos, Gray and Sharpe were supreme up front, Peter Reid was the midfield master, Kevin Ratcliffe was a rock in the centre of defence with Neville Southall, arguably the best keeper in Britain at the time. The signs looked bad, Everton were newly crowned English Champions and winners of the European Cup-winners Cup when they took to the field in the 1985 F.A. Cup Final against my Manchester United side who had been hammered 5-0 at Goodison in the league that season and four days later Everton removed them from the Milk Cup 2-1 via an unlucky John Gidman own goal late in the game, after United had been the better side. So imagine my horror when fate transpired against us on that sunny May 18th, When a clumsy but not malicious challenge by Kevin Moran up-ended Peter Reid and resulted in the centre half's dismissal, the first in an F.A. Cup Final. I must admit I cried. But somehow galvanised by this infamous moment, United seemed to feel a sense of injustice and with the game into extra time, the young prodigy Mark Hughes fed Whiteside with a perfect pass. Norman seemed to have little support as he gathered the ball, but in a twinkling of an eye turned just outside the 18 yard box and curled a delicious shot into the far corner of the net, past the despairing dive of Southall. I just sat in my chair stunned, no celebration, nothing. It was like I was watching something straight out of fiction. Even by Whiteside's romantic script, this couldn't be happening. When the final whistle blew to indeed confirm that Norman had written another fairytale chapter into his (sadly brief) career I was on my knees, head in my hands, just weeping with sheer joy and disbelief.

Ian Bartlett, Avon

Monty

It is one of my earliest memories, aged nearly thee and sitting on my Nana's knee watching the 1973 Cup Final. My father was a participant on the preceding televised 'It's A Knockout' show, between the two sets of team supporters. I vaguely remember the game, the goal Ian Porterfield scored to put Sunderland ahead in the first half, and then the most famous save in Wembley's history. Jim Montgomery's double stopper in the second half. Of course, over the years I have seen the stand-out match incidents replayed a million times, and I still get a lump in my throat when, at the final whistle, the Sunderland manager Bob Stokoe, dressed in hat and mac, sprints over the Wembley turf, a grin as wide as the River Wear on his face to hug the Sunderland goalkeeper, Jim Montgomery.

Paul Dixon, Durham

Beasant

Just getting to the final was a fairy tale in itself, but to be leading Liverpool after 60 odd minutes was fantastic enough. Then the ball was played into the Wimbledon box, and even from my position at the back of the Wembley stands I could tell Clive Goodyear made a clean tackle. I was furious when the ref pointed to the spot,then John Aldridge took his kick, I was telling my mates he'd go to the keeper's left like he did in the semi - and sure enough he did - but Beasant read the kick superbly and tipped it round the post. After that - we knew we'd win.
Tony Sollers, Surrey

Your F.A. Cup
Charlie George
Arsenal 2:1 Liverpool, 1971

George

Shankly's Liverpool had held us for 90 minutes. I was a nervous 12 year old Arsenal fan watching on the telly. Bob Wilson let in a Steve Heighway shot on his near post in extra time, I cried so much thinking the dream may be over. Feeling sick and blinded through my tears, I went to the bathroom and, despite being a non-believer, I prayed whilst kneeling on the floor with my elbows on the toilet pan! As I did I heard a roar, Eddie Kelly had equalised. Now we had the momentum, I dried my sore red eyes and keenly watched as Radford passed to Charlie George who hit a screamer past Clemence. Like Charlie, I lay on my back and took the moment in. Winning a domestic trophy for the first time since I was born was incredible, especially as it became 'the double' with the Championship won at Spurs. I'm 44 now but the desperation of praying for a goal, and the coincidence of the equaliser is still remembered in the back of my mind as a minor miracle!
Chris Cleave, Kent

Ricky Villa's magical goal
Barnaby Hunt, Middlesex